Child Rorschach Responses

Developmental Trends
from Two to Ten Years

Also from the Gesell Institute of Child Development

Adolescent Rorschach Responses

Rorschach Responses in Old Age

CHILD RORSCHACH RESPONSES

Developmental Trends from Two to Ten Years

LOUISE BATES AMES, Ph.D.

Co-Director, Gesell Institute of Child Development;
Past President, Society for Projective Techniques
and Personality Assessment

RUTH W. MÉTRAUX, M.A.

Speech and Rorschach Consultant

JANET LEARNED RODELL, Ph.D.

Formerly Director of Preschool Service

RICHARD N. WALKER, Ph.D.

Director of Research

BRUNNER/MAZEL Publishers • New York

Third Printing

Library of Congress Catalog Card No. 72-93599
SBN 87630-042-5

Contents

List of Tables

1952
Institut Jean-Jacques Rousseau
Université de Genève, Geneva, Switzerland

My dear friends,

Your book is the first American publication on the Rorschach test following the so-called "Swiss" method which continues as faithfully as possible the tradition of Rorschach without confining itself to a sterile traditionalism. The important study that you have carried out will prove of great service because it will fill a lacuna felt by numerous specialists of the test. In fact we know but very little about the performance of young children with the blots and while I agree with you that the results of the very young children offer an interest more scientific than diagnostic, it is useful to have these results taken systematically and with so much perception on so great a number of children.

Your findings will be without doubt a valuable contribution to the psychology of preschool children and will permit the application of the test as a diagnostic technique in any case for children from 5 to 6 years on. Secondly, and it is here that I see the most important interest of your research, the knowledge of the reactions of the younger children will permit us a finer nuance in the diagnosis of older persons including adolescent and adult. From now on the reactions occurring more frequently with the children and diminishing, even disappearing, with age can be taken as an indisputable sign of inharmonious psychic evolution when they appear in the results of older children or adults.

I think particularly of such things as color naming, Clob interpretation, and the interpretations given because of position. Following the context in which such reactions are found we can conclude that a certain evolutional stage has not been surmounted or that there is a regression due to momentary or permanent disturbance. In this sense certainly your study will aid to consolidate the diagnostic value of the Rorschach. Your findings can even contribute to clarify by means of the Rorschach certain psychogenic problems in the domain of Psychiatry.

Cordially,

Marguerite Loosli-Usteri
(Vice President, International Society for Rorschach Research)

Foreword to First Edition

The Developmental Aspect of
Rorschach Research

It is gratifying to learn from no less an authority than Madame Loosli-Usteri of the Institut Jean Jacques Rousseau, that the present American volume is faithful to the principles of the "Swiss method" without narrowing itself to "a sterile traditionalism." The originality of Hermann Rorschach opened a vast domain with a psychodiagnostic technique which proves to have great import for the study of normal as well as of abnormal behavior. Perhaps no single test during the past ten years has been more widely applied in research and in practice. In this same decade the literature of psychology and psychiatry has shown a marked tendency to correlate the dynamics of perception and of personality. Such correlation demands an increasing attention to the factors of ontogenetic development.

It is difficult to make a sharp distinction between developmental and dynamic psychology, for the simple reason that development is itself a process, an inclusive dynamism, which comprises the total growth complex. With his liberality of outlook Rorschach was quite aware of the importance of developmental factors in his frame of reference. In a section of the original report which summarizes his research results, he offers a cogent commentary on "The Development of the Experience-Type." The optimal goal of development, he states, is "the harmonious relationship of three principles—rationality, capacity for 'inner life,' and emotional willingness to adapt. . . . The development of the experience-type is, then, a process of coartation conditioned by the growth of disciplined thinking, and taking place within certain optimal limits." Using the terminology of his experimental method, Rorschach briefly characterizes the probable experience type of a small child of between two-and-a-half to three years of age.

Interestingly enough, the authors of the present volume begin their delineation of thirteen progressive developmental levels with the age of two years as the first stepping stone. Even this early age is not entirely devoid of Rorschach phenomena! Indeed we can safely assume that the basic perceptual mechanisms and patterns of visual behavior undergo their primary organization throughout the first two years of life. In great measure these primary patterns must prefigure the eventual reactions to the ink blots. But the eventualities are slowly built up. The authors demonstrate the presence of underlying maturational factors for each of thirteen age levels from two to ten years. It is suggested that comparable maturational mechanisms continue to operate to the age of twenty. To gain an impression of the force of maturation one needs only to read in rapid forward moving sequence the consecutive chapters on 2- 2½- 3- and 3½-year-oldness.

Although the concept of "oldness" may seem a bit mystical, the reader can look forward to a wealth of concrete data in the chapters which follow. The senior author, Louise B. Ames, has given no less than a thousand Rorschachs to children, many of whom are well known to her through associated studies of their behavior development at progressive ages.

There seems to be no way to circumvent the concept of oldness, growing and maturity. Behavior and psyche alike are subject to laws of growth—of developmental morphology. Whether applied to child or to adult, one of the critical tasks of the Rorschach technique is to aid a differential diagnosis of immaturity, abnormality and individuality. The present publication, based on close collaborative developmental studies, makes a significant contribution toward this end. I believe it will be appreciated both in terms of theory and of application.

But intricate skeins do not easily untangle, as Rorschach wisely hinted in his basic book: "If the origin or genesis of experience-type were known, it might be possible to give a more complete discussion of this topic . . ." The incompleteness is constructive. It will long be a challenge to continuing research.

ARNOLD GESELL

Preface to Second Edition

It is now over twenty years since the first edition of this book was published. It is good to have it back in print and good to have the chance to make some changes.

The core of the book is essentially the same: it is a study of 650 Rorschach records of children aged 2 to 10 years. While we have not changed the core sample itself we have added to our evaluation of it in a number of ways. First, we have made some refinements of scoring, particularly of location, and so we rescored all the records and rewrote all the pertinent sections, particularly Chapter Five, which is entirely new. Second, in our discussion of the Rorschach variables the introductory material is less tentative, less buttressed with citations of authorities and more a product of our own enlarged-by-20-years experience. More importantly, the chance to follow longitudinally a number of the subjects who were part of the core sample has resulted in a chapter on the stability of Rorschach scoring over time and on the developmental patterning of scores.

A real problem in our first edition was the specialness of our sample—mostly bright, healthy children of mostly highly educated parents. We have now supplemented our statistical findings with a comparative study of three other samples, at different levels of socio-economic status. These nearly 900 records have not been averaged in with those of the core sample in the body of the book but are compared with one another and with the core group in a separate chapter. It is our hope that inclusion of these additional sets of norms will make this edition more widely usable than our earlier version.

A final chapter updates the list of "danger signals" we proposed in the earlier edition, testing its revised form by contrasting matched groups of normal and disturbed boys, and also compares the early Rorschach performances of children who later became good and poor readers.

Two chapters from the earlier edition have been dropped. The Summary chapter seemed redundant and too compressed to be of practical use. And the Review of the Literature got beyond us. The earlier edition made a fairly systematic survey of the American literature up to 1950, citing about 90 references. To make a similar survey of the hundreds of publications since 1950 seemed like more of a chore than we could face—even if our publisher were not already patiently waiting for a manuscript two years beyond the promised delivery date. Rather than preserve an inadequate chapter, we dropped it. (We have retained a number of the more useful older references in our bibliography, and added a number of more recent ones, even when they are not referred to in the text. An unusually complete bibliography to 1964 is presented by Lang [50]).

We have the help of many people to acknowledge. Our first and foremost thanks go to the many children, parents, and teachers whose cooperation made the study possible. Of the many educators who contributed, we would like most particularly to thank the following: Dr. Edward Ricciuti, Ralph Carrington, Charles Twyman, Edward Summerton, Charles St. Clair, Mildred Wakeley, and Elizabeth Doyle. We wish also to thank the directors and teachers at the following nursery schools: the Betsy Ross Nursery School, Miss Gailer's School, Hamden Hall Preschool, Lincoln Street Nursery, and the Walt Whitman School.

Dr. Helen Thompson of New York City made available Rorschachs on subjects from her clinical practice. Judith August assisted in the "danger signals" study.

We are especially grateful to Dr. Frances L. Ilg, Director Emeritus of the Gesell Institute, for continuing advice, inspiration, and practical assistance throughout the duration of this study.

We thank the editors of the following journals for permission to reprint portions of our papers in those journals: *Journal of Educational Psychology, Journal of Personality Assessment, Journal of Genetic Psychology,* and *Genetic Psychology Monographs.*

The Viking Fund of New York (now the Wenner Gren Foundation for Anthropological Research) generously contributed to financial support of the original research.

The current revision is the work of Louise Bates Ames and Richard N. Walker. Dr. Ames collected and scored all the nearly 900 supplementary records at different socio-economic levels and did a portion of the statistical analysis of each new section. Both authors obtained about equal numbers of the 300 longitudinal follow-ups. Dr. Walker proposed the new location scoring and rescored the core group's records, did the final statistical analyses, and wrote the final drafts of the material new to this edition.

L.B.A.
R.N.W.

Part One

CHAPTER ONE

Introduction

The Developmental Point of View with Regard to Projective Techniques

The developmental point of view suggests that the behavior of the child as well as his physical organism develops through a sequence of structured, patterned stages. This basic development comes from within. Its potentialities lie in the infant at the moment of birth and in fact have already expressed themselves by the time of birth, since the behavior of the fetus has already unfolded in a patterned, predictable manner.

Since the child's behavior does appear to develop in such a lawful, patterned manner, it is possible, within limits, to predict what reactions a given child may make in a given situation. Cinema and other studies have amply documented this fact, particularly in relation to such behaviors as vision, locomotion, drawing, and the manipulation of simple objects.

Our studies have further shown "that the higher psychical manifestations of child life also are profoundly subject to laws of development. . . . Psychically the child inherits nothing fully formed. Each and every part of his nature has to grow—his sense of self, his fears, his affections and curiosities, his feelings toward mother, father, playmates, sex, his judgments of good and bad, ugly and beautiful. . . ." (Gesell, 26).

This basic and lawful development of intellectual and emotional functions appears in broadest outline to remain fairly consistent from child to child, though it seems to be at every stage inflected and colored by the individuality of each individual child. The stages of behavior are roughly the same from child to child, but each child expresses these stages at his own tempo and in his own way. A further factor which shapes the child's behavior is, of course, the environmental situation in which he finds himself, and his adaptation to that situation: his experience.

It seems probable that projective techniques, if carefully administered and skilfully interpreted in the perspective of adequate age norms, can throw light on each of these three factors: 1) the child's level of development, 2) his innate individuality, and 3) the kind of adjustment he is making to his life situation.

However, without concrete information as to age factors, that is without knowing what kind of response to expect from a 3- or 4-, or 7- or

3

8-year-old child, the clinician is in danger of attributing too entirely to the child's own unique individuality, or to his life situation, behavior which actually is merely characteristic of his age level. True, if a child has made a certain response it is presumably at that time characteristic of him. But it will have different implications with regard to his personality if it is a response shared by 90 per cent of other children of his age level, or if it is a behavior not ordinarily seen at that age and therefore presumably more uniquely characteristic of him.

If it is true that all aspects of the child's behavior, including the higher psychic manifestations, are subject to the laws of development, then it should be useful to apply the developmental approach in the field of projective techniques. The need of such an approach in this field may be considered to be twofold:

1. In studying the workings of any perfected structure or function, it is generally conceded that a knowledge of the early development of that structure or function is essential. Embryology is studied not only for itself but to give a better knowledge of the mature organism. Similarly, in trying to gain insight and understanding into the behavior of the adult human, we believe that a thorough knowledge of the stages of developing child behavior is essential.

A thorough and specific knowledge of the developmental stages through which the organism customarily passes in attaining a normally mature performance, can be of considerable use to the clinician in assessing the behavior of the adult. It is a fairly common occurrence for an adult performance on some one projective technique to contain some or many responses typical of adolescent or even pre-adolescent performance. If such deviant signs can be identified as characteristic of a certain earlier stage of development, they are of course much more useful clues to the clinician than if they are merely recognized as atypical of adult performance.

2. The most immediate and practical use of a developmental approach to the study of projective techniques, however, is that it makes effective their use with children. Opinions as to the value of various projective techniques, particularly the Rorschach, in the study of the young child vary. Some research conducted without a knowledge of normative child responses as different from adult responses has led to the conclusion that the use of the Rorschach with children is invalid insofar as there is found to be no relationship between single personality variables—such as insecurity—as measured by the Rorschach method, and behavior considered clinically to be symptomatic of this variable (Swift, 69, 71).

Both lack of confidence in the Rorschach as a useful tool for exploring the personality of younger children, and failure to correlate Rorschach findings with clinically established signs of certain personality variables are based, we believe, on a lack of knowledge of what may be expected of children of various ages in projective test performance, and therefore upon the judging of child performance merely in terms of known adult norms. Practical experience leads us to believe that such a procedure is not only inadequate, but that it frequently yields completely incorrect results.

Clinical practice has for some time made it increasingly clear that many children whose performance on standard intelligence tests shows them to be well above average in intelligence, who live in presumably favorable home environments, and who appear to be reasonably "well-adjusted" in their environments (that is, do not appear to be "emotionally disturbed"), nevertheless do poorly in both school performance and home adjustment. Particularly have we noted these signs in adopted children whose early performance on standard tests has been excellent, yet who do not live up to expectations in actual everyday performance even though subsequent intelligence tests show them to be of continued good intelligence.

It would seem that if standard intelligence and developmental tests could be supplemented by projective tests such as the Rorschach, which is aimed at revealing the actual structure of the individuality, we might have a more adequate basis for understanding why a child's actual performance may not be keeping step with his supposed abilities. We might also reach a better understanding of why he behaves as he does and of whether or not he is actually living up to his innate potentialities. But before projective tests can become a useful part of a battery of tests for children, we need practical age norms.

The present study is directed chiefly toward supplying such norms for the Rorschach test. We have analyzed data which include fifty records at each of the following age levels: half-yearly age levels from 2 through 5½ years, yearly age levels from 6 through 10 years, in a relatively homogeneous group of children of above average intelligence.

The present analysis yields the same type of information found in earlier studies by other writers, but has the advantage of presenting this material in systematic detail for a rather wide age range. It will indicate in which, if any, direction and to what extent the customary determinants change with age. Thus, briefly, it will tell how many responses we may expect at any given age; to what extent color and movement responses occur; what type of color responses we may expect; whether movement is of humans or animals. Also to what extent shading responses occur; what part of the blot is used in responses; and to what extent the content of responses, found by some investigators to be but slightly related to age, changes.

These are but a few of the questions which need to be answered at a simple normative level. However, a thorough developmental study should go beyond this. It is our belief that the child's behavior at any time is not merely the sum of many part-behaviors, but that behavior at any given age has an essence or characteristicness which distinguishes it from all other ages. Thus, we speak of 5-year-oldness, 6-year-oldness, and the like.

Behavior at each age may, we believe, be described in qualitative as well as in quantitative terms.

Thus, it seems plausible to expect that in responses to the Rorschach test we may get clear indications of characteristic age changes which must be taken into account and then to some extent discounted in an accurate characterization of the unique individuality of the child making the response. We would anticipate that Rorschach findings would agree with and would supplement the developmental picture of each age level which has been arrived at independently (Gesell & Ilg, 27, 28).

Maturity versus Individuality Factors

In the study of the child we must at all times keep in mind both the maturity changes which the child undergoes, *and* the enduring, consistent thread of his own individuality. We have found that in regard to many functions, there are certain sectors of the life span when maturity factors are so all-pervasive that the unique individuality pattern of any individual child cannot always be clearly discerned. It is always present, but at certain ages it appears to be overlaid and to some extent obscured by the age factors.

Thus, for example, 28-week-old infants of normal intelligence, regardless of individuality factors, when presented with a small object such as a cube, tend to grasp this cube, bang it on any convenient flat surface, and transfer it from hand to hand. At 40 and 44 weeks, normal infants, regardless of temperament, tend to poke at objects; at 15 months tend to cast them. Each child will perform these activities in his own way and at his own tempo, but the similarities of behavior from child to child tend to be greater than the individual variations.

In responding to the Rorschach cards, it appears that subjects, whatever their age, assuming that they do accept the test and give verbal responses, reveal to us a good deal about themselves. They give clues as to their intelligence, their thought content, their emotional adjustment, their manner of perceiving visual stimuli, their basic personality structure and above all, according to Rorschach, how they experience.

However, developmental or maturity factors as they affect Rorschach performance appear to be extremely strong and rapidly changing in the early years of life, certainly throughout the first ten years, probably even through adolescence. Thus, any two 2-year-olds may express more strongly the "magic repetition" of some one-word concept such as "doggie" or "tree" characteristic of the 2-year age zone, than anything which is uniquely revealing of their basic individuality. Two 7-year-olds with their emphasis on the morbid, their stressing of decay, damage, and mutilation, may be expressing 7-year-oldness more clearly than they are revealing their own individuality patterns. As Piotrowski and Lewis have commented (63):

It is possible that visual images or percepts, the basis of the perceptanalytic Rorschach method, express less of a child's personality than of an adult's. . . . The Rorschach method detects many traits pertaining to dynamic psychosocial inter-relationships, but the total personality in the strict meaning of the word eludes it as it eludes every experimental psychological procedure. Rorschach records of children reveal less than records of adults because the role of children in the interactions between them and the world is less varied, their perceptions less comprehensive, their activities less independent, and their experiences less anticipated in the imagination.

If it were true that the Rorschach revealed only the child's maturity status with regard to others of his chronological age, it would still be a useful tool. We believe, however, that it not only serves this function but, increasingly as the child matures, that it does throw light on the individual personality structure which it is generally believed to reveal in the adult.

At some age, perhaps in the early twenties, it is probable that individuality factors emerge as showing themselves more clearly than age factors. At some later age, possibly in the late seventies or early eighties, we hypothesize that maturity factors may once again play the predominant role in determining Rorschach responses.

Age Changes in Any One Child

An extremely important aspect of the Rorschach, which a developmental approach has revealed, and one which only long-term longitudinal studies can finally clarify, is the fact that any individual child changes markedly in his Rorschach response from age to age, in ways for which it is difficult to account purely on the basis of what may have happened to him environmentally. A child may change, in a year's time, from conspicuous introversivity to marked extratensivity, or from an experience balance which is rich and full to one which is conspicuously constricted. Many subjects who at 6 years of age give no shading or Clob responses, for example, give many such responses at 7 years of age, and then again at 8 years give records quite free of these determinants.

We have noted the same type of age changes in the performance of individual children on Lowenfeld's Mosaic test. Eleven-year-olds, for example, often make what are usually considered "normal" designs. These same children at 12 years of age frequently make designs of a type considered neurotic in the adult, and then again at 13 years of age make "normal" designs—in the absence of environmental or experiential changes which would ordinarily be adequate to account for such variations. In such instances, we question that the so-called "neurotic" Mosaic performance of the 12-year-old actually expresses a neurotic individuality makeup as we understand it in the case of the adult. Similarly we must be guarded in our evaluation of some Rorschach factors which appear at certain ages in our subjects, especially when they occur in many subjects of the same age.

Only further detailed study, and great familiarity with normative age trends, will allow us to evaluate properly the changes which we customarily find in the Rorschach records of any one child who is tested on successive occasions. But even though we cannot fully evaluate or explain these age changes in individual records, we must remember that they ordinarily take place. The mere factor of marked fluctuation in type of response from year to year may itself be one clue to the individuality pattern, since some subjects present a much more consistent picture from age to age than do others.

Scope of this Volume

It should be noted that this volume is not presented as an introductory manual on Rorschach procedure. Though we shall present in some detail our scoring system, we assume familiarity on the part of the reader with at least one or other of the more common scoring systems. Similarly we shall discuss methods of administering the Rorschach to young children, but would refer the reader who is looking for specific instruction in testing procedure to some one of the standard Rorschach texts.

Furthermore, we shall not here present detailed or "deep" interpretation of the records on which we have based our findings, beyond giving brief comments on several illustrative cases for each age level under discussion. The individual reader may wish to make his own interpretation of the meaning of the individual sample cases presented, but the authors do not feel that the material warrants detailed interpretation at this time.

Though the Rorschach test is considered by some investigators to be a test for the imagination, Rorschach himself has stated (66, pp. 16–18) that there "can be no doubt that this experiment can be called a test of the perception power of the subject." We so consider it here. Unlike Murray, we do not consider projective techniques in the psychoanalytic sense of implying projection into test material of elements of personality of which the subject is unconscious. We consider them in the sense of Lowenfeld and Frank:

A projection method involves the presentation of a stimulus situation chosen because it will mean to the subject not what the experimenter has arbitrarily decided it should mean but rather whatever it must mean to his personality. . . . He will then respond to his meaning of the stimulus situation by some form of action and feeling that is expressive of his personality. (25).

CHAPTER TWO

Subjects and Methods

Subjects

The children who served as the main subjects in this study were 650 boys and girls, nearly all from the Connecticut cities of New Haven and Waterbury. Fifty children, 25 boys and 25 girls, were seen at each of thirteen different age levels: half-yearly levels from 2 to 6 years, and annually thereafter through 10 years of age. The great majority of these children are above average in intelligence and in social class status.

TABLE 1. SOURCE OF CASES

		Number	*Percentage*
New Haven:	Clinic of Child Development	330	51
	Nursery schools	141	22
Waterbury:	Public schools	137	21
New York:	Nursery school	6	1
	Dr. Thompson	20	3
Miscellaneous:	gathered individually by authors	16	2
TOTAL		650	100

The core of the sample—just over 50 per cent—consisted of members of the research group which has been followed for many years at the former Yale Clinic of Child Development. We supplemented this group with children of similar intelligence and social class levels. The composition of the total sample is shown in Table 1.

At the preschool ages, subjects were obtained from various New Haven nursery schools: the Betsy Ross Nursery School, Lincoln Street School, the preschool groups at Hamden Hall and Miss Gailer's, and the Yale Clinic of Child Development. We also used a total of six children at two ages from the Walt Whitman Nursery School in New York City.

At the school ages, our New Haven group was supplemented by children from the public schools of Waterbury. In selecting subjects, we chose children comparable to the core group on an intelligence level basis. The socio-economic level is slightly below our New Haven sample, and at 5 years and thereafter there is a downward shift in over-all socio-economic status.

Finally, we used 20 cases from the files of Dr. Helen Thompson, a New York practicing psychologist, formerly of our staff. These children had been referred for psychological advice, but the only cases used were those presenting essentially "normal" problems: "mother doesn't feel she under-

TABLE 2. MINNESOTA
OCCUPATIONAL SCALE DISTRIBUTION OF FATHERS
(Percentage in each group)

Age	Number	I: Professional	II: Semi-professional, managerial	III: Clerical, retail business, skilled	V: Semi-skilled	VI: Slightly skilled
2	49	67	20	10	2	0
2½	50	68	22	10	0	0
3	48	69	19	10	2	0
3½	46	65	24	9	2	0
4	50	64	18	14	2	0
4½	41	56	24	15	5	0
5	44	45	20	25	9	0
5½	42	45	21	26	7	0
6	50	42	20	24	12	2
7	50	44	26	20	10	0
8	45	42	33	18	7	0
9	42	40	33	14	12	0
10	48	40	25	23	10	2
TOTAL	605	53	23	17	6	0

stands the child very well," "fearful in gym," "absent-minded, tense," "jealous of brother,"—that is, the same kinds of problems which are met in our own normal research group.

SOCIO-ECONOMIC STATUS   The Minnesota Scale of Paternal Occupations was used as an index of social status. SES ratings were available for 93 per cent of the cases. Table 2 presents the percentage of children falling in each scale class for the ages separately, and for the whole group.

Despite a downward shift in SES level from year 5, there is quite a consistent SES distribution of subjects in the different age groups, and within the preschool and school age groups the distributions are highly similar from age to age. Over-all, this is a high-level population, with more than half the children in the professional group, and three-fourths in the professional and managerial groups.

INTELLIGENCE LEVEL   Because of the correlation between socio-economic status and intelligence test scores, the socio-economic distribution serves as the main index of intelligence level of the group. For two-thirds of the children some sort of intelligence rating was more directly available.

For the core group, this was in the form of a developmental rating based on one, or more often a series, of developmental examinations, using a battery of tests. The rating considered many aspects of performance, and was given in terms of a general verbal description, rather than in I.Q. figures.

TABLE 3. "INTELLIGENCE RATING" DISTRIBUTION
(Percentage at each level)

Age	Number of subjects	Low average (86–95)	Average (95–105)	High average (106–115)	Superior (116–125)	Very superior (Above 125)
2	42	2	12	31	31	24
2½	38	5	18	21	37	18
3	31	0	13	13	58	19
3½	28	0	11	7	57	25
4	21	0	9	14	52	24
4½	16	6	13	25	37	19
5	29	10	14	24	38	14
5½	33	9	21	18	36	15
6	41	5	29	15	39	12
7	41	7	24	5	46	17
8	40	8	20	13	52	8
9	47	4	11	26	36	23
10	38	5	21	24	40	11
TOTAL	445	5	17	18	42	17

Ratings in the form of group I.Q. test scores (Pintner-Cunningham) were available for the Waterbury Public School children, and Stanford-Binet I.Q.'s were available for Dr. Thompson's New York children. These were equated crudely with our developmental ratings, and counted along with them. Thus the distribution of "intelligence ratings" given here is a conglomeration of scores, and serves only to identify roughly the intelligence level of the sample. The distribution for the total group and for each age separately is indicated in Table 3. The median and modal rating is *superior*; ratings for three-fourths of the children are above the *average* category. For the small number of cases involved, the distribution is quite similar from age to age.

Six additional groups of subjects are referred to in later chapters of this book. One is a group of 22 boys and 11 girls tested longitudinally from 2 to 10 years. Individual children contributed from six to 11 records apiece over the 13 half-yearly and yearly age levels considered here, the median subject giving 10 records. Most of these children have one or more of their tests included in our main body of records—all at preschool ages (except for three records at age 6), and never more than three records from one child. Their full sets of records were used for longitudinal evaluation of ideas arrived at from cross-sectional treatment of our main sample, in Chapter 23.

Three samples of subjects aged 5 to 10 years were collected from schools in neighborhoods differing in socio-economic level. The sample designated Suburban I consists of 313 children from a school in a residential suburb of New York. The modal father's occupation in Suburban I was managerial or semi-professional. The Suburban II sample consists of 350 children from a residential and manufacturing town near New Haven, and has a modal father's occupation at the skilled trades and retail business level. An inner-city sample consists of 219 children, all black, from a New Haven neighborhood where the modal father's occupation is slightly skilled. A comparison of Rorschach scores in these three groups and in our main sample is presented in Chapter 24.

Finally, two groups are used to relate Rorschach characteristics to other criteria, as described in Chapter 25. One group consists of 50 boys aged 6 to 12 years, seen on our clinical service and classified as clearly emotionally disturbed, matched with 50 normal subjects of the same age, intelligence, and socio-economic status. These subjects were used for evaluation of Rorschach indicators of emotional disturbance. Another group consists of 54 children first tested in kindergarten on the Rorschach and evaluated for reading ability at the end of fifth grade.

Methods of Administration

Since the Rorschach is a purely verbal test, its administration to young children requires some degree of finesse on the part of the examiner in establishing rapport. A preschool child even though ill at ease with an examiner will often successfully perform a test of purely manipulative nature. Eliciting verbal responses from an uncooperative child is a much more difficult task. For this reason, it is important for the Rorschach examiner of young children to be perceptive and able to adapt to the child's abilities and tempo.

In the present investigation, a member of the nursery school staff examined the children under 5 years of age, most of whom were well acquainted with her. For the children over 5 years, many of the Rorschachs were given during the course of a developmental examination.

Rorschachs were administered in regular testing rooms, or in rooms provided by the public schools of Waterbury. The children under 5 were approached in the nursery school by the Examiner with the comment, "I have a new game to play with you. You could come with me and I'll show it to you." When the older children were approached in the classroom, the Examiner stated, "I have something to show you. Let's go to my room and see it." In almost every case the child went willingly with the Examiner, at once or after a minimum amount of reassurance from his teacher. Occasionally with the youngest children, the teacher walked to the examining room with the child. In many instances, after a few children in a group had been tested, the rest of the children were eager volunteers to go with the Examiner.

The subject was seated at a low table with the Examiner seated at his left, and in most instances a recorder at his right. Generally, sufficient rapport had been established by conversing with the child on the way to the examining room to allow immediate administration of the test.

The Examiner stated, "I have some things to show you," care being taken to avoid mentioning the word "pictures." The first card was presented in an upright position and given to the child to hold. The Examiner then asked, "What do you see?" If the child hesitated, the Examiner added, "Tell me all about it," or "What does it look like to you?" These were usually adequate directions, but when the child refused, or answered, "I don't know," the Examiner explained, "People see all sorts of things, and I want to know what this might look like to *you*." No further directions were needed. When the child had given one response, the Examiner said, "Yes, fine. Can you tell me anything else?" Throughout the test the Examiner attempted to be spontaneous in interest and encouragement, avoiding stereotyped approval after each card. The timing factor was particularly important in eliciting responses from the preschool children. Some responded slowly and needed to be given plenty of time to think about the cards, while with others, interest and rapport would have been lost if the cards had not been presented at a rapid tempo.

If the child's response was in the form of an inquiry, for instance "Is that a duck?" the Examiner replied, "Yes, it could be a duck." In all instances the child's own words were turned back to him so that the Examiner's replies would in no way influence his further responses.

In this investigation, the inquiry was conducted as follows. Most of the information necessary for scoring was obtained by asking *safe* questions immediately after the full response to each blot. Preschool children were instructed: "Put your finger on the ————." In many instances, it was felt that any checking would disrupt the flow of the test, therefore the inquiry was not forced, and the exact location was judged by content, or direction of the child's regard.* When it appeared that a determinant other than form

---

* Klopfer (49, p. 20) takes exception to our procedure, stating that "guesswork has no place in the inquiry, regardless of whether our subjects are adults or children." To this remarkable statement we can only suggest that guesswork plays quite a large role in scoring the records of a great many subjects, adults as well as children. The guesswork should be as well informed as possible, but good inquiry is not a cross-examination, as Klopfer recognized four pages earlier in describing his own procedure: "If the child sees an animal . . . the examiner needs only to ask where its body, head and legs are; if he sees a mountain, the examiner merely has to ask for its top and its bottom. In the majority of cases, where the child responds at all in an understandable way, the reaction will convincingly demonstrate to the examiner that the response was meant as an arbitrary whole, a confabulatory whole, or a confabulatory combination whole response, no matter what part of the card the child's finger touched previously" (49, p. 16). Informed guesswork!

was present, this was usually elicited by, "Tell me about the ———," or "What made you think of ———?" "What reminded you of a ———?" or "How could you tell it was a ———?" suiting the question to the age and intelligence of the child. With the older children, however, a few *necessary* leading questions such as inquiry concerning the role of color, shading, or movement were saved until the conclusion of the entire test series.

By combining the initial presentation and the inquiry, the restlessness and loss of interest often found with young children when a complete inquiry follows presentation of the cards were eliminated. Ford (22) reports that "the younger children were apt to become impatient with the inquiry and to lose interest in the material, often asking to stop or leave." Piotrowski and Lewis (63) find that "when the child's spontaneous Rorschach reactions are followed by an inquiry, the child is more likely to give a new response, or to accept any suggestions made by the Examiner, than to explain his primary response about which he is questioned."

In this test series, no preliminary trial blot was used, as in the studies of Hertz and Ford. Although such a blot provides an orienting introduction to the test, it was felt that a more complete sample of the child's reaction would be obtained by including in the record his initial reaction to the test. When children were unable to respond to the first card or cards, the later cards were presented and after completion of the series, the earlier cards which the child had rejected were re-presented. Included in the formal scoring summary were those responses obtained in the retrial up to the point where the first scorable response in the original presentation occurred. For example, if the child gave no response to Cards I, II, and VI in the first presentation, but responded to all of these on the retrial, Cards I and II would be included in the scoring summary, while Card VI would not. When the child refused a card, he was urged to regard it for just a minute longer; and if no response was forthcoming, the card was re-presented later.

Also contrary to Ford's procedure, the children were allowed to turn the cards at will. Excessive motor manipulation of the cards, which led Ford to forbid rotation, was found in our group only in a few extreme cases. In this study, card turning was allowed and was considered a significant and revealing behavior.

After the child had completed the entire series, all of the cards were spread out on a table. The child was then asked to identify the ones that he liked best and least, and if possible to give reasons for his choices. Best and least were difficult concepts for many of the preschool children, and several substitutions of simpler words had to be made, such as *the good one,* or *your favorite,* for best; and *the worst, the bad one,* or *the one you don't like,* for least. Frequently with the youngest preschool children there appeared to be a complete lack of ability to make such choices, or an indiscriminate choosing of many cards. However with the older children this procedure often yielded information valuable in scoring questionable points.

In the older group, the Examiner recorded responses on the Rorschach location chart; and in most instances a recorder, seated behind a one-way-vision screen made a more detailed recording. However, with the preschool children it was found that rapport with the Examiner could be maintained on a much higher level if the Examiner could give full attention to the subject. Therefore a recorder, who was somewhat familiar to most of the children, was seated in the room to the right of and behind the child's chair when the Examiner and subject entered. The child was casually introduced to the recorder, then his attention was quickly drawn to the business of being seated and proceeding with the test. Generally the child welcomed the presence of the recorder. On the rare occasions when her presence seemed to inhibit his behavior, the recorder retired behind the one-way-vision screen.

All responses and their location were recorded verbatim and also on a Rorschach location chart. The child's spontaneous comments and actions, particularly any turning of the cards, were also recorded. Timing for the total performance was recorded but timing for individual cards was not taken. However, indication was made of any abnormal length of time in responding.

Scoring was often done while the record was being taken, especially with the younger children, in order to take immediate advantage of all clues provided as the child responded. When this was done, movements, expressions, and inflections could all be taken into account.

CLINICAL VARIATIONS The following procedures are not desirable when gathering statistical data, but can be used clinically to break into refusals or perseveration:

1. If complete refusals occur on the first three cards, the Examiner may point to center red on Card III saying, "What could this be?" or "What is this?" If the child does not respond, Examiner can say, "Where is the bow?" or "Where is the butterfly?" Or Examiner may prefer to delay any direct questioning of this type until Card V, and if by then no spontaneous response has been obtained, may ask, "Does this look like a butterfly to you?"

2. If there is a perseverative response on the first six cards, Examiner may say on presenting Card VII, "Now this is going to be a *different* one."

3. If the child perseverates on all ten cards on the first trial, Examiner can re-present the series with the comment, "Sometimes people see all different things on these cards. See what you can see that is *different*."

Comments on Use of Rorschach with Young Children

It is the opinion of some clinicians that the Rorschach is not of value for use with young children, particularly for those under 7 years of age. Some would even restrict its use to children 10 years old or older. Objections to use of this test with the very young for the most part are based on three arguments: 1) the test is difficult to administer to young children; 2) results are not particularly valid, that is, determinants which indicate disturbance appear in children who on other grounds are considered quite undisturbed; and 3) even when the test is administered successfully the child's responses tend to be meager and his visual percepts do not as in the case of the adult reflect fully his individuality.

So far as the administration of the test to young children is concerned, we have found that simple techniques such as those just described make its administration to children 2½ to 3 years old and older perfectly feasible in most cases. In many instances it can be given successfully to 2-year-olds. We did not find, as did Ford, that the child's manipulation of the card interfered seriously with the giving of the test and we did not find it necessary to restrict such manipulation. We did find it necessary, as Ford suggests, to keep instructions clear, simple, and brief and we also found that considerable encouragement, frequently nonverbal, was helpful.

So far as the second problem goes, we have already suggested that adult standards are not valid for judging children's performance on the Rorschach and it is for this reason that we are here presenting norms which will, we hope, be helpful in the accurate evaluation of children's Rorschach responses.

As to the third objection, when data are available for many children of an age in question and of surrounding ages, even a meager response can be evaluated and can reveal both individuality and developmental status.

We have been able to obtain reasonably full responses from children 3 years of age and under. It is true as discussed above (p. 7) that visual images or percepts reveal less of the child's personality than of the adult's, but increasingly as the child matures they do reveal his dynamic psychosocial interrelationships even though the total personality may at the earliest ages elude us in the Rorschach responses. They also reveal a good deal as to developmental status even though with very young children the Rorschach alone is not an adequate measure of development. If only one test can be given we prefer such a one as the Gesell Developmental Schedule. However as one item in a battery we find that the Rorschach, even with a child as young as 3 years of age, throws considerable light on developmental status. It is particularly useful when combined with other projective techniques based on manipulation rather than verbal performance—as for example the Lowenfeld Kaleidoblock or Mosaic tests.

CHAPTER THREE

Scoring

General Scoring Approach

As we have already indicated, this text is not an introductory manual. We do not aim to give basic, step-by-step instruction in how to score a protocol. Such information may be found in the publications of Beck, Bochner and Halpern, Hertz and Klopfer. But because there is such variation in scoring practices among different "schools" of scoring and from individual to individual, we have set down our own scoring procedure as explicitly as possible.

When the Rorschach method was introduced for clinical use at the former Yale Clinic of Child Development it was taught to the psychological staff, including the present authors, by Mrs. Ruth W. Métraux, who had studied the method with Mme. Loosli-Usteri in Switzerland. Consequently, it was Loosli's system of scoring that was followed in the early part of this study, and a great many of the records were scored by this system.

A primary aim of our work has been to evaluate the responses of each child on the basis of their relationship to the responses of other children of the same age, rather than to follow the usual procedure of scoring children's records by adult norms. To do this we had first to establish group norms for several scoring categories. Furthermore, as we proceeded we discovered that we had made some mistaken assumptions due to general lack of knowledge about children's Rorschach responses. We thus decided, after all records had been gathered and scored, to rescore the entire series, and before doing this to define for ourselves as clearly and simply as possible the criteria for each score. In this we found Dr. Hertz's work invaluable in its concise definition of the Rorschach scoring symbols, and in its eclectic approach which nevertheless stays close to Rorschach basic principles. The system we present here is a comparatively simple one which has been developed in actual work with children. Using this system, it is possible* to score records with a high degree of agreement between two workers scoring independently.

---

*Such a check has been made by two of the authors, and is presented on pages 31 and 42. Most of the correlations were found to be in the .90's.

In scoring a record, each response is considered separately, and is scored on four primary dimensions: area, determinants, content, and popularity. The categories in each of these dimensions are as follows:

Area		Determinants		Content	
W	Whole response	F	Form response	A	Animal figure
		M	Human move-	Ad	Animal detail
D	Normal detail		ment	H	Human figure
		FM	Animal move-	Hd	Human detail
Dd	Rare detail		ment		
Do	Oligophrenic	m	Inanimate		(For other content
	detail		movement		categories see pages
S	White space	FC	Form-color		76 ff.)
		CF	Color-form		
		C	Pure color		
		F(C)	Non-dysphoric		*Popularity*
			shading	P	Popular
		Clob	(FClob, ClobF)	O	Original
			Dysphoric		
			shading		

The "score" for any response, then, is actually a brief abstraction of the essential features of the response.

SINGLE RESPONSES It is sometimes difficult to determine what constitutes a single response and to differentiate remarks and descriptive comments from responses. Independent concepts must be scored separately, while elaborations are considered part of the original concept. Generally, individual responses are clearcut and separate, but sometimes several items may seem to be loosely combined. In such a case, Klopfer's concept of *accessories* may be helpful as a guiding principle.

REMARKS AND DESCRIPTIONS Spontaneous exclamations often occur in children's responses. Often apparently stemming from current popular jargon and from the comics, these remarks—"ulp," "oh horrors," "mph," "grrr," "eeyow," and the like—should be recorded faithfully and noted in scoring, by underlining or marginal notes.

Sometimes, instead of interpreting, the child describes the blot. A description is not formally scored, but is always noted—*descr.*—in the margin of the protocol. Some comments seem to be on the borderline between description and response—"a big spot," or "a hole" to a white space. When such responses occur in a succession of scorable responses they are usually scored, while when they occur in a stream of description, they are not. The child's intention should be judged as far as possible—whether it is "like a hole in something" or is merely an objective description of the blot.

DENIALS Sometimes a child will correct, or completely deny, a response once he has given it. When a response is corrected, the score is changed according to the child's dictates, but a note is made of the response as it originally stood. In the case of a complete denial, the response as originally given is scored, then crossed out or the comment *denial* noted in the margin. The denied response is not included in the totalling of scores, but must be noted so that it may later be taken into consideration.

ADDITIONAL SCORES As is soon evident in scoring, many responses do not have a single determinant, but several. A response determined primarily by form may be enlivened only hesitantly or vaguely by an additional determinant, or only a small part of the concept may be involved, as when the new determinant is added as embellishment—red hats for the bears on Card II. Or two determinants may both play an important role in shaping the concept. In any of these cases, the examiner scores the primary determinant of the response as usual, and scores the other determinants as *tendencies*. For example, "bright flames—seem to be falling" would be scored CF, tendency to m, and the whole score would be written D CF fire

m . In totalling the responses, these tendencies are not added to the primary responses, but are noted separately. It sometimes seems impossible to determine which determinant is primary, which secondary, in which case an arbitrary decision may have to be made by the scorer. In general, in case of such a tied decision, we would probably tend to give M responses precedence over color, and color responses precedence over shading. Most frequently such close decisions are between color or shading and minor movement (flames leaping, smoke billowing, etc.). We have no simple rule for making such decisions, but can only obtain the best possible inquiry and then call them as we see them.

Scoring D, F+, and P

In the scoring scheme for individual responses on the Rorschach, most categories may be termed absolute—that is they are scored on the basis of the response alone. Certain categories (D, F+, P) are more relative in that they must be scored with reference to group frequency. "Normal details are those selected most frequently by a normal group of subjects" (Rorschach); a good form perception is a response given by a majority of normal subjects; a popular response is one given very frequently by normal subjects. Several authors (Beck, Hertz) have published lists of D, F+, and P, quantitatively determined from large groups of adult Rorschachs, to be used in scoring adult protocols.

As children's records were collected, the question arose as to whether they might be scored by these same lists. Klopfer and Ford felt the adult lists to be adequate for scoring children's records. In the present study we wished rather to be able to compare individual children with others of a similar age, and, as Ford had suspected, it turned out that several details rarely responded to by the adult occur with such frequency as to be scored *normal details* for these children. Many forms scored F— in adults must be scored F+ in children, and there is only partial overlap between lists of P for adults and children.

In determining our lists for scoring D, F+, and P, we followed as closely as possible the careful statistical work of Dr. Marguerite Hertz. It was evident that we could not formulate different lists of D, F+, and P for each different age level in our series, so for convenience we arbitrarily divided the series into three age groups: 2 to 3½ years, 4 to 6 years, 7 to 10 years, with 200 cases in the first and last groups and 250 cases in the middle group. Then for each of the groups, the following procedures were followed to determine D, F+ and P:

1. *D*: The actual number of times specific details were selected for interpretation was tabulated for each blot, and frequency tables were prepared. Following Hertz, all details with a frequency above the twentieth percentile were considered normal details; all other details, rare details.

2. *F+*: One of the most difficult and most subjective problems in scoring is determination of what is accurate form. In order that children responding with forms highly typical of their age might be scored as perceiving accurately, while children giving rarer, but more adult-like forms might not be penalized, the following criteria determined F+:

   a. Responses occurring with high frequency among each group of children were scored F+. Hertz, in scoring F+ for a group of 300 adolescents, considered all forms with a frequency of 13 or more to be good form. In the present study, forms given by more than 1/20 of the group were considered F+. Forms which received a low frequency but which belonged to a similar class were scored as that class was scored.

   b. Forms which are usually scored F+ for adults were scored F+ when given by the children. Hertz's *Frequency Tables* were used to determine adult F+.

   c. Forms of low frequency, and not included in Hertz's tables were classed as "better" or "poorer" than other responses scored F+. Classification was made by at least two and often three judges during

TABLE 4. NORMAL DETAILS

		Age in years	
Card	2–3½	4–6	7–10
I	Upper center detail, "hands"	Upper center "hands"	Upper center "hands"
	Small top center "bumps"		Small top center "bumps"
	Center figure, "Woman's body"	Center figure, "body"	Center figure, "body"
			One whole side
	Any one white space		One top "wing" only
II	One side black alone	One side black alone	One side black alone
	Top reds	Top reds	Top reds
		Lower red	Lower red
			(Whole white center)
III	One man		One man
	Center red	Center red	Center red
	Top reds	Top reds	Top reds
		Lower center blacks	Lower center blacks "Person's leg"
IV	"Boot" figure (one or both)	"Boot" figure	"Boot" figure
	Top corner projections, "arms"	Top corner "arms"	Top corner "arms"
	"Stump" figure, lower center	Lower center "stump"	Lower center "stump"
			Top center "flower"
V	Center figure, "rabbit"	Center "rabbit"	Center "rabbit"
	Lower center projections, "feet"	Lower center "feet"	Lower center "feet"
	Top center projections		Top center projections
			Side projection, "alligator head"
VI	Top projection, including "wings"	Top including "wings"	Top including "wings"
	Center column, top to bottom	Center column, top to bottom	Center column, top to bottom
		Lower, larger part of blot	Lower, larger part of blot
			Top "wings" only
VII	Light gray center bottom "house"	Center bottom "house"	Center bottom "house"
	Top tier	Top tier	Top tier
	Top plus center tiers	Top plus center tiers	Top plus center tiers
	Bottom tiers	Bottom tiers	Bottom tiers
			Center tier
VIII	Side "animals"	Side "animals"	Side "animals"
	Top gray section		Top gray section
		Gray *plus* blue sections	Gray *plus* blue sections
	Top blue section	Top blue section	Top blue section
			Pink section only
	Pink *plus* orange sections	Pink plus orange	Pink plus orange
			White center "ribs"

TABLE 4. NORMAL DETAILS (*Continued*)

Card	2–3½	Age in years 4–6	7–10
IX	Orange section	Orange section	Orange section
	Pink section	Pink section	Pink section
	Green section	Green section	Green section
		Green center column	Green center column
			White (light blue) center
X	Side blues	Side blues	Side blues
	Pink or pinks	Pink or pinks	Pink or pinks
	Whole lower green	Whole lower green	Whole lower green
	Whole top gray	Whole top gray	Whole top gray
		"Face" part of top gray	
	Side gray-browns	Side gray-browns	Side gray-browns
	Center orange "seeds"		Center orange "seeds"
			Center yellow "dog"
			Top green

the scoring of the entire record, the latter judges checking the scoring of the first. Occasionally the score F± was used, allowing more confidence in scoring certain mediocre forms, or forms given rather vaguely by the child which yet seemed better than F−.*

As it turned out, the majority of forms could be scored from our own list or from Hertz's. Of the remaining forms, most were quite clearly F+ or F−. There was very high agreement between the judges in the more subjective scoring.

3. *P*: Averaging the eightieth percentile values for the test cards, Hertz arrived at a criterion of 50 responses from her group of 300 for a response to be scored P. This is the one-in-six criterion used in most studies which we ourselves follow. All forms given by one child in six were scored P.

Because these particular forms which constitute D, F+, and P in our scoring are an optimum weighting for the particular sample we used, we would expect that the mean values for D, F+, and P would be slightly less in any similar sample, using the forms determined for this group. For this reason, a cross-validating study would be helpful and desirable. In a study using a similar sample of children, and the *same lists* of D, F+, and P, mean values should be slightly less, but age trends should remain the same.

Tables 4, 5, and 6 present our findings as to normal details, good form, and popular responses.

---

* When F± is used, F+% is considered to equal $\dfrac{F+ \ +\frac{1}{2}F\pm}{\text{Total } F}$

TABLE 5. LIST OF F+ RESPONSES DETERMINED STATISTICALLY

Card	Age in years		
	2–3½	*4–6*	*7–10*
I	(W) Dog		
	Bird	(W) Bird	(W) Bird
		Bat	Bat
		Butterfly	Butterfly
		Tree	
	Tree		
	Face, mask, pumpkin	Face, mask, pumpkin	Face, mask, pumpkin
		Map	
		Leaf, leaves	
		House, building (whites as windows)	
			2 people and a third in center
			(Center) Person
II	(W) Tree		
	Church, house		
	Elephants		
	Whole animal face, front view (doggie, kitty)	(W or WS) Whole animal face, front view, with top reds as ears or eyes	
		(W) 2 animals (bears, monkeys) with top reds as heads	
		(W or D) 2 animals (dogs, bears, elephants) with or without top reds as hats	(W) 2 animals, especially dogs, bears, elephants
		(W) 2 people (witches, clowns)	(W) 2 people
		Butterfly	Butterfly
		(One side) Animal as above	(One side) Animal as above
		(Top reds) Hats	(Top reds) Fire
		Socks, feet	(Bottom red) Fire
			Blood

TABLE 5. LIST OF F+ RESPONSES DETERMINED STATISTICALLY (*Continued*)

Card	2–3½	4–6	7–10
III	(W) Birds, ducks	(W) Birds, ducks	(W) Birds, ducks
	Monkeys	Monkeys	Monkeys
		Four-legged animals (esp. sheep, horses)	People
	Man or men	People	Skeletons
			(W or WS) Face, front view
	(Middle red) Bow tie or ribbon	(Middle red) Bow tie or ribbon	(Middle red) Bow tie or ribbon
	Butterfly	Butterfly	Butterfly
IV	(W) Tree	(W) Tree	(W) Animal
	Animal: dog, wolf, fox	Animal: head at top. Dog, bear, wolf	
		Animal: head at stump. Dog, wolf, bull	
	Man	Person, giant, clown, scarecrow, etc.	Person, clown, scarecrow, giant (with club)
			Animal skin
			Bat
	(Boot figure) Feet, legs	(Boot figure) Feet, legs	(Boot figure) Boots, feet
			(Stump) Animal's head
V	(W) Tree		
	Dog		
	Fly, bug, bee	(W) Fly, bug, bee	(W) Bird
	Bird	Bird	Butterfly
	Butterfly	Butterfly	Bat
		Bat	

VI (W) Tree

Butterfly	(W) Butterfly	
Fly, bug, bee, mosquito	Fly, bug, bee, mosquito	
Cat, Kitty	Animal, head at top: cat, dog, wolf	(W) Animal
		Animal skin
		Bird on something
(Top projection) Butterfly, fly	(Top projection) Butterfly, fly	(Top projection) Some kind of insect
		Bird

VII

(W) Smoke, clouds	(W) Smoke, clouds	(W) Smoke, clouds
	2 rabbits or dogs on something	2 rabbits or dogs on something
(Top section or top two sections)	(Top section or top two sections) Rabbits or dogs	(Top section or top two sections) Rabbits or dogs
Rabbits or dogs		
(Light gray bottom) House, church	(Light gray bottom) House, church	(Light gray bottom) House, church
		(Top sections) Heads of people
		(Middle sections) Elephants
		(Bottom sections together) Butterfly

VIII (W) Tree

Flower	(W) Flower, flowers	(W) Animals climbing something
Animals climbing something	Animals climbing something	
	Boat, sailboat	
(Side animals) Bear, lion, elephant	(Side animals) Bear, lion, mice, dogs, "animals"	(Side animals) Some animals, esp. bears
(Gray top) Tree	(Gray, plus blue) Tree, Christmas tree	(Gray, alone or combined) Tree
	(Pink plus orange) Fire	(Pink plus orange) Fire
	Butterfly	Butterfly
		Rocks
		(Center white) Ribs, bones

TABLE 5. LIST OF F+ RESPONSES DETERMINED STATISTICALLY (*Continued*)

Card	Age in years		
	2-3½	4-6	7-10
IX	(W) Tree	(W) Tree, trees (V∧), Flower, flowers (V∧), Butterfly	(Middle green) Tree
	(Middle green) Tree	(Pink) Flower, blossom (Orange) People, clown, witches	(Orange) People, witches Deer, reindeer
X	(W) Flower	(W) Flowers, flower, colored leaves Tree with flowers, with colored leaves Tree (no color implied) "Many animals," "Many insects" of diff. kinds	(W) Flowers
			Design Ocean scene, or sea things
	(Top gray) Tree	(Top gray) Tree	(Top gray) Bugs
	(Green lower) Bunny	(Green lower, face part) Rabbit face	(Green lower, face part) Rabbit face
		(Side blues) Spider, crab (Tube part of top gray) Stick	(Side blues) Spider, crab (Lower green, all) Rabbit's head Worms
			(Side gray) Deer (Center yellow) Dogs

TABLE 6. LIST OF POPULAR FORMS

	Age in years		
Card	2–3½	4–6	7–10
I	Tree	Bird, butterfly, bat..........Bird, butterfly, bat Face, mask, pumpkin........Face, mask, pumpkin	
II	Two animals: bears...... Kitties, doggies, etc.	Two animals: dogs, bears.....Two animals Elephants	
III	Two animals............ Bow, ribbon, tie........	Two four-legged animals Bow, ribbon, tie.............Bow, ribbon, tie Two people.................Two people	
IV	Tree Animal.................	Animal (head at top)........Animal Person, giant...............Person, giant	
V	Bird, butterfly..........	Bird, butterfly, bat.........Butterfly, bat	
VI	Tree	—	—
VII	Dog, rabbit.............	Dogs, rabbits..............Dogs, rabbits	
VIII	Animal.................	Animals: bears, lions, mice, dogs	Animals, static or in action
IX	—	—	—
X	—	Side blues: spider, crab......Side blues: spider, crab W: tree with flowers or colored leaves (color *must* be men- tioned)	

The Scoring Categories

This section lists the scores used in the present study, with a description of each score.

R   Total number of scorable responses.

W_0   Gross, global response to the whole card, where content is inherently vague or formless and subparts are not distinguished. *Also,* any perseverated W response. (See Chapter 5 for fuller descriptions of W levels.)

W_1   Response to the whole blot as a single figure.

W_2   Response to the whole blot, differentiated into two major portions.

W_3   Response to the whole blot, differentiated into three or more distinct portions which are interrelated.

W_x   Response to the whole blot which cannot be classified as W_0, W_1, W_2, or W_3.

WS   Response to the whole blot in which the white spaces play a role. WS are subscripted WS_1, etc., like W.

$\not W$ "Cut-off" whole response: the intent is to include the whole blot but a small portion is omitted. $\not W$ are subscripted $\not W_1$, etc., like W.

D   Response to a normal detail, scored according to the details listed in Table 4.

Dd   Response to a rarely selected detail. Any response which is to a detail of the blot not listed in Table 4 is a Dd.

Do   Response to an 'oligophrenic' detail. Only a part of a body is seen where most normal children see whole bodies. Relative frequencies of perception of whole and parts of bodies were determined in this study from the frequency distributions of all responses.

S   Response to white space within or adjacent to the blot.

W%   Total number of whole responses (W+WS+$\not W$) divided by R.

D%   D divided by R.

Dd%   Total Dd (Dd+Do+S) divided by R.

F   Responses in which form is the sole determinant of the interpretation. The subject responds to the shape alone of the blot.

F+,   Quality and accuracy of form perception. Scored primarily from statis-
F±,   tically determined lists. The following summarizes our scoring proce-
F—   dures for F+:

     a) See list of statistically determined F+ for children, in this study. If the response, or a response essentially the same, is found for any age, it is F+.

     b) See Hertz's *Frequency Tables to Be Used in Scoring*. If the response occurs there as F+, it is so scored.

     c) If not found in either list, judge the response as *more* or *less* accurate than other responses scored F+. (If convenient, it is desirable to have several judges make this decision.)

     d) In case of borderline, mediocre, or vague forms, which seem clearly better than F—, the score F± may be given.

F%   Total F divided by R.

F+%   (F+ +½F±) divided by total F.

M   Human figures seen in movement, or animals (bears, monkeys) in human activity. Theoretically, the movement is actually felt and experienced by the subject. Because of the difficulty of eliciting introspective reports from children, we have had to rely on initial, spontaneous responses for scoring M. We have followed Rorschach's practice of scoring the human figures in III as M, whether or not movement is described, so long as the blot is described as specifically human figures.

FM   Response determined by animal movement. The animal perceived is described as being in action.

m   Response indicating inanimate objects in movement. The movement is generally brought about by an outside force.

F(C)   Response defined or differentiated by shading values. Form and light-dark values both play a role in determining the response; shading may be primary or secondary. Because of the infrequency of shading responses from children, all the following types of shading are included in the single category:

     a) Fine differentiation. Responses determined by well-differentiated lines and shading in the black-gray areas.

     b) Surface shading. Shading giving texture to the response.

     c) Vista. Nuances of shading giving perspective and depth.

     d) Non-dysphoric diffusion, with some element of form.

ClobF,*   Response based on a diffuse impression of the blot, stemming from its
FClob   darkness. Unpleasant contents, dark, diffuse, gruesome, dismal, threat-

---

* Clob is pronounced Clōb—from the French *clair-obscur*. We have used this term since no commonly used American term is quite equivalent.

ening. Darkness or blackness is the primary quality. Includes use of black as color. (Form may be primary or secondary.)

FC Form-color response. Response is determined primarily by the form, with color incorporated in the response. The response implies an object of definite shape.

CF Color-form response. Response is determined primarily by the color, but some form is present. Generally the response implies an object of rather indefinite shape, or one which can take many forms—e.g.,"Flowers" on X.

C Pure color response. Response determined by the color alone of the blot, with no reference to the form.

Cn Colors merely named, as a response, but with no attempt at interpretation. Not included in ΣC.

ΣC Sum C, or weighted C score. Determined by adding ½ total FC + total CF + 1½ total C.

A, Ad Animal responses. Content of response is an animal form, either the whole animal, A, or part of an animal, Ad.

H, Hd A human form, either whole, H, or part of a human, Hd.

( ) Imaginary forms are enclosed in parentheses. I.e. a dragon would be (A), a witch (H).

P Popular responses, those given by one out of every six children. Scored according to the lists of populars for each age, presented in Table 6.

CHAPTER FOUR

Statistical Analysis

A number of different statistical methods have been used to describe the frequency of occurrence of the variables at different age levels. This chapter presents the main comprehensive tables, covering each of the important variables at each age, and also describes an estimation of scorer reliability.

Score Frequencies

Mean scores for the important variables at each age are presented in a master table, Table 7. Because only a few children make use of some of the determinants, mean values are not always representative of the whole group. Supplementary statistics are therefore included. Table 8 lists for each determinant the percentage of children who use the determinant one or more times. An indication of the dispersion of scores, as well as the central tendency at each age, is presented in Table 9, which gives the median, the twenty-fifth and seventy-fifth percentiles, and the range of scores for the major variables at each age. The data in this table are also presented in graphic form in Figures 1 to 5, which show the middle 50 per cent of scores as a gray band, with the median drawn inside and the total range at each age drawn outside the band. Table 9 and Figures 1 to 5 should be of clinical value, showing as they do the delimiting values for a population of normal children.

Scorer Reliability

Though all the protocols used in this study were scored cooperatively, one scorer checking another, we felt it desirable to obtain some estimate of the consistency with which workers could score the same records when working independently. For this purpose two of the authors* exchanged a group of 40 records of 6- and 7-year-old children which had been collected independently, in addition to the records included in this study. Each

---

* L. B. Ames and R. N. Walker.

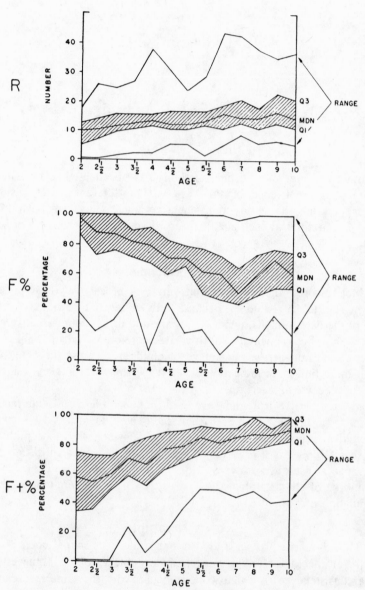

FIG. 1.   Median, Quartiles, and Range for R, F%, and F+%.

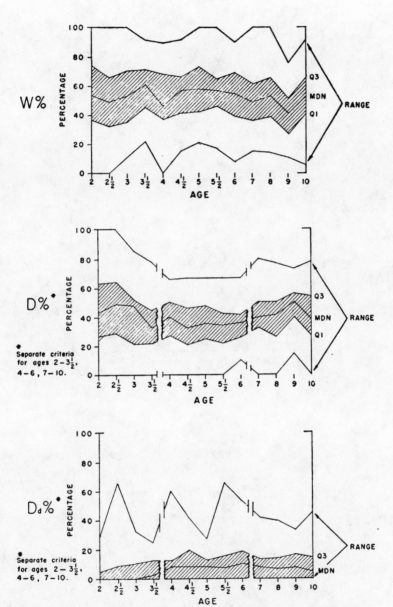

FIG. 2.   Median, Quartiles, and Range for W%, D%, and Dd%.

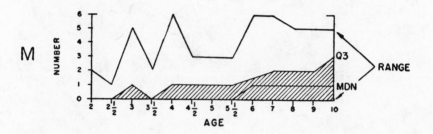

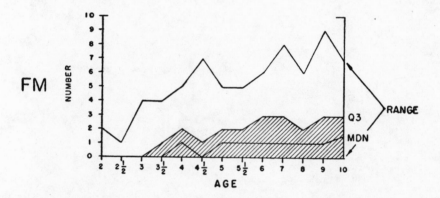

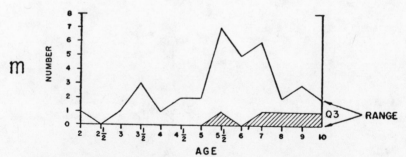

FIG. 3.   Median, Quartiles, and Range for M, FM, and m.

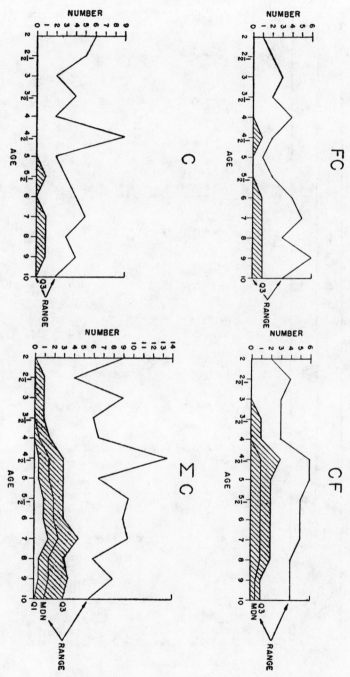

FIG. 4.   Median, Quartiles, and Range for FC, CF, C and ΣC.

TABLE 7. MASTER TABLE

MEAN SCORES FOR THE MAJOR VARIABLES AT EACH AGE

Variable	Age in years												
	2	2½	3	3½	4	4½	5	5½	6	7	8	9	10
R	9.6	10.8	12.9	13.5	14.7	14.2	13.9	13.6	15.8	18.3	15.9	18.6	16.3
Refusals	2.4	1.8	.8	.3	1.1	.6	.6	.7	.5	.3	.5	.5	.6
W%	53%	50%	55%	60%	52%	56%	58%	55%	51%	51%	55%	42%	52%
D%	42%	44%	39%	34%	38%	33%	34%	33%	34%	41%	37%	48%	40%
Dd%	4%	6%	6%	6%	10%	11%	8%	12%	15%	8%	7%	9%	8%
M	.1	.1	.2	.3	.5	.3	.6	.4	1.0	1.4	1.3	1.4	1.7
FM	.1	.1	.3	.7	1.2	.7	1.1	1.3	1.6	1.9	1.5	1.6	1.7
m	.1	.1	.1	.2	.2	.1	.2	.5	.4	.8	.5	.5	.4
FC	.1	.1	.3	.3	.2	.3	.2	.2	.4	.7	.5	.7	.5
CF	.1	.5	.4	.6	.6	1.3	1.2	1.4	1.5	1.3	.9	.7	.8
C	.4	.2	.1	.3	.2	.3	.2	.5	.3	.8	.4	.7	.3
ΣC	.7	.9	.8	1.1	1.0	1.9	1.6	2.3	2.2	2.9	1.8	2.1	1.5
Cn	.1	.5	.4	.2	.1	.1	.0	.1	.2	.0	.0	.0	.0
F(C)	.2	.3	.6	.4	.5	.6	.4	.6	.7	1.1	.9	.8	.6
FClob+ClobF	.1	.2	.1	.1	.1	.2	.2	.5	.3	.5	.2	.2	.1
A%	50%	41%	47%	48%	56%	44%	44%	41%	48%	42%	45%	48%	49%
H%	3%	4%	7%	10%	9%	8%	9%	11%	11%	14%	17%	16%	16%
F%	90%	83%	84%	80%	75%	72%	70%	62%	60%	52%	58%	67%	63%
F+%	54%	54%	60%	67%	67%	75%	78%	84%	81%	82%	87%	84%	89%
P	1.0	1.5	1.9	2.1	2.3	2.6	3.0	3.0	3.6	3.7	3.7	3.9	3.8
P%	10%	13%	15%	15%	15%	19%	22%	25%	23%	27%	24%	22%	25%

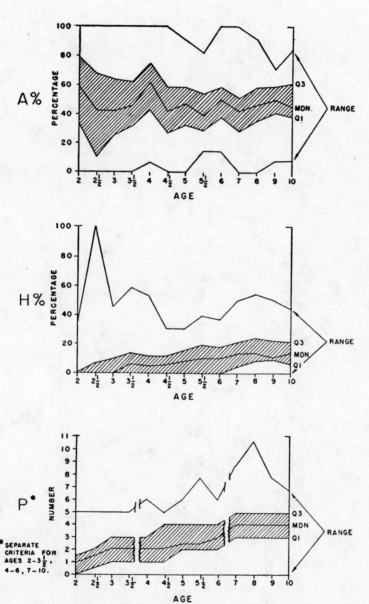

FIG. 5. Median, Quartiles, and Range for A%, H%, and P.

TABLE 8. PERCENTAGE OF CHILDREN USING CHIEF DETERMINANTS ONE OR MORE TIMES

	2		2½		3		3½		4		4½		5		5½		6		7		8		9		10	
	G	B	G	B	G	B	G	B	G	B	G	B	G	B	G	B	G	B	G	B	G	B	G	B	G	B
M	11	4	4	12	12	8	28	24	20	24	16	32	32	40	20	36	56	60	56	80	52	72	52	80	60	80
FM	11	4	20	4	8	24	24	64	52	64	20	40	44	56	60	68	64	68	68	80	72	64	52	72	64	88
m	5	4	8	4	12	0	12	20	16	12	12	12	12	12	28	24	20	28	28	48	24	36	20	32	16	48
FC	11	4	8	8	28	0	12	12	0	28	16	32	20	12	20	20	32	28	44	32	44	32	56	28	16	48
CF	11	9	20	20	24	16	40	32	32	40	64	60	64	60	60	80	76	72	56	76	52	48	48	52	40	60
C	11	13	16	8	12	8	8	20	12	12	20	16	8	32	32	40	12	20	28	52	32	20	32	24	20	20
F(C)	4	24	8	20	36	32	28	36	32	20	36	28	32	32	44	44	32	48	52	52	40	56	48	36	20	60
FClob	4	0	0	0	0	4	4	4	8	12	12	12	8	0	28	16	4	24	24	26	24	8	16	16	12	12
ClobF	4	0	4	8	8	8	4	0	0	0	4	4	8	12	8	32	8	16	4	28	8	4	8	0	0	0

Age in years

TABLE 9.   PERCENTILES FOR MAJOR VARIABLES
MEDIAN, QUARTILES, AND RANGE FOR EACH AGE
(Boys and girls combined)

Variable	Percentile	Age in years												
		2	2½	3	3½	4	4½	5	5½	6	7	8	9	10
R	99	18	26	25	27	38	31	24	29	44	43	38	35	37
	75	13	14.5	16	16	16	17	17	17	19	21	18	23	21
	50	10	10.5	12	13	14	13	13	14	16	15	15	17	15
	25	5.5	7.5	10	11	12	11	11	12	11	13	11	13	11
	1	1	1	2	3	3	6	6	2	5	9	6	7	6
W%	99	100	100	100	91	90	91	100	100	90	100	100	77	91
	75	74	66	70	72	69	67	75	65	70	62	67	52	66
	50	54	49	53	61	47	57	58	57	56	49	54	41	53
	25	37	33	36	47	38	42	43	47	40	37	40	28	41
	1	0	0	12	21	0	16	20	17	8	15	14	11	5
D%	99	100	100	86	78	65	67	67	67	67	80	77	73	78
	75	63	64	53	45	50	46	48	43	42	50	50	57	54
	50	43	49	48	33	40	33	36	34	36	40	41	50	39
	25	26	29	21	22	27	21	25	22	25	33	26	40	28
	1	0	0	0	0	0	0	0	0	10	0	0	16	0
Dd%	99	31	66	33	25	55	42	28	66	54	41	40	34	45
	75	5	8	10	12	12	19	12	15	18	13	13	16	14
	50	0	0	0	3	8	8	8	7	9	7	6	7	4
	25	0	0	0	0	0	0	0	0	0	0	0	0	0
	1	0	0	0	0	0	0	0	0	0	0	0	0	0
F%	99	100	100	100	100	100	100	100	100	100	97	100	100	100
	75	100	100	100	90	92	84	80	78	73	65	74	78	76
	50	98	89	88	82	80	71	72	62	61	48	60	71	61
	25	87	72	76	71	67	60	65	47	43	40	46	52	52
	1	33	20	28	45	7	40	20	23	6	18	16	33	20

TABLE 9. PERCENTILES FOR MAJOR VARIABLES (*Continued*)

Age in years

Variable	Percentile	2	2½	3	3½	4	4½	5	5½	6	7	8	9	10
F+%	99	100	100	100	100	100	100	100	100	100	100	100	100	100
	75	75	73	73	81	85	89	90	93	92	92	100	92	100
	50	59	55	61	72	68	79	80	86	82	86	88	88	92
	25	36	37	50	60	53	65	70	75	75	78	78	81	84
	1	0	0	0	25	8	20	37	50	50	45	50	41	43
M	99	2	1	5	2	6	3	3	3	6	6	5	5	5
	75	0	0	0	1	0	1	1	1	1½	2	2	2	3
	50	0	0	0	0	0	0	0	0	1	1	1	1	1
	25	0	0	0	0	0	0	0	0	0	0	0	0	0
	1	0	0	0	0	0	0	0	0	0	0	0	0	0
FM	99	2	1	4	4	5	7	5	5	6	8	6	9	7
	75	0	0	0	1	2	1	2	2	3	3	2	3	3
	50	0	0	0	0	1	0	1	1	1	1	1	1	1½
	25	0	0	0	0	0	0	0	0	0	0	0	0	0
	1	0	0	0	0	0	0	0	0	0	0	0	0	0
m	99	1	0	1	3	1	2	1	2	0	6	2	3	2
	75	0	0	0	0	0	0	0	0	0	1	1	1	1
	50	0	0	0	0	0	0	0	0	0	0	0	0	0
	25	0	0	0	0	0	0	0	0	0	0	0	0	0
	1	0	0	0	0	0	0	0	0	0	0	0	0	0
FC	99	1	2	3	2	4	2	1	2	4	5	3	6	3
	75	0	0	0	0	0	1	0	0	1	1	1	1	1
	50	0	0	0	0	0	0	0	0	0	0	0	0	0
	25	0	0	0	0	0	0	0	0	0	0	0	0	0
	1	0	0	0	0	0	0	0	0	0	0	0	0	0
CF	99	2	4	3	3	3	6	6	5	5	5	4	4	4
	75	0	0	0	1	1	3	2	2	2	2	2	1	1
	50	0	0	0	0	0	1	1	1	1	1	1	½	½
	25	0	0	0	0	0	0	0	0	0	0	0	0	0
	1	0	0	0	0	0	0	0	0	0	0	0	0	0

C	99	2	4	3	5	4	3	2	9	2	4	2	5	6
	75	0	1	1	1	0	1	0	0	0	0	0	0	0
	50	0	0	0	0	0	0	0	0	0	0	0	0	0
	25	0	0	0	0	0	0	0	0	0	0	0	0	0
	1	0	0	0	0	0	0	0	0	0	0	0	0	0
ΣC	99	5½	8	6	9½	9	9½	6½	13½	6½	6	9	4	9
	75	3	3½	3	4½	3	3	3	3	1½	1	1	1	0
	50	1	1½	1½	2½	2	2	1½	1½	¼	0	0	0	0
	25	0	¼	¼	1½	1	1	¼	¼	0	0	0	0	0
	1	0	0	0	0	0	0	0	0	0	0	0	0	0
F (C)	99	4	4	5	8	5	4	2	5	4	3	4	4	5
	75	1	1	1	1.5	1	1	1	1	1	1	1	0	0
	50	0	0	0	0	0	0	0	0	0	0	0	0	0
FClob + ClobF	99	1	3	3	5	3	2	2	2	1	1	2	3	3
	75	0	0	0	1	1	1	0	0	0	0	0	0	0
	50	0	0	0	0	0	0	0	0	0	0	0	0	0
A%	99	84	71	92	100	100	82	91	100	100	100	100	100	100
	75	60	58	58	51	58	53	58	58	74	61	63	66	79
	50	45	50	46	42	50	39	47	42	61	45	41	41	60
	25	39	40	35	28	37	28	32	27	43	31	24	9	32
	1	8	8	0	0	15	14	0	0	0	7	0	0	0
H%	99	45	50	54	50	37	39	31	30	54	58	45	100	37
	75	21	22	24	21	18	20	16	12	12	15	9	7	0
	50	13	11	15	13	10	11	9	6	5	7	0	0	0
	25	7	10	9	5	0	0	0	0	0	0	0	0	0
	1	0	0	0	0	0	0	0	0	0	0	0	0	0
P	99	7	8	11	9	6	8	6	5	6	5	5	5	5
	75	5	5	5	5	4	4	4	4	3	3	3	2	1.5
	50	4	4	4	4	3.5	3	3	2	2	2	2	1.5	1
	25	3	3	3	3	2	2	2	1	1	1	1	.5	0
	1	0	0	0	0	0	0	0	0	0	0	0	0	0

Child Rorschach Responses

scored all records independently. The narrow age range was chosen to avoid spuriously high correlations, and the 6- to 7-year period, it was felt, was as difficult an age level to score as any, lacking the simplicity of the preschool level and the more clear expressive ability of the later childhood period. Pearson product-moment correlations between the scoring summaries obtained by the two workers for each child are given in Table 10.

TABLE 10. SCORER RELIABILITY
CORRELATIONS BETWEEN INDEPENDENT SCORINGS
OF 40 RECORDS AT AGES 6 AND 7

Variable	Correlation	Variable	Correlation
R	.98	FC	.83
		CF	.81
		C	.82
W	.93		
D	.92	ΣC	.92
Dd	.92		
		F (C)	.79
F%	.93		
F+%	.86	A	.99
		H	.97
M	.96	P	.96
FM	.91		
m	.81		
		Median r	.92

As the table shows, quite a high degree of agreement can be achieved using such a scoring system as has been used in this study. Certain variables are less reliably scored than others: minor movement, color, and shading in particular. This is partly because of a certain arbitrariness in separating FC from CF and CF from C scores, and partly because m and F(C) or color elements may occur in the same response, so that where one examiner would score movement with additional color, the other might score color with additional movement. Reliability of the F+%, considering its largely subjective determination, is quite high.

CHAPTER FIVE

Area

We consider a subject's area scores in an attempt to see what kind of *work* he did in taking the Rorschach: how did he construct his responses? To what extent did he let parts of the blot catch his eye seemingly at random, or let general, vague impressions of the blot determine his reactions, and to what extent did he actively shape his responses? How much did he take the blot apart and how much did he then reassemble it? Did he respond with single figures, whether actually choosing details or treating the whole blot as one big detail, or were his concepts articulated?

As a start in evaluating such questions, we analyzed records into the traditional scores of whole responses, "normal" or commonly seen details, rare details, and white space responses. Whole responses make up such a large part of young children's records and are themselves so varied that further classifications of W were made. Any scoring, however elaborate, can provide only a start for individual evaluation—a means of grouping together somewhat similar responses so that they can be examined more closely. Qualitative descriptions therefore supplement the more statistical presentation.

An overview of the proportions of W, D, and Dd (Dd+Do+S) responses in children's records is provided in Figure 6. While some age-to-age fluctuations and some slow overall trends appear (notably a very gradual decline in W%), the area proportions are most striking for their persistence around 50%W, 40%D, 10%Dd. This ratio contrasts with the classical "normal adult expectancy" of about 25%W, 65%D, and 10%Dd.

A more detailed analysis of area scores is given in Table 11, which presents mean number of responses of each variety for each age, along with mean percentages of total W, D, and Dd responses.

Before considering the varieties of area response, we should note the importance of differences in inquiry and scoring practices among Rorschach workers. Only divergence in aim and practice could account for the size of differences found in different studies of normal children. For example, Beck and his co-workers (Thetford, Molish, & Beck, 72) reported mean

TABLE 11.   MEAN NUMBER OF OCCURRENCES PER CHILD OF DIFFERENT AREA RESPONSES

Area	Age in years												
	2	2½	3	3½	4	4½	5	5½	6	7	8	9	10
W_0	2.8	2.2	1.8	1.8	1.7	1.7	1.7	1.7	1.0	1.3	1.1	.8	.7
W_1	2.1	2.4	3.2	3.9	3.3	4.1	3.7	3.7	4.3	3.9	4.0	3.3	4.0
W_2	.1	.7	.9	1.0	1.2	.7	1.0	.8	1.0	1.3	1.0	1.0	1.3
W_s	.1	.0	.1	.4	.6	.4	.7	.8	.7	.9	1.1	1.2	1.3
W_x	.0	.0	.2	.3	.6	.3	.3	.7	.6	.8	.8	.8	.6
All W	5.1	5.3	6.2	7.4	7.4	7.2	7.5	7.7	7.6	8.3	8.0	7.1	7.9
D	4.0	4.9	5.8	4.8	5.9	5.1	5.1	4.7	5.7	7.9	6.6	9.4	7.0
Dd	.3	.3	.3	.4	1.2	1.2	.8	1.1	1.6	1.6	.6	1.1	.9
S	.2	.1	.4	.1	.1	.4	.4	.6	.5	.3	.3	.3	.3
Do	.1	.2	.2	.4	.5	.2	.1	.2	.4	.4	.4	.6	.3
All Dd	.5	.6	.9	.9	1.8	1.8	1.2	1.9	2.5	2.2	1.3	2.1	1.6
W%	53	50	55	60	52	56	58	55	51	51	55	42	52
D%	42	44	39	34	38	33	34	33	34	41	37	48	40
Dd%	4	6	6	6	10	11	8	12	15	8	7	9	8

area scores of 13%W, 76%D, 13%Dd for normal children aged 6 to 9 years —very different from our means of 50%W, 40%D, 10%Dd for those ages. In inquiring for whole responses we have tried to determine the child's general intention, rather than pushing inquiry too far concerning inclusion or rejection of particular parts of the blot. Too searching an inquiry, we believe, distorts the child's original intent and introduces a spurious precision into area choice. In scoring, we group "cut-off wholes" (Klopfer) with total W and we do not score all sub-parts separately when a child

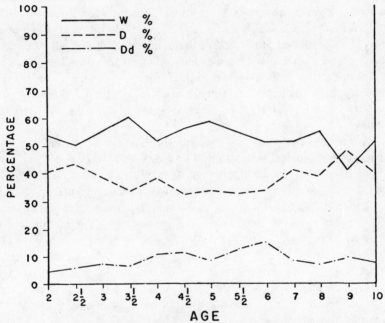

Fig. 6.   Mean Values for W%, D%, and Dd%.

clearly intends that they go together to form a total concept. For Beck it is evidently essential that the "meaning" of W be preserved: "The perception of whole responses involves concept formation, the ability to form abstract relationships" (Thetford, Molish, & Beck, 72, p. 62). It would follow naturally that he would pursue detailed inquiry and maintain strict scoring standards for W. Such differences in practice, for which Beck and we probably represent the extreme poles, need not lead to discrepancies in interpretation if both groups could look at the *actual responses* of the children, but they would certainly lead to discrepancies if scoring alone were considered. Our norms (and anyone else's) will make sense only for records obtained and scored in the same way the norms were collected.

Whole (W) Responses

Traditionally, the W response has been taken as an index of the individual's intelligence, his capacity for abstract thinking, his ability to order and organize his thoughts. The finding that throughout childhood the proportion of W responses is much higher than in adulthood and that it is at its very highest in the preschool period calls for at least qualification of such interpretation. Clearly, some different varieties of W must be involved.

Rorschach (66) described several kinds of W, including simple, immediate W, confabulated W, contaminated W, successive-combinatory and spontaneous-combinatory W, and confabulatory-combined W. Following Rorschach and Loosli-Usteri (54), in our first edition of this book we scored DW for all except the first of these, including in DW all W responses put together from details. This was misleading to some readers, since most American scoring systems reserved DW for confabulated wholes, which frequently have pathological significance. In addition, it failed to discriminate adequately the quite different kinds of thinking that led to W responses.

A variety of scoring schemes has been used for differentiating W. Rapaport (65), for example, uses W+, Wo, Wv, W−, DW, etc., and other authors have used similar groupings, formally or qualitatively. We have adopted a scheme that seems simple but useful, based primarily on degree of differentiation of the W: how many major portions the blot is broken into before it is reassembled. Its starting point is W_1, a one-piece figure of definite form, such as the bat on V. At a level below this, W_0 are gross, unrefined percepts where the content is inherently vague: cloud, design. And at levels above W_1 are W_2 and W_3, where the blot is broken into two parts, or into three or more parts. A W_x category was used to cover the whole responses that did not fit appropriately into any of the other categories.

This scheme, developed first as a teaching device for evaluating responses of school-age children, met with some difficulties when first applied to preschool records. Two modifications take care of the difficulties: 1) perseverated W responses are scored W_0 from the point where they become perseverated, on the grounds that they accord only vague attention to the blot; 2) "odd combination" W responses—confabulated or contaminated W, fabulized combination, etc.—are all grouped with the W_x and are later discriminated qualitatively.

Although these W levels have already been described briefly in Chapter 3, they are presented in expanded form here, since they are not well known scores.

W₀   A gross, undefined, global response to the whole card, where the content is inherently vague, formless, or diffuse, and where sub-parts are not distinguished, or only incidentally so. *Examples:* mud, paint, clouds, design, big pile of sand, mountain, rock, map (if not further elaborated), insides (if vague, unspecified), pile of feathers, leaves (but not "a leaf"), flowers (but not "a flower").

Also, any W which is perseverated. Ordinarily a concept is considered perseverated on its third mention, and, if W, scored W₀ from there on. However, concepts of high specificity may be considered perseverated on their second mention (example: "a fractured moose"), and so also may responses perseverated throughout the entire record (example: if all ten blots are "doggie," from the second one on they are scored W₀).

W₁   ONE-piece figures which are definite objects. These are single, global forms, with sub-parts distinguishable (spontaneously or on request), but the whole thing is essentially *a* thing: a man, a bat, a face, etc. "A man: he has arms, legs, hat," etc., would still be W₁: all the details are considered as "accessories" to the single basic figure.

W₂   The blot is differentiated into TWO major portions, then recombined. Usually it is split laterally into two sides: 2 elephants, 2 people clapping hands, lady seeing her reflection, etc. "Accessory" items may be included: "Two bears fighting—they have blood on their paws." Horizontal rather than vertical cleavage is also included here ("A man sitting on a stump," "Bee coming out of a flower," etc.)

W₃   The blot is differentiated into THREE OR MORE distinct portions and recombined. The pieces are definite in form; often two of them are duplicated. Examples: "Two bears climbing up a mountain," "Two men dancing around a woman," "Two women bending over pots," "Two rabbits on two rocks."

Wₓ   "The above scale cannot handle this W." This wastebasket category was included for the W that do not fit into the W₀-W₃ scale and that should not be forced into it. For example, it is used for "collection" W's—multiple details grouped only loosely into a W (most undersea scenes on Card X). Also includes responses in which a large area is at one level, often W₀, but another area is more defined (VII: "A tiny church steeple down here and all clouds around it."). Inherently vague forms described in detail, such as map responses elaborated with bays, peninsulas, etc., are included here.

Also, the "combination" responses of contamination, confabulation, fabulized combination, and their intermediate varieties, are grouped here.

(Note that WS and W̸ responses are also rated for W level—for example, most faces on Card I are WS₁; "Rocket ship shooting through clouds

Child Rorschach Responses

toward two red planets" is WS₃; "Bearskin, not counting this part" is W̸₁; "Two cannibal women bending over a pot" is W̸₃.

Note also that form level is not considered, except that W_0 is ordinarily F±. A W_1, for example, may be F+ or F−.)

The percentage of all W responses at each age level falling into each of the categories just described is presented in Table 12. Also in Table 12 is the percentage of responses falling in levels $W_2+W_3+W_x$ combined, the more complex levels. Table 13 gives the percentage of children using any

TABLE 12. PERCENTAGE OF ALL WHOLE RESPONSES
AT EACH W LEVEL FOR TOTAL SAMPLE
AND AT LEVELS 2+ 3 + X COMBINED FOR BOYS AND GIRLS

Age	Level of W						$W_2 + W_3 + W_x$		
	W_0	W_1	W_2	W_3	W_x	Total	B	G	All
2	55	40	3	1	1	100	2	8	5
2½	41	45	13	0	1	100	8	21	15
3	30	52	15	1	2	100	24	14	19
3½	26	53	11	6	4	100	26	18	22
4	24	46	17	8	5	100	33	27	30
4½	24	56	10	5	5	100	26	13	20
5	23	48	11	9	9	100	30	32	31
5½	22	48	10	10	10	100	31	28	30
6	13	57	13	9	8	100	29	30	30
7	17	47	15	11	10	100	38	35	36
8	13	50	13	14	10	100	37	38	37
9	12	46	14	17	11	100	49	35	42
10	9	50	16	16	8	100	38	44	40

of each type of W and also the percentage using two or more of each type of W. Following are the principal trends in W responses.

W_0. The W_0 response is essentially a young response. From making up more than half of all W given by two-year-olds, it declines to less than 10 per cent by ten years. Perseverated response as a source of W_0 drops rapidly from about two thirds of all W_0 at two years to a fifth of all W_0 by six years. Most children include W_0 responses in their records until about 7 years; thereafter a minority do, and few include more than a single W_0.

After the preschool period, W_0 represent essentially regressive responses. We suggested, in the revision of our *Adolescent Rorschach Responses* (12), that one W_0 or so may be absorbable in the record of an older child or adolescent. A subject may even use such regression of perception constructively, "in the service of the ego," if the rest of the record is strong and creative, indulging in some form-free, sensuous, impression-istic responses. But several W_0 in older children and adolescents more often indicate problems of loss of form, de-differentiation of the personality, passivity of coping under stress, more serious regressions.

W_1. W_1 is the most common sort of Rorschach W response; in effect, it treats the whole card as one big detail. From age three on, it makes up very close to half of all W responses and nearly all subjects give such responses.

Giving W_1 is a quite adequate way for a child to make up much of his record (provided the form level is adequate), though it alone is not an indicator of high intelligence or conceptualizing ability. In view of the atten-

TABLE 13. PERCENTAGE OF CHILDREN USING ONE OR MORE
OR TWO OR MORE OF EACH TYPE OF W RESPONSE

Age	W_0		W_1		W_2		W_3		W_4	
	1+	2+	1+	2+	1+	2+	1+	2+	1+	2+
2	78	60	92	68	20	2	4	0	2	0
2½	60	44	84	60	40	18	0	0	12	0
3	78	44	96	90	48	26	4	2	10	2
3½	74	46	100	92	62	24	38	6	18	4
4	60	34	98	88	76	30	40	12	24	6
4½	70	56	98	84	52	20	24	10	22	10
5	60	40	92	90	58	30	48	16	46	16
5½	70	50	96	88	48	20	52	12	40	18
6	54	22	98	94	56	26	48	18	32	16
7	52	30	98	86	68	42	54	26	50	20
8	48	24	98	88	56	32	66	30	50	20
9	40	18	94	88	66	26	54	34	44	22
10	40	18	98	94	68	42	62	36	48	12

tion that has been given to exotic kinds of W in early childhood, it is important to recognize that about half of all children's W are simple, gar-den variety W_1.

W_2. For many adults, the Rorschach blots break easily into their two mirrored halves and these provide a source of many W responses. The same is true for children, and at a surprisingly early age. From very little occurrence at two years, the increase in use of W_2 is very rapid in the pre-school period. For our total sample, two to ten years, 55 per cent of sub-jects use W_2 responses; this proportion is already exceeded by 3½ year olds.

To be able to conceive of the blot as divided and yet still whole seems to represent a real step in intellectual development. It is not as big a step as constructing the more complex W_3, but it shows important beginnings of the analysis-synthesis process.

W_3. Just discriminating one more main part in a whole response turns a W_2 into a W_3. This seemingly small step turns out to be quite a big one;

W$_3$ appear much later than W$_2$. Virtually no W$_3$ are produced before 3½ years, and not until children are well out of the preschool period do a majority produce at least one W$_3$. Only by 7 years can this complex form of W be considered an expectable sort of response.

The W$_3$ response is an indication that the individual has done some real intellectual work in its construction. The younger the child giving it and the more it varies from the most "blot-given" W$_3$ (people bending over pots, bears climbing a mountain) and the more W$_3$ he gives, the more intellectual power it portrays. The presence of even just one really well seen W$_3$ in a child's record suggests good thinking potential, however little it may appear in everyday use.

W$_x$. The W$_x$ score has no meaning in itself; it is a signal that the response so scored needs closer qualitative attention. Such scores are found infrequently in the early preschool period. From about 4 through 5½ years they increase considerably, and it is during this period that all the "odd combination" responses occur most—contaminations, confabulations, fabulized combinations, and the like. Even in the 4 to 5½ period these are not common, but they merit some comments and examples.

Confabulations—overgeneralizations from a detail to the whole—are actually the most difficult to detect in children, since it is often not possible to tell whether the difficulty lies in the child's percept or in his limited ability to explain or justify it. For example, VI: "A cat, because it has these little whiskers," is a classic DW verbalization, but cat is a near-popular percept for VI and its whiskers are a salient detail for many children. In *any* Rorschach response, a few particular parts suggest the percept and not all details can be appropriate—it is an inkblot, not a photograph. We consider a response confabulated only when it is clearly F—.

Contaminated responses are more unambiguous, though never common. Clear instances occurred between 3 and 5 years. For example—3G, IV: "That's a furniture house, a furniture log house"; 3B, IV: "Old man on a barber pipe, a cow barber pipe"; 5G, V: "That's another map—a butterfly map"; 5B, VIII: "Inside of a bear." The last example is more arguable, a good instance of the more subtle "slippage" of thinking characteristic of older children's contaminations.

Fabulized combinations are the most common of these "odd combination" responses, and the most defensible in a sense—V: "A bat with alligator heads on its wings" *does* look like a bat with alligator heads on its wings. With older children, such responses often represent a pseudo-abdication of responsibility for actions—"I'm just reporting what I see"; with younger children more of a cognitive problem of concept separation is probably involved. The peak ages for these responses are clearly 4½ and 5 years. Besides such classic responses as "A bridge with wings," "Donkeys standing on a butterfly," are many responses where human-like features are given to other figures: "A tree—the branches, the arms, the foots"; "A board—its arms and eyes"; "Leaf—leaf's nose, leaf's mouth." Which responses are the child's fabulized combinations and which are the culture's is a question as responses become Disneylike: "Dog with his shoes on," "Bunny that could fly, bunny with wings."

Other "odd combination responses" combine the above categories. Both contamination and confabulation are involved in I: "Camel face— eyes, nose, cheeks; camel because it has humps (tiny upper center bumps)." Still others defy categorization, involving positional cues, size cues (X: "The big ones are daddy and mommy, the little ones are children"), absurdities of proportion, etc.

The occurrence of these "odd combination" responses from 4 to 5½, when W_3 responses are starting a rapid increase, is no coincidence. Similar discoveries are involved in both. Children are moving away from more global generalizations and finding more complexity in the blots. As multiple possibilities for multiple blot areas emerge, it is not surprising that the details of the combination are not always well separated or ordered. And even through the 4 to 5½ year period, when they occur most, "odd combinations" are still a distinct minority of W_x responses, which are much more often loosely put together assemblages of parts, more like W_3 than like textbook DWs. Klopfer's statement (47) that "the five-year-old child is normally expected to use confabulation and confabulatory combinations for at least half of his responses" differs considerably from our findings.

From 6 to 10 years the clearly contaminated, confabulated, or fabulized combination W response has virtually disappeared, only five out of 250 records showing such responses. Loosely linked asemblages are most common. One kind of response that has been called "confabulation" does occur with some frequency. This is a story-telling approach, in which parts of the blot are tied together by spinning a tale around them rather than by direct perceptual relationship; the child goes outside the bounds of the blot, introducing unseen constructs, to justify his response. (Elements of this process are common in many W_3, particularly those with movement; only where it is quite flagrant do we score it W_x and term it "fabulation.")

$W_1 + W_3 + W_x$. Summing the more differentiated W levels gives a kind of index of W complexity. As table 12 shows, this index increases steadily, composing 5 per cent of responses at age 2 and 40 per cent by age 10. Only at 4½ years is there an apparent turnback in this rising trend, when W_1 increases instead. Since this occurs at the same time that seeming confusion appears in both verbalizations and constructions, it may represent an effort at control on some children's part.

Normal Detail (D) Responses

The normal detail response indicates a kind of concrete perception, based on the more obvious possibilities offered by the cards. We know that they are the obvious possibilities because they were selected as the parts of the card children chose most often.

For our sample of 2 to 10 year olds, the mean proportion of D responses ranged from 33 to 48 per cent of all responses, with an overall average close to 40 per cent. A suggestion of declining D% appears in the early preschool years, followed by a low period from about 3½ to 6 years, then by increasing use of D thereafter, with a peak at 9 years.

After the preschool period, children are clearly moving in the direction of the "normal adult expectancy" in use of detail responses, but not until 9 years does mean D exceed mean W. Even then the ratio of W to D is still a long way from the W:D of 1:3 expected in adulthood.

Rare Detail (Dd) Responses

The roughly 10 per cent of responses that are not wholes or normal details are of three main kinds: Dd, response to areas infrequently chosen for interpretation; S, responses to white spaces in the blot; and Do, fragments of responses ordinarily seen in more complete form. All these are combined in computing the Dd%.

Dd. When an area rarely interpreted by other subjects is chosen for response, it may be indicative of an ability to refine judgment to a marked degree and to make an interpretation which demands fine and critical observation, if the form is good and there is good quality to the response. If the form is poor and the quality is stereotyped, we may surmise that the critical ability is not well developed or that there is an intellectual or emotional factor operating to lower the form precision. A high number of Dd in relation to the total R is usually indicative of uncertainty, insecurity, anxiety, compulsiveness.

The number of Dd, as shown in Table 11, is very low in early childhood but rises sharply around 4 years of age. Thereafter, it averages close to one per child, with decreases at 5 and 8 years and with a peak at 5½ and 6. All the varieties of rare details described by Klopfer (46) are represented, the most common ones being tiny details, inside details (often emphasizing the midline), and responses which are D at older ages but which occur rarely in childhood. Edge details and those which cut across the usually perceived boundaries of the blots are less common.

Do. The fragmented Do response is described by Loosli as an "index of inhibition of thought due to affective disturbance." It seems, in older individuals, to represent a premature termination of thought at an incomplete stage or a retreat from a thought which has developed, and generally to indicate the use of repressive or denying styles of defense. In young children, it seems likely that the giving of fragments of responses is part of normal perceptual development, particularly around 3½ and 4 years, when it appears with some frequency. Often, around that time, children seem to denote a response by its parts rather than by its total concept, especially on card IV: "Feet, arms, body, head." In its later appearance, from 6 to 10 years, peaking at 9, it may be reflecting more individual inhibitory functioning. The most common Do by far is the giving of just "boots" or "feet" on IV—a response which becomes the normal expectancy by adulthood but which as late as 16 years is still greatly outnumbered by the total human figure, making it a Do.

S. Interpretation of the white space instead of the surrounding blot has traditionally been viewed as indication of "oppositional tendencies." As Fonda (21) has pointed out, two quite different kinds of response have been scored S. In one variety, where usual figure and ground are reversed so that the white area becomes the figure and the blot itself the background, the individual does indeed seem to be determinedly expressing his variant way of perceiving, and in effect to be asserting his concern for defense of his autonomy. In the other, the white area is not a figure but a gap, a hole, something missing. The implication is of a sense of lack, of inner emptiness.

S responses are most prominent in children's records from 4½ to 6 years, with a peak at 5½—a classic age for oppositionality. By far the greatest number of S use the space as a figure—a candle, a church, a ghost, teeth. Only occasionally does S standing alone represent a hole or gap.

WS responses, where the S is an important feature of a larger W, are tabulated with W responses and distributed across the different W levels. Considered separately, some WS show the clear distinction mentioned above between the S part as figure ("rocket traveling through space") and the S part as open area ("rock with a hole in it"), and have corresponding implications. In many cases, however, the S is used to mark out areas within the W (eyes in a face, spots on a butterfly) and has little clear interpretive significance.

Few WS appear before 4½ years. From 4½ to 10 its mean occurrence ranges from .6 to 1.0 per child, first increasing to its peak at 7 years and then declining. The face on I makes up close to half of all WS responses.

Succession

Rorschach found the order or disorder in the individual's sequence of W, D, and Dd responses on the cards to provide insight into the orderliness of his thinking processes. We attempted to analyze our records for succession and arrived at a clear finding: you cannot determine succession when there is a mean of just one response per card. Only at 7 and 9 years did as many as half the subjects provide records long enough to determine succession. The procedure appears useful clinically for full records, but we can offer no normative guidelines.

Sex Differences in Area

Differences between the sexes in choice of area are not marked, nor are they highly consistent from age to age. Findings are a bit more consistent if we ignore those at 2 and 2½ years, where sex differences in maturity seem especially to confound more "temperamental" sex differences. For the sample as a whole, 3 to 10 years, boys have a slightly larger percentage of W responses, girls of Dd responses, as follows:

Girls: 51% W; 38%D; 11%Dd

Boys: 54%W; 38%D; 8%Dd.

Girls exceed boys in mean W% at five ages, boys exceed girls at six. Girls exceed boys in mean Dd% at seven ages, boys exceed girls at four.

Besides giving a slightly greater proportion of W, boys construct more complex W. For boys, the mean proportion of all W responses, 3 to 10 years, at levels $W_2 + W_3 + W_x$ is 33 per cent; the corresponding mean for girls is 28 per cent. Boys particularly appear to exceed in W_3 and W_x, many of them seemingly willing to sacrifice neatness of concept for the sake of complex assemblages. The goofy inventiveness in many boys' Rube Goldberg-like W_x is rarely encountered in girls' constructions.

CHAPTER SIX

Determinants

FORM

In most adult records, more responses are determined by the *shape* of the blot than by any other determinant. These *form* responses reflect the degree of the subject's intellectual control. The form responses provide some indication of the intellectual ability of the subject, of his reasoning powers, of his critical faculties. It is generally expected that responses determined solely by form will constitute less than 50 per cent of the adult subject's responses. Klopfer (48) states, "The control of any subject of more than average intelligence, whose record contains more than 50% F, can be called constrictive. Among presumably normal adult subjects, any F% between 50 and 80% invariably corresponds to signs of inflexibility, or in clinical terms, constriction with compulsive elements. . . . The same conclusions seem to be valid for children of school age." However, as noted elsewhere, we have not found this to be the case with our subjects.

At every age, in our sample, the mean F% remains *above* 50 per cent. F% is at its highest at 2 years (90 per cent), from which point the percentage declines steadily to a low point of 52 per cent at 7 years. Only at this age does the mean F% even approach the usually accepted critical limit for adults. (The median at this age is 47.5 per cent; at all other ages it is over 50 per cent.) Thereafter, F% again rises to a mean of 63 per cent at 10 years. Even considering that quarter of the children with the lowest F%, only at ages 5½, 6, 7, and 8 does the lowest quartile fall entirely below 50 per cent.

From this F%, which is extremely high as compared with the adult, we may conclude that the emotional activity of the young child is not directly indicated by the usual "enlivened" Rorschach determinants. The spontaneity of the 2-year-old is not reflected in his Rorschach record, at least in its traditional interpretation. However, with increasing maturity, the child's responsiveness to other than form-determined qualities more and more nearly approaches the adult's, until by 7 years, just half of the children fall within the normal adult limits, though thereafter the F% again increases.

Form-determined responses differ in the accuracy and sharpness with which the concept matches the actual blot area. Rorschach has stated that the requisites for "good" form perception are: ability to maintain attention; possession of clear, definite engrams; ability to call these engrams into consciousness; and ability to select from these the most fitting image. Thus, F+% (in the adult record) "is an indicator of the clarity of the associative processes and, at the same time, of the length of the span of attention and the capacity for concentration." (Rorschach, 66.) To some extent, this meaning of the F+% must be modified in our results, at least by adding the phrase, "as compared with other subjects *of his own age*," because in determining form accuracy, we have compared the child's concepts with those of his contemporaries, rather than directly with those considered "good form" for adults. Even so, it is clear that there is a gradual, direct increase in the percentage of "good" forms given at successive ages, the mean rising in almost straightline progression from 54%F+ at 2 years to 89% at 10.* As the mean percentage rises, the range of percentages given at an age tends to narrow. By 5½ years of age, all but the lowest quarter of the children give above 75%F+ and by 9, all but the lowest quarter give 80% F+ or above.

It is clear, though hardly surprising, that with age there is a direct increase in clarity of associative processes, in attention span, and in capacity for concentration. What is more surprising is the fact that F+% so early approaches adult limits, even when one discounts for our method of scoring F+ (which increases F+% as compared to adult scoring.)

Figures for both F% and F+% are given in Table 7 on page 36.

Sex Differences in Form

There is a slight, but very consistent tendency for girls to exceed boys in the amount of their record which is determined by form alone. At 2 and at 3 years, F% for boys and girls is virtually equal; at every age thereafter girls exceed boys. The average F% for the total range for girls is 73 per cent, for boys 68 per cent.

As to F+%, it appears that at the earlier ages the girls have the superiority in formal accuracy, while later the boys excel. Up to 4½ years,

---

* In a cross-validating sample, we would expect to find slightly lower F+%, but the same direct increase. This rise in F+% with age, despite our intragroup comparison method, seems to obtain for several reasons, two of which are: 1) we have used adult norms to some extent in scoring responses given infrequently by the different age groups; 2) it appears that of the responses not given frequently enough to be statistically scored F+, more have been scored F— at earlier ages than at later ages. That is, of the more original responses, more tend to be F— at the earlier ages, more tend to be F+ at the later ages.

girls have a greater F+% at every age but one (3½ years); while from 5 on, boys have a higher F+% at all ages but 6 years.

MOVEMENT RESPONSES
Human Movement (M)

M responses are an index to the richness of the inner life of the individual. In their quantity, they evidently reflect the accessibility to the individual of his own "inner workings"—his fantasies and images. The person with M activity seems able and likely to imagine events, to form plans, to feel a personal role in forming his own fantasies, to have some development of a concept of self.

TABLE 14. CLASSIFIED TABLE OF M RESPONSES
(Total number per age)

							Age in years							
		2	2½	3	3½	4	4½	5	5½	6	7	8	9	10
I.	Static	2	4	2	8	7	11	13	11	13	24	24	23	20
II.	Total Extensor	1	0	8	6	15	3	11	9	32	26	29	30	46
	Moderate	0	0	6	5	7	3	9	3	20	14	13	14	20
	Strong to violent	1	0	2	1	8	0	2	6	12	12	16	16	26
III.	Total Flexor	0	0	0	0	1	0	4	2	6	19	14	17	19
	Flexor, passive	0	0	0	0	0	0	2	0	2	11	4	7	6
	Lifting, holding	0	0	0	0	1	0	2	2	4	7	10	10	13

In quality, the content of the M may suggest the nature of important fantasies, involving such central areas as role concepts and identity. M seems to relate to the individual's most conscious, deliberate self concepts, as if he were saying, "Here is what *people* do (as opposed to *animals* or *things*); this is part of my role as a person." Rorschach (66) noted associations between projected extensor movements in M and self-assertiveness, between flexor M and compliance, blocked M and indecisiveness. This typology forms just one dimension of self concept; particular M responses often depict other individual aspects of self concept.

The number of M responses found in the adult record may normally range from 0 to 15, depending on the intelligence of the subject and the degree of emotional freedom. Two or three M responses are expected in subjects of average intelligence; five or more are usually considered compatible with superior intelligence. In children, M responses are usually reported to occur minimally and to be exceeded at least in the early years by FM responses.

We have found the average number of M responses to increase in an almost steady progression from 2 to 10 years, except for 4½ and 5½ years (see Tables 7, 14, 15). During this period the increase is from an average of .1 to 1.7 per child, M more than doubling from 5½ to 6 years. The number of M responses observed during the first ten years is therefore obviously small, but steadily increasing.

We have classified the M responses given by our subjects as static, extensor (moderate and "strong to violent"), and flexor (passive, and lifting or holding) (see Table 14). We find that static responses predominate at 2 and 2½ years, at 3½, and at 4½ through 5½ years; extensor move-

TABLE 15. UNCLASSIFIED TABLE OF M RESPONSES
(Total number per age)

	Age in years												
	2	2½	3	3½	4	4½	5	5½	6	7	8	9	10
Just 2 people	2	3	1	7	2	2	7	1	6	13	7	11	5
Sitting	0	0	1	0	4	1	3	3	4	4	2	6	4
Standing	0	0	0	1	0	4	2	1	2	1	6	1	0
Walking	0	0	0	1	2	0	1	0	4	3	0	3	1
Running	1	0	0	0	0	0	0	0	0	1	0	1	0
Climbing	0	0	0	1	2	0	0	1	1	1	0	0	0
Dancing	0	0	0	0	2	0	0	1	3	4	6	6	11
Fighting	0	0	1	0	1	0	1	1	0	1	7	2	0
Talking	0	0	1	1	0	0	1	0	1	0	0	2	2
Looking	0	0	0	1	1	0	0	1	0	2	0	0	7
Holding, carrying, lifting	0	0	0	0	1	0	2	2	4	7	10	16	14
Kissing	0	0	0	0	0	0	0	0	0	2	1	1	0
Placing something	0	0	0	0	1	1	1	1	2	3	0	0	0
Cooking	0	0	0	0	0	1	1	0	2	4	0	4	2
Shaking, touching, or posturing hands	0	0	5	0	1	1	1	1	2	4	3	4	9
Other	0	1	1	2	6	4	8	9	20	19	25	13	28
TOTALS	3	4	10	14	23	14	28	22	51	69	67	70	85

ments at other ages, especially from 6 through 10 years. Of the extensor movements, moderate extension prevails at the earlier ages, strong to violent extension from 8 years on. Flexor movements increase after 5 years, reaching their high points at 7 and 10 years but never predominating.

An unclassified table of M responses (Table 15) indicates exactly how many subjects at each age respond with each of the more common specific movement responses such as standing, walking, running, dancing, fighting, and the like. In brief summary of these findings by ages, we find that just *two people existing* leads from 2 to 3½ years. *Sitting* leads at 4 years; *standing* at 4½. At 5 years just *two people* again; at 5½ years, *sitting;* at 6 and 7 years, just *two people.* However at 8, 9, and 10 there is a shift to *holding, lifting,* or *carrying;* and at 10 years, *dancing* is also strong.

Thus, if we may assume that the M responses do reflect the individual's role in life or the nature of his psychic activity, then it would seem from our data that this role becomes increasingly active and increasingly capable of expression as the child matures.

Animal Movement (FM)

Animal movements, like M, represent the inner life of the individual, but at a more spontaneous, impulsive level. The images and impulses represented in a person's FM come easily into his awareness and are recognized by him as his own, but they apparently play little role in planning or more deliberate ideation. The quality of the FM given suggests some contents of the spontaneous impulses. These are impulses that come into the individual's awareness with less acknowledged identification, as if he were

TABLE 16. CLASSIFIED TABLE OF FM RESPONSES
(Total number per age)

	Age in years												
	2	2½	3	3½	4	4½	5	5½	6	7	8	9	10
Static*	1	1	7	11	14	12	15	12	16	18	21	21	30
Moderate extension	0	1	1	5	11	4	14	7	12	15	24	14	13
Strong extension	2	4	7	18	32	18	25	39	50	46	27	34	33
Holding, carrying	0	0	0	0	2	1	0	1	1	3	1	3	10
Flexor, passive	0	0	0	1	2	0	0	4	2	12	4	9	1

* Key: *Static* includes: Sitting, standing, biting, vocalizing, looking at.
Moderate extension includes: Walking, stepping on something.
Strong extension includes: Running, jumping, climbing, fighting, flying, dancing.

saying, "This is how *animals* behave—and how I behave when I am more an animal self and less a controlled person." FM is accordingly more vigorous, often more aggressive, than M, but a wide range of actions (and self concepts) can be portrayed, from passive and cowering to violent and predatory.

In our subjects we find that FM, like M, increases steadily from 2 to 7 years except for a drop at 4½ and 5 years. There is a slight drop at 8 years, then a slight increase at 9 and 10 years. The range is from an average of .1 FM at 2 years to 1.9 at 7 years, with a slight decline to 1.7 at 10 years (see Table 7).

We have classified FM responses along approximately the same lines as M responses, that is, into total number of static, moderate extensor, strong to violent extensor, holding and carrying, and flexor-passive responses. We find from such a classification (Table 16) that strong extensor movements predominate at all ages. Thus, FM is, for this age range in general, consistently more active than is M.

As in the case of M responses, we have also presented a detailed unclassified table of all FM responses at each age (Table 17), showing how many of the subjects at each age respond with the more common specific animal movement responses such as jumping, climbing, flying, and the like. Here we find a very marked central tendency. At every age but 2½, when responses are extremely dispersed, *climbing* responses are outstanding. Through 5 years they definitely overshadow all other kinds of animal movements. At 5½, 6, and 7 years, *flying* responses occur conspicuously. At 8 years, *sitting* is strong. *Fighting* comes in at 9 and 10 years; *putting noses or paws together* at 7 years following.

TABLE 17. UNCLASSIFIED TABLE OF FM RESPONSES
(Total number per age)

	Age in years												
	2	2½	3	3½	4	4½	5	5½	6	7	8	9	10
Sitting	0	1	0	2	1	2	1	3	1	3	8	6	3
Standing	0	0	1	0	4	5	5	3	7	8	3	4	7
Walking	0	0	0	0	3	1	2	1	2	3	4	3	2
Running	0	1	2	1	3	0	3	3	3	2	1	0	2
Jumping	0	0	0	0	1	0	0	2	4	5	0	2	2
Climbing	2	1	4	14	20	11	16	20	17	21	18	14	12
Fighting	0	1	0	2	1	0	0	2	4	1	0	6	9
Biting, eating	1	0	1	3	0	1	2	0	4	2	2	2	0
Flying	0	1	0	2	4	6	3	11	18	22	4	4	6
Pulling something	0	0	0	0	1	0	0	0	0	0	4	0	4
Vocalizing	0	0	4	0	2	1	0	1	1	2	0	0	4
Noses or paws together	0	0	0	1	0	1	2	0	1	5	6	6	8
Carrying, holding	0	0	0	1	1	1	0	1	1	2	2	4	6
Hanging from something	0	0	0	0	0	0	0	1	2	2	0	5	1
Looking at, regarding	0	0	0	0	5	2	1	1	2	1	2	2	1
Dancing	0	0	0	0	0	0	3	1	2	1	0	0	1
Stepping on something	0	0	0	0	1	0	3	4	0	1	1	2	0
Other	0	1	3	9	14	4	13	9	12	13	22	21	19
TOTAL	3	6	15	35	61	35	54	63	81	94	77	81	87

Comparison of M and FM

At the very beginning and the very end of our age range, children give just about equal amounts of M and FM—at the beginning because they give hardly any of either, and at the end because M has nearly caught up with FM. But in between, from 3 to 9 years, mean FM consistently exceeds mean M, and from 3½ to 5½ years FM is given at least twice as often.

Table 18 presents an age-by-age comparison of M and FM. The greater vigor of FM is noted in a series of summary statements within the table. Sex differences are also indicated, and will be summarized in a later section.

Inanimate Movement (m)

Like all movement responses, m represent fantasies and partial identifications. In m, however, the fantasy has been disowned and projected outward: "This is not what people or animals do; this is what *things* do or

TABLE 18. M AND FM COMPARED*

(Including sex differences)

FM	M
2 years:	
Girls (2): eating, climbing	Girls (2): people, daddy (makes fist)
Boys (1): climbing	Boys (1): man run
Very few of either type of response. FM a little more active than M.	
2½ years:	
Girls (5): running, sitting, fighting, climbing, flying	Girls (1): baby lying down
	Boys (3): men, men, ladies
Boys (1): washing	
FM is conspicuously more active than M which is extremely static.	
3 years:	
Girls (3): running, climbing, crying	Girls (3): 2 babies, talking, fighting
Boys (12): 3 climbing, standing, eating, running	Boys (7): sitting, doing "this"
FM is considerably more active than M, which is largely static or moderately extensor.	
3½ years:	
Girls (7): 4 climbing, 2 biting or eating	Girls (7): men, daddies, witches, standing up people
Boys (28): 9 climbing, 2 flying, 2 fighting, 2 sitting, eating, running	Boys (7) people, men, talking, seeing
Nearly three times as many FM as M. FM is conspicuously more active than M which is extremely static.	
4 years:	
Girls (17): 7 climbing, 2 flying; others kick, look, step, sit, stand	Girls (13): 2 existing, 2 somersaulting, 1 fighting, 1 climbing, 1 dancing, 4 static
Boys (44): 14 climbing, 4 looking, 3 standing, 2 running, 4 catching or chasing, 1 flying	Boys (10): 3 existing, 1 dancing, 1 shooting, 4 static
Nearly three times as many FM as M. FM and M both extremely active. This is one of the most active ages for M, though there is still great variety from child to child.	
4½ years:	
Girls (12): 4 climbing, 2 flying; others hold on, peek out, bark, sit, eat, press noses	Girls (7): sitting, standing, talking
Boys (23): 7 climbing, 4 flying, 5 standing, 2 crawling; others sit, walk, stand on head, look	Boys (7): clapping hands, putting fish into pot; static
Twice as many FM as M. FM decidedly more active than M which is much more static or passive than at 4 years.	
5 years:	
Girls (24): 6 climbing, 2 flying, 3 running, 2 standing, 2 dancing; others sit, eat, play	Girls (12): 5 static; 4 moderate activity (tipping hats, etc.), 1 diving, 1 fighting, 1 bending

*Not every M and FM listed here. For complete listing see Tables 15 and 17.

TABLE 18.   M AND FM COMPARED (*Continued*)

FM	M
Boys (30): 10 climbing, 2 swimming, 2 stepping, 2 standing; others cry, smell, hop, stand on head, boast, fly, eat	Boys (16): 7 static; 7 moderate (crawling, walking, lifting, cooking, trying to hide)

Twice as many FM as M and FM decidedly more active than M. Still very little similarity from child to child in M. FM is more uniform from child to child.

5½ years:

Girls (30): 9 climbing, 2 fighting, 2 jumping, 2 sitting, 2 flying, 3 perform, 3 stand; others hide head, hop, hang on, hold hat	Girls (8): 1 static; 3 moderate (shining shoes, etc.); others dance, climb, push
Boys (33): 11 climbing, 9 flying, 2 running, 3 stepping; others stand, crawl, smell, sit, sing, swim	Boys (14): 10 static, 1 squirting and 1 picking up, 1 boxing, 1 playing tag

Nearly three times as many FM as M. FM the more active, but M is becoming more active than earlier. Static leads but "strong to violent" activity comes second.

6 years:

Girls (40): 11 climbing, 7 flying, 2 jumping, 2 sitting, 2 kneeling; others chatter, walk, bite, look, dance, eat, fight, run, perform.	Girls (24): 8 static; 11 moderate (walking, picking up, working, playing violin); 3 active (flying, jumping, climbing)
Boys (41): 6 climbing, 11 flying, 3 fighting, 2 standing, 2 hanging, 2 jumping, 2 eating, 2 running; others dance, swim, eat, argue	Boys (27): 5 static; 13 moderate (walking, cooking); 8 strong extensor

M is approaching FM in incidence; 81 FM, 51 M. FM the more active but M is quite active, especially in boys. There is still little similarity in M from child to child.

7 years:

Girls (38): 9 climbing, 8 flying, 3 standing, 2 sitting, etc.	Girls (25): 6 just two people, 2 sitting, 2 holding, 2 dancing, 2 putting things
Boys (56): 5 standing, 14 flying, 10 climbing, 2 running, 2 dancing, 3 jumping	Boys (44): 8 just two people, 6 holding, 3 dancing, 2 picking something up

Again M is more than half as many in number as FM. FM, however, is much more active than M. Flexor responses in M occur here the most of any age. Lifting and holding are also conspicuous.

8 years:

Girls (33): 4 sitting, 2 standing, 8 climbing, 2 flying, 3 pulling apart	Girls (27): 3 fighting, 4 holding something, 2 standing, 1 dancing, 1 kissing, etc.
Boys (44): 10 climbing, 4 sitting, 2 flying, 2 looking at each other, 1 standing	Boys (40): 4 fighting, 5 dancing, 4 standing, 5 holding

M occurs almost as extensively as FM. They are also much more nearly equal as to amount of activity than at 7 years. Both are fairly active. Climbing predominates in FM, fighting in M. There is now considerable similarity from child to child.

TABLE 18. M AND FM COMPARED (*Continued*)

---

9 years:

Girls (40): 3 sitting, 4 climbing, 3 jumping, 2 springing, 4 fighting; others stand, lie, walk, swim, fly, hide, look, eat, nod head, pick flowers, carry, kiss

Girls (30): 8 static, just two people; 4 sit, 6 hold-lift-carry, 4 dance; others pull, pick up, hang by feet

Boys (41): 3 standing, 3 walking, 3 sitting, 7 climbing, 3 flying, 5 hanging onto things; others lie, fight, argue, smell, eat

Boys (40): 3 static, just two people; 2 sit, 1 lies, 1 stands, 10 hold-lift-carry, 2 dance, 2 bow, 2 bowl, 2 quarrel, 2 fight; others cook, fall, bend knees, whirl, escape

FM and M occur about equally. There are here marked sex differences. In girls FM is more active than M. In boys both are about equally active. Boys, in FM give "hanging onto things" responses not seen in girls, and indicate less fighting than do girls. FM is more active in girls than in boys; M is more active in boys than in girls.

10 years:

Girls (42): 6 climbing, 7 standing, 3 flying, 3 fighting, 3 pulling, 3 carrying

Girls (44): 15 hands in action, 6 dancing, 5 holding something, 5 sit or stand on something, 3 look, 2 pull apart, 2 talk, 2 pray

Boys (45): 6 climbing, 2 flying, 2 fighting, 2 running, 3 kissing, 1 pulling, 1 carrying

Boys (41): 12 hands in action, 5 dancing, 4 hold something, 2 sit or stand on something, 4 look at something, 2 pull apart

FM and M occur about equally in number. Both are active but FM is the more active. Strong to violent extension leads, moderate extension comes second. Central tendencies are stronger—there is much less variety from child to child. Dancing occurs 11 times, holding something in hands 10 times, sitting or standing 10 times, looking at something 7 times.

---

what happens to things." The impulse or fantasy involved is, for whatever reason, unacceptable to the person and is changed into a sense of being acted upon rather than acting. The associated feeling—angry, explosive, tense, dependent, longing—is somehow experienced but rejected as "not me." At most it might be acknowledged in: "This (feeling, fantasy) happens to me" rather than "I am like this" or "I have this wish." When many of a person's movement responses are in m, an important part of his fantasy is inaccessible to him for constructive use, even though it may significantly determine his overt behavior. Nevertheless, the m may represent a kind of reservoir of movement potentiality, which might be brought to greater realization by changes in inner balance. The quality of the feeling or fantasy is often represented in the activity portrayed.

In our young subjects, m was one of the less frequent primary determiners of response, but as many as a third of the children used primary m at 7 to 10 years. Mean m does not exceed .2 throughout the preschool period, but increases after age 5 up to a peak of .8 m per child at age 7, thereafter dropping back to about .5 m. Inanimate movement is implicit or explicit in many responses where it is not scored as the primary determinant—either because it was given as a past action ("cat that was squashed") or because

TABLE 19. CLASSIFIED TABULATION OF PRIMARY AND SECONDARY
m RESPONSES
(Total number and percentage at each age)

Quality of m	Age in years												
	2	2½	3	3½	4	4½	5	5½	6	7	8	9	10
Active quality													
Upward—blazing, spouting, burning up, etc.	1	1	2	4	5	4	5	11	9	19	7	4	8
Outward—exploding, shooting, fireworks, etc.	1	0	0	0	0	2	2	8	7	16	8	8	2
Forward—sailing, flowing, driving, etc.	0	0	1	1	1	0	0	0	0	4	0	1	0
Passive quality													
Downward—falling, hanging, pouring, burning down, etc.	1	2	3	3	7	3	1	17	16	17	15	11	8
Acted on, disintegrating—cracked, torn, smashed, etc.	7	2	11	7	6	7	4	10	13	23	12	6	7
Conflicted quality													
In place—spinning, rocking, stretched, stuck, etc.	1	1	1	4	3	3	1	0	4	6	7	4	2
Total m	11	6	18	19	22	19	13	46	49	85	49	34	27
Percentage of total m													
Active	18	17	17	26	27	32	54	41	33	46	31	38	37
Passive	73	66	77	53	59	53	38	58	59	47	55	50	56
Conflicted	9	17	6	21	14	15	8	0	8	7	14	12	7

another determinant was primary ("red flames leaping up"). When secondary m were added to primary m in computing means, much more use of m was apparent. The trend of development was similar in form but more marked: relative scarcity of m through the preschool period, a rapid increase after 5 years up to a peak of 1.7 at 7 years, then a steady decline to .5 at age 10.

A tabulation of the principal kinds of primary and secondary m responses is presented in Table 19. The classifications are of course arbitrary —m within any one category differ considerably, some m might equally well have gone into another category than where they were classified, and the distinction of "active," "passive," and "conflicted" movements is only a rough one. Still, these grouping do allow several developmental trends to emerge. The early m are largely classified as passive, and mostly consist of things broken, cracked, etc. After 3 years m become increasingly active. Nearly all kinds of m are at their absolute peak at 7 years, but those classified as passive are at their relative lowest, and more violent m are both absolutely and relatively frequent. After 7 the violence declines along with sheer number of m.

Sex Differences in M, FM, and m Responses

Girls get an earlier start in using all varieties of movement responses, more girls than boys giving M, FM, and m responses at the earliest ages tested. The proportions then change, at different times for the three variables. After age 2½, more boys than girls give FM responses at every age; after age 3½, more boys than girls give M at every age; after age 5½, more boys than girls give m at every age. Though starting later, boys altogether produce many more m than girls—a mean of .4 primary m for the total sample of boys, .2 m for girls.

Differences in the intensity of activity portrayed are not striking in the case of M and FM; the activity is about equally strong at most ages, and the number of ages where girls project more active M or FM is matched by the number of ages where boys project the more active movement. In quality of m, boys tend to go to extremes, giving more of the most violent m and also more of the most damaged m (cracked, broken, cut off).

COLOR

Color responses reflect the person's openness to stimulation from his surroundings. Depending on the extent of the individual's control over this openness, color responses can indicate affectivity which ranges from sensitivity to the actions and feelings of others, leading to adaptive warmth, all the way to a wide-openness and vulnerability to seemingly stray environmental stimuli, leading to violent emotional response. The degree to which control is imposed on the emotional response is roughly gauged by the degree to which form is integrated with the color response. FC responses represent color most delayed and restrained by form; their presence suggests affective adaptiveness. CF interpretations suggest less delay, more impulsive, direct reactivity. In pure C reactions the stimulus produces the response directly, with no intervening self process, and the behavior is nonadaptive, poorly integrated, "emotional" (though often emotionally shallow).

Tables 7 and 8 show the extent to which our subjects used color as a primary determiner of their Rorschach responses. Few children used color in the early preschool period, but their numbers increased until nearly half used color by age 3½ and nearly two thirds by age 4½. To reason either that 2-year-olds are unresponsive and unemotional or that color responses do *not* signify emotional responsiveness would be fallacious. For the very young child, verbal response to ink blots is simply not an appropriate medium for expression of affectivity. (The developmental findings should serve as a warning against too facile ascription of "emotional coldness" to all older subjects who use no color. Coldness is one possible reason for absence of color, but so is marked immaturity and poor differentiation of the personality, often accompanied by impulsiveness and pronounced "emotionality.")

CF is the form of color response most often used by children throughout our age range—by twice as many children as use either FC or C. Mean CF increases in plateaus, from near absence at 2 years, to about .5 from 2½ to 4 years, to about 1.3 from 4½ through 7 years. Thereafter it slowly decreases. Pure C response shows less marked change with development but does increase slowly to a peak at 7 years, when 40 per cent of subjects use C; then it declines. (Note that C does not, as some summaries suggest, start out high and decline steadily. Relative to other color scores, which are increasing more rapidly, it becomes less prominent, but it too increases for many years.) FC response is never strong in childhood but it shows a clearly increasing trend, from virtual absence at 2 years to use by about a third of subjects from 7 years on.

Total responsiveness to color, as indexed by the weighted color sum, ΣC, shows quite a smooth inverted-U curve increasing from a mean of just .7 at age 2 to 2.9 at age 7, then declining gradually to 1.5 by age 10. Rorschach considered ΣC to represent the extratensiveness of the individual, as balanced against his introversiveness, represented by number of M. While this ratio of M:ΣC is a rough, heuristic index, with weighting assigned on the basis of adult records, it is of interest to see how children's records would be classified.

Figure 7 depicts mean values for M and ΣC, showing the clear predominance of the latter until near the end of our age range. Only at 10 years did mean M exceed ΣC. Interestingly, ages of greatest increase in mean ΣC are usually accompanied by relative or absolute decreases in mean M, and vice versa. In a later study (Ames, 1965), which included 130 subjects aged 2 to 13 years in a semi-longitudinal design (many of them also subjects in the present sample), the shift to an introversive balance occurred earlier, at least in boys. Judging by mean scores, boys were introversive by 5 years and following, girls by 8 years and following. Judging by experience balance in individual subjects, a majority of boys was classified as introversive by 7 years. A majority of girls was still not introversive by 10 years (but three fourths of the girls were introversive by 13).

To conclude from the early predominance of color that "Young children are more extratensive than introversive" would be meaningless, since there is no zero point on the scale, no way of knowing where the point of balance between movement and color would be, other than by comparisons among subjects within ages. Still, it seems plausible that young children seem more "turned outward" than do adults, less directed to inner events.

In general, the findings for color suggest an increase with age in children's responsiveness to external stimuli, a widening range of emotional response. Judging from FC, we see a tendency to increasing adaptability to others. But the CF progression suggests at all ages the child's relative impulsiveness, egocentricity, and suggestibility. In color responses, as in

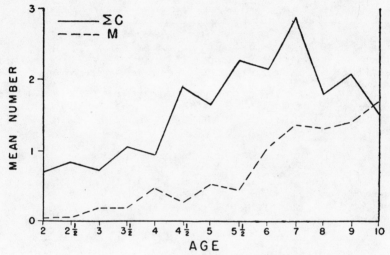

Fig. 7.   Mean Values for M and ΣC.

other determinants, age 7 seems to represent a peak and a turning point in development. It appears as a time of particularly intense feeling, which has been increasing over preceding years and which lessens in succeeding ones.

In evaluating individual Rorschach records, knowing the sheer numbers of each kind of color response—FC, CF, and C—is not enough; the responses themselves must be examined. Strength or depth of feeling appears in the content quality of the color associations as well as in their number and relation to form. More elemental, natural color associations (fire, blood, grasshopper) ordinarily have greater intensity than imposed or arbitrary ones (red hat, colored stones, painting). Warmth or coolness, whole-heartedness or restraint may be suggested in color reactions. A first step in grouping frequent CF and C responses of our subjects appears in Table 20.

In pure C responses, *paint* is the earliest kind of content. Its rapid decline indicates its immaturity when it is used at later ages. *Nature* responses appear later, increasing and then decreasing again. *Blood* and then *fire* responses appear still later and show less decrease by our oldest ages.

Among CF responses, *flower* is the most common content at nearly every age, though most flowers are given between 4½ and 6 years. Butterfly is also given at many ages and strongest from 4½ to 6. *Fire* responses are frequent only between 5½ and 7 years. CF *nature* responses rarely occur in the preschool years but increase thereafter.

TABLE 20.　QUALITATIVE ANALYSIS OF COLOR RESPONSES

					Age in years							
	2	2½	3	3½	4	4½	5	5½	6	7	8	9	10
TOTAL NUMBER OF CF RESPONSES AT EACH AGE												
Flower	4	8	2	18	12	38	14	27	26	13	5	6	13
Butterfly	0	6	2	3	4	10	7	9	8	3	3	1	3
Tree or leaf	0	1	0	2	3	3	4	7	8	10	6	7	1
Design, painting	0	4	2	2	1	2	3	2	3	0	2	3	2
Anatomy	0	0	1	0	0	1	11	0	4	2	5	5	6
Clothing, etc.	0	0	0	0	0	1	3	4	5	6	0	0	0
Fire (flame)	0	0	0	0	4	5	2	12	12	12	2	0	1
Nature	0	0	0	0	2	4	7	7	2	6	6	3	5
TOTAL NUMBER OF C RESPONSES AT EACH AGE												
Paint	11	6	1	3	3	2	1	3	2	0	5	5	0
Nature (sun, sunset, sky, grass, rainbow, etc.)	0	0	4	0	3	0	1	1	5	15	1	0	0
Blood	0	0	0	1	1	10	2	2	2	3	6	10	4
Fire	0	0	1	2	0	5	7	9	4	15	10	9	7
Food	0	0	0	0	1	0	1	1	0	3	0	1	0

Color naming, in which the subject simply offers the names of colors as responses, represents a very inadequate response in older children and adults. In our subjects, such response was given almost exclusively from 2½ to 3½ years of age, and even then was infrequent. At these early ages, Cn carries little connotation of stimulus-bound behavior but represents a pride in being able to identify color names—a task little children are often called on to perform. The absence of Cn after 6 years in our normal sample points up its significance when it does appear in older children's records.

Color shock is a concept used by Rorschach to describe the reaction of individuals whose responses are disrupted upon the introduction of the colored blots. He believed that subjects who show unmistakable shock "are always 'emotion-repressors,' neurotics of varying grades of severity. 'Emotion-controllers' show the phenomenon to a lesser extent" (66, p. 35). The disruption may be indicated in a number of different ways. There may be a sudden diminution of response on Card VIII which may continue through IX and X. (This may have been foreshadowed by a diminution of response at Card II, where the first red appeared.) The response time may be longer on the color cards, or the quality of response may be suddenly different. Refusal, dysphoric exclamations, hesitation, long verbalization before response, sudden or excessive turning of the card may all be considered as indicators of color shock. If there is complete absence of color response or if the subject interprets only the more pale and neutral colors, avoiding red and orange, one should look for other signs which might confirm color shock. If color interpretations are given on Cards II and III and none are given on the remaining color cards, we must consider the possibility of color shock. When the total number of responses on Cards VIII to X is less than 30 per cent of total R, we may suspect that the response is made more difficult by the color or that the subject is self-protectively avoiding it, and this may be evidence of color shock.

Loosli distinguishes between color shock and red shock, which is produced only at Cards II and III, but which is determined by many of the same signs as color shock. She indicates that red shock may be present without color shock and comments: "I see in the red shock, often very violent, a sign of repressed hostile feelings accompanied by a feeling of guilt" (Loosli-Usteri, 53).

For each of the subjects in our sample, we attempted to determine the presence of color shock and red shock (as well as initial shock, Clob shock, and space shock). The subjectivity of this determination and the small numbers of subjects classified as showing any of these varieties of reaction make our findings too inconclusive to warrant detailed presentation. As will be indicated in the age chapters, there seems to be more red shock at 5½, 7, and 10 years, and more color shock at 8 and 10 years, but no clear-cut age trends were observable. At no age do more than a fourth of the children give positive indication of any kind of shock.

Sex Differences in Use of Color

Differences between boys and girls in use of color are not marked and they vary from age to age. In general, girls appear to use slightly more of the color responses combined with form, boys to use more of the color responses with little form control.

FC responses: at seven of the ages studied, more girls than boys used FC responses; at just three ages more boys than girls did so. Girls' mean scores were also higher than boys' at seven ages, boys at just four ages. The differences are never marked, however, and the mean FC across the whole age range is only slightly higher for girls than boys.

CF responses: more girls than boys use CF responses at seven of the ages studied, more boys than girls at five. However, boys who use CF use slightly more than do girls who use CF, so that the overall mean is slightly higher in boys (.9 CF for boys, .8 for girls).

C responses: more girls than boys give C responses at five ages, more boys than girls at six. Differences are not large or consistent except from 5 to 7 years, when boys consistently exceed girls in use of C, with an overall mean of .6, compared with the girls' mean of .3.

ΣC: the weighted color sum is slightly higher in boys than girls, because of their greater use of the more heavily weighted C and CF. After age 3, boys exceed girls in mean ΣC at seven of the ten ages. The overall mean difference is very small, however: 1.5 ΣC for girls, 1.6 ΣC for boys.

In quality of response, no systematic differences were observed except that girls used more colored *flower* responses.

SHADING RESPONSES

In our scoring of shading we have followed Loosli, using only two major categories: *F(C)* and *Clob*. It is necessary, in studying an individual response, to determine more finely the exact nature of the shading, and in Table 21 we present a breakdown of the important subcategories. However, because so few of the young child's responses involve shading, an elaborate system of scoring does not seem necessary. As the scoring we have used differs from the more common American system, it is here presented in some detail, along with an outline of its rationale and interpretation.

Loosli's scoring and interpretation derive from Binder's investigations. Of the different types of responses to gray-black values, the F(C) category contains the finely differentiated responses to nuances of shading, the Clob category contains the diffuse responses based on the dark character of certain blots.

F(C)

F(C) is the score Loosli gives to most forms of true shading responses. Shading used for discernment of detail within the blot, for the play of light and shadow, and for texture, all fall in this F(C) category (as would vista, had any of our subjects given such responses). All the foregoing are Binder's F(Fb). In practice, Loosli also scores as F(C) the use of shading as nondysphoric diffusion—that is when darkness or unpleasantness is not mentioned or directly implied as a feature of the diffusion: for example, "clouds" or "smoke" on VII would be F(C).

Most investigators would agree that "the shading category in general appears to represent a careful, cautious, highly sensitive approach to the environment" (Hertz, 36). It is Loosli's belief that in every sort of shading response, the gray-black provokes uneasiness in the subject. His method of dealing with the anxiety-arousing situations is shown by the type of shading response that he gives. Loosli (53) states,

All F(C), it seems to me, whether given with pleasure or not, is to be considered as a vigorous (and successful) reaction against the painful reaction provoked by the gray. If the gray were not perceived as such, F(C) would be impossible. But the elaboration of that perception is quite different from the Clob: instead of abandoning himself passively to the diffuse impression, the subject takes a more active attitude. Rising above the initial reaction of displeasure, he studies the blot more closely, distinguishes shadings, and usually succeeds in making very fine interpretations.

The F(C) responses indicate that the subject is concerned with adapting to the environment. Binder believes that shading responses given with pleasure, and given to the lighter parts of the blot indicate a "gently accommodating and delicately submissive adaptation to the environment, which is accompanied by positively toned emotions," while responses given anxiously and to darker portions show "an anxious, cautious, painfully conscientious form of adaptation to the environment" (Binder, 17). The F(C) seems to be less connected with the deeper emotional life of the subject than the Clob, representing a more "peripheral" emotional adjustment, and appears to be related to the FC, denoting an affective disposition still finer than FC.

As we first scored and summarized our children's records, it appeared that F(C) was rarely used as a determinant. Only at 7 years of age is there a mean of more than one F(C) per child. Looking more closely, however, we find that although the *mean number* of F(C) is small, many individual children do use this type of response, usually giving a single F(C) response in an entire record. In fact, at 2 years of age more children use F(C) than use any other single determinant except form. Gradually more children use other determinants, but at *every* age more children use F(C) than use m, FC, or pure C.

In general, there is an overall increase in the number of children using F(C) from 14 per cent of the subjects at 2 years to 52 per cent at 7, then a gradual drop to 40 per cent at 10 (see Table 8). At every age from 4 years on, between a third and half of the children give shading responses. The mean number increases from .2 F(C) per child at 2 years to 1.1 at 7, then drops to .6 at 10.

The nature of the shading responses which make up these averages changes markedly with age (see Table 21). At the earlier ages, the impression created by shading is largely one of diffusion. Diffusion responses predominate at every age up to 5½, except at 2½ and 3, where they hold second place. At 2½ years, water responses predominate, apparently suggested by the play of light and shade on the blot; at 3 years texture predominates. At no age after 5½ is shading used mainly for diffusion. At 5 years diffusion and fine differentiation responses share second place while texture responses lead. The real transition from diffusion to differentiation of details within the blot comes at 7 years, and shading is used primarily for differentiation of details at 7, 8, and 9 years. Texture responses are the second leading category at 7 and 8 years, they equal inner discrimination by 9 years, and by 10 they are the leading category. Thus, in general, shading is used as diffusion up to 5½ years; by 7, it is used much more for differentiation of details within the blot, and by 10 years it is used to discern texture.

These developmental trends indicate that at different age periods the child changes in the sensitivity and cautiousness of his approach to his

TABLE 21. CLASSIFIED F(C) RESPONSES

	Age in years											
	2	2½	3	3½	4	4½	5	5½	6	7	8	9	10
Diffusion: clouds, smoke	8	5	8	*11*	*13*	10	9	*18*	9	14	2	4	7
Light-shade: lights, shadow, reflections	1	*8*	1	2	1	4	4	2	3	3	4	2	1
(water)*	1	*8*	0	2	0	2	2	2	2	2	2	0	0
Differentiation within blot: eyes, path, etc.	1	0	5	6	4	4	3	2	9	21	25	14	9
Texture:†	2	4	*14*	5	5	9	4	8	*13*	19	9	*14*	10
hard surface	1	0	1	1	3	8	2	1	3	4	7	3	3
soft surface	0	0	6	1	0	1	2	6	4	8	2	9	5
fine differentiation	0	0	2	1	2	0	0	1	5	9	0	2	2
snow	1	4	5	2	0	0	0	0	1	1	0	0	0

* Water is included in light-shade total.
† Hard and soft surface, fine differentiation and snow included in texture total.

environment. At some ages he shows caution, uncertainty, and even anxiety in his approach to the outer world; at other ages he is less concerned in his advances. Furthermore, the nature of the shading suggests that at some ages, especially earlier, the anxiety is diffuse and undefined, while with increasing age it becomes clearer, more specific, perhaps more peripheralized, and the child has more successful methods of coping with anxiety.

Clob

Responses based on a diffuse impression of the blot, stemming from its darkness, are scored Clob (in combination with F, that is, FClob, ClobF, Clob). Darkness is the primary quality of Clob, and almost invariably the contents are unpleasant. This category includes the use of black as color (Klopfer's C′). This inclusion was made, for this age range, because of the small number of responses of both kinds which occurred, and because of the difficulty of distinguishing between them in the young child. At later ages, after 10 years, in our clinical practice we distinguish between Clob and C′. C′ is black used as color but without explicit threatening or unpleasant connotations.

Binder explains the Clob response in the following manner: the sight of a large surface of uniform and diffuse color releases in each of us a mood. However, the degree of reactivity varies a great deal from one subject to another, and in order for the small black surface of the ink blot to release such a strong, morbid reaction in the subject, he must have an abnormal susceptibility to profound disturbance. "The Clob indicates that the subject abandons himself without resistance to the disagreeable impression of the dark character of the blots. Unable to mobilize forces of defense, he abandons himself passively" (Loosli). In contrast to the F(C) responses, the Clob responses are "related to the central emotional life and express diffuse and deep emotions" (Hertz). The sensitivity to the darkness, the surrender to passivity, the gruesome content of the Clob responses, point out the sombre, depressive, minor strain in the subjects' psyche.*

At nearly every age, Clob is the determinant used least frequently by our subjects. Altogether just 10 per cent of the children give one or more FClob responses, while 7 per cent give ClobF responses. Taking FClob and ClobF together (and referring to them as Clob), the mean is just .1 to .2 from 2 to 5 years. It increases to about .5 from 5½ to 7 years, then drops again to .1 to .2 from 8 to 10 years.

As shown in Table 22, most responses scored Clob were so scored at nearly every age because of the child's use of the qualifying adjective "black." Because of the very small number of responses involved, it would be difficult and unreliable to draw fine age distinctions for the other types of Clob response. However, there is a suggestion that at the earlier ages, the Clob responses are mainly concerned with dark, ominous places—dark mountains and caves, and then are concerned more with death and dead

---

*Piotrowski's system of scoring shading is nearly identical with the one used here, his c′, which contains interpretations of the very dark nuances of the blots, corresponding to our Clob, and his c, which contains non-dysphoric interpretations of shading, corresponding to our F(C). It appears at first that his interpretation of the shading categories is quite opposite to Loosli's, the c′—our Clob—indicating "a need for doing something actively in order to relieve a disturbing anxiety,"—the c—our F(C)—pointing to "a tendency to assume a rather inactive attitude of withdrawn watchfulness if the feeling of anxiety becomes disturbing." Actually Loosli and Piotrowski agree on the basic meaning of shading. Piotrowski's statement that "all shading responses are considered to be signs of anxiety, of uncertainty, of a feeling of being exposed to danger, of doubt concerning the most suitable method of controlling a potentially hostile environment" is a clear statement of Loosli's basic view also. Further, "the Fc and c—our F(C)—point to a submissive and conscientious adaptation to the environment." With this too we agree, perhaps viewing the adaptation aspect of F(C) as a more active, rather than submissive, process. In regard to Clob, perhaps Piotrowski's interpretation is one step further removed from the subject's verbal response. In the Clob response, the subject's "core" of personality is shaken, he abandons himself without resistance to strong dysphoric moods. Apparently, according to Piotrowski, thus swayed, the subject would intensify activity, perhaps in a rather uncontrolled manner. This explanation is supported by the greater incidence of Clob in psychopaths than in normals.

people, and then with alive and threatening monsters. Death appears more at 5 and 7 years; more overtly threatening people and animals seem to predominate at 4½, 5½, 6 years and at the later ages. At 9 and 10 years there seems to be a shift, with more children seeing monsters and threatening animals than mere "black" things.

TABLE 22. CLASSIFIED Clob RESPONSES (INCLUDING C')
(Total number at each age)

	Age in years												
	2	2½	3	3½	4	4½	5	5½	6	7	8	9	10
"Black"	3	9	4	1	2	5	6	15	9	13	8	5	1
Darkness; dark, ominous places	1	0	1	2	1	0	0	1	0	8	0	1	0
Dead people or animals, bones showing, etc.	0	0	0	0	1	0	2	0	2	5	2	0	0
Monster, ghost, animal— alive and threatening	0	0	1	1	1	3	0	7	4	4	2	6	5

Age Trends in Shading

The findings on children's responsiveness to the shading and the darkness of the blots at different ages suggest some developmental trends. At 2 and 2½ years, the Rorschach gives as little indication of children's experiencing through shading as it does through movement or color responses. Such anxieties as are hinted at appear to be diffuse and nonspecific. At 3 years a sharp increase appears in expression of sensitivity to the environment, with a conscientious, cautious adaptation to it. From 3½ to 5 years the moderate level of cautiousness persists, expressed in a more diffuse form. At 5½ a considerable change occurs, and this intensifies until 7 years: all forms of shading response increase and, for the first time, a number of children show a more pervasive anxiety. The 5½-year-old appears to show sensitivity and concern over his adaptation to his environment, but his anxiety seems diffuse and nonspecific, as if his feelings were uncertain and his means of coping with his anxiety were undependable. Many, boys especially, are concerned with blackness; some see threatening creatures in the shading. At 6 years concern over adaptation continues, but more children appear to have found successful ways of dealing with anxiety; it seems more objectified and the gloomy moods indicated by Clob are less evident. At 7 years these increase again, with all indicators of unease and anxiety reaching a peak, especially in boys. Comparatively many children talk of darkness, death, and threatening figures. Attempts at coping with anxiety through intellectualizing efforts appear with frequency for the first time. From age 8 to 10 a steady decline appears in expression of anxiety, more controlled and less diffuse reactions appear, and children seem less deeply moved by feelings of uncertainty or of sadness.

Sex Differences in Shading

F(C): Sex differences in shading are not great, and occur quite irregularly, now boys and now girls giving the larger number. At six ages more boys utilize shading than girls, at four ages girls exceed boys. At the ages where $F(C)$ is highest, it is nearly always the boys who exceed.

Clob: More girls than boys give Clob at five ages; boys exceed girls at six ages. As with $F(C)$, at the ages where Clob responses are strongest—5½, 6, and 7 years—many more boys than girls give Clob. At these ages, form plays a secondary role in the boys' Clob responses; with girls, form is more often primary.

CHAPTER SEVEN

Content

Classifications of content have been relatively uniform among different investigators with only minor variations. Our selection of content categories was determined after the data were gathered, and includes all types of responses given. The following categories have thus been employed in the present study:

Animals (A); Animal detail (Ad); Humans (H); Human detail (Hd); Plant (Pl); Flowers; Object (Obj.); Nature (Nat.); Architecture (Arch.); Painting; Paint; Food; Reflection (Reflect.); Map; Abstract (Abstr.); Scene; Fire; Blood; Anatomy (Anat.)

Table 23 shows the average number of times that each type of content response occurs per child at each age level. (Categories are listed in order of their total occurrence for the whole sample.) This table shows that with the child, as with the majority of adults, the outstanding content response at every age is the *Animal* response. A% ranges from 41% to 56%, its high points occurring at 2 and 4 years of age; its low points at 2½, 5½, and 7 years. The range from 2 through 10 years is from 50% at 2 years to 49% at 10 years. The occurrence of A% in the child is therefore at most ages near the usual top limit for the normal adult in whose record A% is expected to fall between 25% and 50%.

At 2 and 2½ years, *plants* is the second leading category, but from 3 through 7 years, *objects* holds second place. Another shift comes at 8 years when *humans* rises to second place, which it maintains through 10 years.

If we consider the four leading categories at any one age (the average number of different content categories throughout this range being usually close to four), we find that at 2 and 2½ years they are: animals, plants, objects, and nature. From 3 through 4½ years they are: animals, plants, objects, and humans. From 5 through 7 years they are: animals, objects, nature, and humans—plants dropping out. At 8, 9, and 10 years they are: animals, objects, anatomy, and humans.

Thus, the outstanding changes are that *humans* becomes a prominent response at 3 years and following; *plants* drops out as a main category

TABLE 23. DISTRIBUTION OF CONTENT CATEGORIES

(Mean occurrence of each category, mean A% and H%, and mean number of categories per child)

Variable							Age in years						
	2	2½	3	3½	4	4½	5	5½	6	7	8	9	10
Animal	4.8	4.5	6.0	6.5	8.3	6.3	6.2	5.7	7.5	7.6	7.3	8.7	8.1
Object	1.3	1.2	2.1	1.8	1.5	1.9	2.0	1.8	2.5	2.7	2.2	2.5	2.2
Human	.3	.5	.9	1.4	1.4	1.2	1.3	1.5	1.7	2.6	2.6	2.9	2.8
Plant	1.3	1.8	1.8	1.0	1.4	1.3	1.0	1.3	.8	.9	.6	.6	.4
Nature	.6	1.0	.0	.8	1.0	1.0	1.2	1.3	.9	1.5	.7	1.1	.6
Architecture	.4	.4	.5	1.0	.9	.7	.4	.5	.4	.5	.1	.2	.2
Anatomy	….	.1	.0	.0	….	.2	.4	.3	.6	.4	.9	1.2	.7
Flower	.4	.3	.2	.3	.2	.6	.1	.3	.4	.3	.2	.0	.3
Fire	.0	.1	.0	.1	.1	.2	.2	.5	.4	.7	.2	.2	.2
Scene	….	.0	.0	.1	….	.2	.3	.2	.3	.4	.2	.3	.2
Paint	.4	.4	.0	.1	.1	….	.1	.1	.1	.1	.2	.1	….
Map	….	….	….	.0	.1	.1	.4	.2	.2	.1	.1	.2	.0
Blood	….	….	….	.1	.1	.3	.1	.1	.1	.1	….	.1	.1
Food	.2	.1	.0	.1	.1	.1	.2	.1	.1	….	.2	.1	.1
Painting	….	….	….	.0	….	….	….	.1	.1	….	….	.0	….
Abstract	….	….	….	.0	….	….	….	….	….	….	.0	.1	….
Reflection	….	….	….	….	….	….	….	.1	….	….	.1	.0	….
A%	50%	41%	47%	48%	56%	44%	44%	41%	48%	42%	45%	48%	49%
H%	3%	4%	7%	10%	9%	8%	9%	11%	11%	14%	17%	16%	16%
Categories	2.6	2.9	3.5	4.2	3.8	4.6	4.7	4.9	4.8	5.2	4.7	5.2	4.8

Note: .0 indicates mean occurrence of less than .05; …. indicates no occurrence.

after 5–6 years; *anatomy* occurs conspicuously at 8 years and thereafter. *Animals* and *objects* are among the leading categories at every age. *Nature* responses occur conspicuously at every age even when not one of the four leading categories, though they are relatively inconspicuous at 3 to 4½ years and at 8 to 10 years.

The following categories occur but do not at any age reach an average incidence of one per child: paint, flower, painting, food, reflection, architecture, map, abstract, scene, fire, blood. Of these only architecture, flower, and fire occur at any age to the extent of .5 response per child.

The number of *different* content categories (including animal and human responses) given by the whole group at any one age ranges from ten at 2 years through seventeen at 9 years—its high point and an age which is also variable with regard to other factors—to thirteen at 10 years. 3½ and 5½ are also ages of rather high variability, there being sixteen different content categories at each of these ages.

The *average* number of different categories used by any one child is, of course, smaller, ranging from 2.6 at 2 years to 5.2 at 9 years and dropping slightly to 4.8 at 10 years when the large number of anatomic responses given by girls reduces the variety of kind of response. There is an almost straight-line increase in the number of different categories throughout the age range from 2 to 10 years except for very slight declines at 4 and 8 years.

With adults it is usually considered (Piotrowski, 61) that the more spread of content the better adjustment we find. Evidence of the cultural level and the quality of the intellect as well as freedom from repression and constriction is thought to be found in spread of content, and in the presence of such responses as map, architecture, scene, art, and the like. Thus with the child we may assume that the steadily increasing number of categories indicates cultural and intellectual responses which growth and experience are steadily enriching.

If we consider that A% indicates stereotypy of response, we find the most stereotypy at 2 and 4 years of age; the least at 2½, 5½, and 7. A certain amount of stereotypy is useful in the successful performance of daily tasks and a too great lack of this factor results in unpredictable and highly variable behavior.

Not only the number but also the type of animal responses is customarily taken into account in analyzing Rorschach protocols. Bochner and Halpern (18) note that:

... some animal responses are less indicative of stereotypy than others. ... An animal with a human expression such as a grinning bear or a sly fox shows more critical thinking and evaluation, less casual acceptance of the obvious, than do the usual animal responses. ... Moreover the type of animal chosen can be significant of the individual's feelings and attitudes. Obviously people who see only ferocious and aggressive animals, such as lions, tigers, fighting bears, etc. do not have the same attitude and outlook as do people who see rabbits, sheep, deer. Nor are either of these two groups like the subjects who see rats and bugs and other generally unpleasant and disliked animals. Still another group includes those who see birds and butterflies primarily. . . . Interpretations consistently dealing with aggressive fighting animals reflect strong feelings of hostility and aggression. Whether this aggression is directed outward or inward will be determined by other factors in the record. Where the mild, timid animals are the rule, the prevailing attitude will be found to be a somewhat insecure, essentially passive one.

Table 24 indicates the age changes which we have found with regard to the type of animals prevalent at different age levels. Table 25 presents these same data verbally. If we assume that different kinds of animals imply

TABLE 24. DISTRIBUTION OF ANIMAL RESPONSES*
(Total occurrence of each category)

| | Age in years | | | | | | | | | | | | |
	2	2½	3	3½	4	4½	5	5½	6	7	8	9	10
Domestic animals	83	61	90	80	53	59	48	55	51	57	49	58	47
Wild animals	44	51	99	109	126	81	104	72	97	114	99	123	95
Butterfly, bird, etc.	49	74	71	93	129	103	99	117	124	127	128	159	148
Water creatures	4	6	8	13	58	25	20	19	45	33	35	41	47
Worm, snake	0	2	1	2	12	9	7	6	7	10	5	13	7
Total number	180	194	269	297	378	277	278	269	324	341	316	394	344
No. of different kinds	22	23	41	46	52	52	52	49	53	53	59	68	63

* Ad not included.

different kinds of attitudes in subjects, we may note that very definite age changes take place in our population as to attitudes thus expressed. At 2 years and here only, *domestic animals* prevail. By 2½ and 3 years they have fallen to second place in frequency of occurrence, and after 3 years they occur even less conspicuously. *Wild animals,* which do not occur extensively at 2 and 2½ years, suddenly reach first place at 3, 3½, 4, and 5 years. After that age they drop to, and maintain, second place. The *butterfly-bird* category reaches and maintains first place from 5½ years following. Water creatures, and worms and snakes, occur minimally at all ages.

Thus the developmental change is from a predominance of domestic animals at 2 years, to wild animals at 3 to 5 years, to butterflies and birds from 5½ years following. Therefore, in evaluating animal responses in the child, though we may feel that the occurrence of wild animal responses indicates possible aggressivity at any age, we must at least recognize that wild animal responses are the predominant animal response from 3 to 5 years of age, and a conspicuous response from 5 to 10 years.

Number of different kinds of animals mentioned by the entire group varies from 22 at 2 years to 63 at 10 years. There is an almost steady increase in number of different kinds from 2 years to 9 years, the high point, and a slight decrease at 10 years.

TABLE 25.   ANIMALS OCCURRING IN RESPONSES TO THE RORSCHACH
(By ages in years)

2:	*Domestic animals* lead and of these kitty (27) and dog (32) are by far the most frequent. Butterfly (18) comes next.
2½:	*Butterfly-bird* leads as a category, and butterfly occurs most (31); bird is 27. Domestic animals are next, with dog leading (26). Elephant (13) and wolf (11) are conspicuous.
3:	*Wild animals* lead for the first time. Bear (18) is most; there are 18 elephants, 13 monkeys. Domestic animals come next. There are 31 dogs, actually the leading single category. Butterflies occur 23 times.
3½:	*Wild animals* again lead. Of these, elephant occurs 16 times, bear 22, monkey 14. Butterfly-bird is next, with butterfly occurring 24 times, bird 42. Dog occurs 36 times, cat 20.
4:	*Butterfly-bird* leads again; 54 butterflies, 40 birds. Wild animals are second: 22 bears, 15 monkeys, 18 elephants, 16 rabbits. Cat and dog are very infrequent at this age.
4½:	*Butterfly-bird* still leads, with 45 butterflies and 22 birds. Wild animals come next: there are 12 bears and for the rest a great variety of different wild animals. There are 29 dogs.
5:	*Wild animals* again lead: 16 rabbits, 20 bears, and 13 elephants. Butterfly-bird is next with 35 butterflies, 32 birds. There are 19 dogs at this age.
5½:	*Butterfly-bird* again leads with 45 butterflies, 43 birds. Wild animals is next with unnamed animals 19 times, bear 13. Dog occurs 20 times.
6:	*Butterfly-bird* leads: 55 butterflies, 34 birds. Wild animals next: 9 monkeys, 11 rabbits, 14 bears. There are 16 dogs.
7:	*Butterfly-bird* leads: 42 butterflies, 43 birds, 27 bats. Wild animals are next: 10 deer, 25 bears, 15 rabbits, 20 unnamed animals. Very few dogs—11.
8:	*Butterfly-bird* leads: 48 butterflies, 24 birds, 20 bats. Wild animals next: 19 unnamed animals, 15 rabbits, 12 bears. There are 17 dogs.
9:	*Butterfly-bird* leads: 57 butterflies, 30 birds, 32 bats. Wild animals next: 25 unnamed animals, 14 rabbits, 16 elephants, 19 bears. There are 18 dogs.
10:	*Butterfly-bird* leads: 55 butterflies, 22 birds. Wild animals next: unnamed animals 25, rabbits 13, 14 bears, 22 dogs.

If we consider that H% indicates interest in persons or in the self, we find that such an interest increases slowly but steadily through this eight-year span. Responses involving such semi-human figures as ghosts, dwarfs, giants, angels, witches are somewhat different in connotation from the usual human responses. They are usually thought to imply a childish, wishful, immature attitude indicating lack of reality, and superstition. Such responses occur minimally at all ages, though they increase steadily, doubling in number from 4½ to 5 years (i.e., from an average occurrence of .12 to an average of .26.) They double again (.54) at 5½ years, and this extent of response is maintained through 10 years.

So far as human and animal details are concerned, we find a conspicuous difference in the relative proportion of whole human figures to human details; and of whole animal figures to animal details. So far as human responses go, we find that a high proportion of such responses is detail

TABLE 26.   OCCURRENCE OF HUMAN AND ANIMAL DETAILS
(Average occurrence per child)

Age in Yrs.	H*	Hd*	Hd:H	A	Ad	Ad:A
2	.10	.05	50%	4.80	.02	—
2½	.26	.12	46%	4.38	.08	2%
3	.64	.22	34%	5.54	.44	7%
3½	.62	.24	38%	5.99	.47	7%
4	.80	.50	63%	7.77	.53	7%
4½	.70	.30	43%	5.42	.88	16%
5	.75	.25	33%	5.63	.57	10%
5½	.85	.40	47%	5.28	.42	8%
6	.85	.40	47%	6.28	1.22	19%
7	1.38	.54	39%	6.72	.88	13%
8	1.48	.56	37%	6.38	.90	14%
9	1.16	.98	84%	7.57	1.13	15%
10	1.60	.60	37%	6.67	1.43	21%

* Exclusive of (H) and (Hd)

rather than whole figure responses. As Table 26 indicates, detail responses are 30 to 40 per cent as frequent as whole responses; high points come at 4 years when detail responses are 63 per cent as frequent as whole responses and at 9 years when they occur as frequently as 84 per cent. With animal responses, the figures are quite different. Animal detail responses range from 2 per cent to 21 per cent as frequent as whole animal responses, the ages when they occur most extensively being 4½, 6, 9, and 10 years.

The expected ratio in adults of H:Hd is customarily given as 2:1. Human detail responses, if found in excess of this number, are thought to indicate an undue concern with body parts, as in hypochondriasis; may stem from feelings of anxiety; or may result from inability to integrate either because of emotional or other difficulties. During the first ten years of life, there are only two ages when detail responses exceed this 2:1 ratio, i.e. 4 and 9 years. The customary relationship of A to H is also usually considered to be about 2 to 1. However, Table 23 indicates that this ratio is not approached in the early years.

Anatomy responses, generally considered to indicate an excessive interest in bodily parts and functions and to reflect a certain amount of morbidity and/or hypochondriasis, come in conspicuously at 8, 9, and 10 years, approximating about one response per child at each of these ages. A few girls at 10 years give *only* anatomic responses.

In the records of some psychopaths, there has been noted an "overemphasis" on scenery and nature interpretations. Such an emphasis, particularly on nature responses, appears normally to characterize the very early years of life.

Sex responses and responses referring to eliminative organs occur so infrequently that they are scored here under anatomic responses when they occur alone. Such responses do not occur conspicuously in the first ten years of life, their frequency of occurrence at the ages here considered being, in age sequence: 0,0,1,7,7,7,1,0,2,0,1,2,0. The high point thus occurs from 3½ years when five different children make a total of seven such responses, through 4 years when four children give seven responses, to 4½ years when three children give seven responses. Fourteen of the twenty-eight responses refer directly to elimination; ten to the genital region; four to the buttocks. This high point of interest in sex parts is in accord with a hitherto observed tendency of 4 and 4½-year-old children to stress sex parts in drawing the human figure (Ames, 10).

Sex Differences in Content

Sex differences are conspicuously lacking with regard to *number of different content categories* employed, on the average, by boys and girls at each age. At three ages out of thirteen the average number of content categories used by the two sexes is identical, and at only four ages is the difference as much as .40. The only conspicuous difference is at 10 years when girls average 4.4 different content categories and boys 5.2. This rather large difference can be attributed to the high number of anatomical responses in 10-year-old girls, which reduces the number of different categories used.

Considering the main *content categories,* we find that sex differences are not for the most part large. We have considered the average number of occurrences for each category per age. So far as A% is concerned, at only six ages are differences of more than 4% found. In every instance this difference is in favor of the boys. H% differs by more than 4% at only two ages, both times in favor of girls.

Conspicuous differences in number of objects occur only at 4½ and 9 years. At 4½ years there are 2.3 object responses in girls, 1.6 in boys; at 9 years, 2.04 in girls, 2.92 in boys. Marked differences in number of plants occur at 3½, 5, 7, and 8 years, boys giving most plant responses except at 5 years.

Conspicuous differences in nature responses occur at 2, 2½, 5, 7, and 8 years, boys giving most at 2, 2½, and 7 years, girls most at 5 and 8 years. Differences in regard to architecture occur most at 3½, 4, 4½, and

7 years, favoring boys at 7 years only, girls at the other ages. Other content categories do not occur extensively enough to make differences noteworthy, and such differences as do exist are small. (Fire occurs twice as much in boys as in girls at 7 years; anatomy occurs much more in boys at 5, 6, and 8 years, and more in girls at 10 years.)

No meaningful pattern is observed in the differences just noted except that in general A% tends to be more in boys, H% more in girls. Thus we may state that in most instances sex differences in content are small and variable.

So far as the *variety of different animals* observed at any one age, the difference between the sexes increases with age, being greatest at 4 years, 5½, 6, 7, 9, and 10 years. At every one of these ages, as already noted, boys have the greater variety. Considering the total *number of animals* reported at any one age, marked sex differences occur at all ages except 2½, 5½, 6, 8, and 9 years. Girls give the most responses only at 2 and 2½ years. At every age thereafter boys definitely exceed in the number of animals reported.

As to *type of animal* reported: girls give the most domestic animals at seven ages, particularly at the earlier ages, and boys give most at six ages. The only conspicuous differences within this category come at 2 years when girls report 23 cats, boys 4; and at 3 years when girls report 22 dogs, boys 9.

As to wild animals, boys exceed girls in this response. At seven ages more wild animal responses are given by boys, and at two ages boys tie with girls. Boys exceed girls or tie with girls at every age until 5½ years. At eleven ages boys give more large wild animal responses than do girls. Performance is about even as as to small wild animals, now boys and now girls being most productive.

Boys exceed girls in number of flying animals reported, at eleven ages. Water animals occur most in boys at ten ages out of thirteen; worms and snakes at eight ages.

As we were gathering our data, it was our clinical impression that on Card V, particularly, girls tended to give more *butterfly* responses, boys more *bat* responses. Final analysis of data gave some confirmation of this impression. At every age but one—5½ years—there are more bat responses in boys than in girls. However, frequently there are also more butterfly responses in boys, since boys give more animal responses than do girls. Boys in all give 324 butterfly responses, 88 bats; girls give 249 butterfly responses, 45 bats. Thus there are nearly 100 per cent more bat responses in boys than in girls; only about 25 per cent more butterfly responses. The ratio of butterfly to bat in girls is approximately 5½:1; in boys, 7:2. Bat comes in a year and a half earlier in this group of boys than in girls. Ages at which boys most conspicuously exceed girls in bat responses are 4½, 6, 7, and 10 years.

CHAPTER EIGHT

Additional Test Factors

Several further aspects of the Rorschach response are described in this chapter. Some of them are traditional Rorschach scores: number of responses, number of popular and original responses. Others, though not scores, are aspects of response commonly considered: timing, refusals, cards liked best and least. Still others relate to children's usage of language in presenting their concepts: formation of plurals, method of identifying concepts.

Number and Length of Responses

The mean number of responses ranges between 9.6, at 2 years (for the 40 children responding at all), and 18.6 at 9 years. A steady increase appears from 2 to 4 years, then a decrease from 4½ to 5½. An increase appears again, with peaks at 7 and 9 years, and decreases at 8 and 10. For the total age range, mean R is 14.5, and this number is already exceeded at 4 years.

A very rough index of children's verbal productivity on the Rorschach was arrived at as follows. The number of lines of children's typed records was determined and the median computed for each age and sex. A record close to the median was selected and the number of words was counted. These "median" word counts are presented in Table 27.

The great increase in children's verbalizations is striking. Children go rapidly from one- or two-word responses at 2 years—"A doggie," "Kittie"—to long, full responses by the end of the preschool period. Girls' peak volubility appears at 6 years, boys' at 7; following these ages both groups become rather steadily less wordy.

Sex differences. Sex differences in number of responses are not marked except at 7 years when girls give a mean of 15.2 responses and boys a mean of 21.3. Boys' means also exceed girls' by more than one response at ages 2½, 4, and 6; girls exceed by more than one response only at 4½ years. The mean number of responses for girls for the total age range is 14.2, for boys is 15.0.

TABLE 27. TOTAL LENGTH OF RESPONSES IN WORDS

Age in years	Girls	Boys
2	22	30
2½	36	34
3	74	76
3½	92	83
4	141	97
4½	175	136
5	197	206
5½	266	263
6	290	270
7	268	546
8	279	322
9	253	353
10	238	225

In word output, girls' "median" word counts exceed boys' at seven of the nine ages before 7 years; boys consistently exceed from 7 years on. The sex difference is most marked at 7 years.

Refusals

Though refusals are not expected in the normal adult record, at all but three ages (3½, 6, and 7 years) more than one fourth of the subjects refuse at least one card. Table 28 presents the percentage of subjects refusing cards at each age. (Mean number of refusals is presented in Table 7.)

TABLE 28. PERCENTAGE OF CHILDREN REFUSING ONE OR MORE CARDS

Age in years	2	2½	3	3½	4	4½	5	5½	6	7	8	9	10
Percentage refusing	46	44	30	14	34	34	30	34	20	18	26	26	42

The highest rate of refusals occurs at 2 and 2½ years, when close to half of all subjects refuse cards. Thereafter the percentage of children refusing remains around 25 per cent until age 10, when it again increases over 40%.

This rate of refusals among bright, apparently normal children seems high. It is our impression that children seen for mild behavior disturbances actually tend to give fewer refusals than our normal sample. It may well be that our research subjects' familiarity with us and ease in the test situation allowed them to refuse more readily. In any case, it seems evident that card refusal, particularly of a single card, is not in itself an indicator of pathology in children's records.

Timing

Duration of total response was not recorded in all cases, particularly after 6 years of age. (When inquiry is conducted card-by-card, total time becomes as much a matter of examiner's tempo as child's, in records of any length.) Through six years, timing was recorded for about three fourths of the records, and Table 29 presents mean scores for boys and girls in this subsample.

TABLE 29. AVERAGE DURATION OF TOTAL RESPONSE IN MINUTES

Age in years	Girls	Boys	All
2	4.4	3.7	4.0
2½	5.6	4.5	5.3
3	6.1	5.5	5.8
3½	5.9	7.3	6.6
4	6.7	7.6	7.1
4½	7.8	6.7	7.2
5	7.7	7.9	7.8
5½	6.7	8.0	7.4
6	8.4	10.0	8.9

Two findings are apparent in Table 29. One is the steady increase in duration of mean response from four to nine minutes as age increases from 2 to 6 years. The other is the brevity of these early responses. Actually, with less than ten responses to give and using less than 30 words to give them with, the 2-year-old has plenty of time to do so in four minutes—much of which is occupied by encouraging and corralling activity by the examiner. Even the nine-minute records at age 6 will seem very brief to examiners used to hour-long sessions with adults. (But we would caution examiners unused to testing young children against trying too hard to obtain more fully elaborated records; extensive coaxing and detailed inquiry commonly lead to rejection of the task by preschooolers, and end up by producing incomplete records rather than fuller ones.)

Commonness of Response

Popular (P) Responses

Although our method of determining populars for children produced somewhat different lists of popular forms for 2 to 3½ years, 4 to 6 years, and 7 to 10 years, the increase in mean number of P is very steady (Table 7). Even when scored by standards appropriate to preschoolers, 2-year-olds give a mean of just 1.0 P. This mean value increases fairly rapidly up to 3.6 at age 6; thereafter the increase continues very slowly. Similarly, mean P%, just 10% at age 2, rises to 25% by age 5½ and remains close to 25% thereafter.

Original (O) Responses

We considered responses whose content for a particular area occurred only once in 100 records to be original. In order to have enough records to determine which responses met this criterion, we considered just three groups of ages, each composed of 200 subjects: 2 to 3½ years, 4 to 6 years (omitting 5½), and 7 to 10 years. All responses were tabulated for each area, and any response which occurred only once or twice was designated original. Table 30 presents the total number of responses so designated, the mean number per child, and the percentage of all responses which are original.

TABLE 30.　ORIGINAL RESPONSES

	Age in years		
Variable	2-3½	4-6	7-10
Total number	951	902	1597
Mean per child	4.8	4.5	8.0
% of all responses	42	31	46

Using this criterion, about 40 per cent of children's responses in the first ten years are original. The proportion of original responses is higher in the first and last thirds of the total age range; from 4 to 6 years a smaller proportion of children's responses are original.

Considering popularity and originality of response together, one gets a picture of marked variability from child to child in Rorschach responses during the early preschool period, with under 15 per cent of responses shared as common percepts and over 40 per cent of responses unique. In the later preschool and early school years, close to 20 per cent of responses are shared, popular responses, and just 30 per cent are unique. From 7 to 10 years, the most common responses make up about 25 per cent of all responses, while original responses increase to nearly half of all responses.

The finding of so many original responses seems surprising, when compared with standards based on the more usual subjective scoring of originality. This is because most responses which *are* original do not *look* original, in the sense of novel and perceptive; many just look miscellaneous. They are original in the sense that other children have not given that response, but they are not very striking and their originality passes unnoticed in usual scoring. (We no longer try to score originality in individual records, except for research purposes, though of course the total effect of originality remains important in appraising individual records.)

Best- and Least-Liked Cards

Each subject was asked at the end of the test to indicate which card he liked best and which he liked least. Table 31 lists the cards most often chosen as best and least liked at each age.

TABLE 31.　Choice of Best- and Least Liked Cards

	Best		Least	
Age in years	G	B	G	B
2	II	II	X	II
2½	X	I	II	II
3	X	X	VI	II
3½	X	X	VI	VI
4	II	X	II, III, IV	I
4½	X	VIII	VI	I
5	X	X	II	I, VI
5½	X	X	VI	I, VI
6	X	X	I, IV, IX	I, IV, VI
7	X	X	II, VI	X
8	X	X	IV	IV
9	X	X	IV	IV
10	X	X	IV	IV, VI
Predominant	X	X	VI, IV, II	I, VI, IV

At nearly every age Card X is preferred by the majority of both boys and girls. Occasional exceptions occur, when Card II, I, or VIII is preferred, but the preponderance of preferences is clearly for Card X.

Which card is least liked shows much more variation, both from age to age and between sexes. Girls most often choose VI, IV, and II as disliked; boys most often choose VI, I, and IV.

Semantic Analysis

How does the young child conceive the task we set for him? Is he identifying pictures, guessing at puzzles, trying to give right answers, or finding resemblances to vague stimuli? He rarely tells us directly, but his phrasing of his response often throws light on his view of the task.

Table 32 lists a number of forms of phrasing responses, grouped into three main categories: simply naming the blot, identifying the blot, and comparing the blot to the concept. The phrasing of every response was tabulated at each age and the frequencies of each category, expressed as a percentage of total responses for the age, are presented in Table 32. Developmental trends in phrasing responses were surprisingly strong.

Simply *naming* the blot—"doggie," "two kitties," "a boy," etc.—is the simplest and clearly the earliest form of response. It is practically the sole

TABLE 32. SEMANTIC ANALYSIS

(Percentage occurrence of each response category at each age)

Response category	Age in years												
	2	2½	3	3½	4	4½	5	5½	6	7	8	9	10
I. Names blot	84	78	73	64	70	62	40	59	45	38	30	30	33
II. Identifies blot													
a. Positive, "That is"	13	19	13	17	9	7	12	6	10	15	7	6	3
b. Extra-positive	0	0	....	....	....	0	....	....	0	1	....	....	1
*c. Questions identity	0	0	1	1	2	3	1	2	2	....	2	....	....
*d. "Might be," "could be"	0	0	1	2	....	2	3	2	1	5	8	6	11
*e. "I guess," "I think"	0	0	....	0	....	....	5	2	....	1	5	3	....
f. Must be	0	0	....	2	0	....	0	....	....	1	....	0	0
g. "I see a . . ."	0	1	2	2	2	1	1	2	1	2	1	1	....
h. Assumes reality	0	....	2	2	0	0	0	3	....	2	1	1	1
Total Level II	13	21	18	24	13	14	22	17	15	26	24	17	16
III. Compares blot to concept													
a. "Looks like"	3	1	10	10	17	24	33	23	38	29	36	41	42
*b. "Does it look like?", etc.	0	0	0	0	....	0	0	0	....	0	....	1	0
*c. Partial resemblance:													
1. "Looks something like"	0	0	0	0	....	....	2	....	1	4	6	8	7
2. "If you cut this off," etc.	0	0	0	0	0	0	1	0	....	2	2	2	1
*d. To-me-ness	0	0	0	0	0	....	3	1	1	2	1	2	1
Total Level III	3	1	10	10	17	25	38	24	40	36	45	53	51
*All qualified concepts combined	0	0	2	3	2	6	14	6	5	14	25	21	20

.... denotes less than 1 per cent occurrence

form of phrasing at the earliest ages, and it declines steadily in usage until, after 7 years, less than a third of responses are so phrased.

In *identifying* the blot, the child indicates that the blot *is* something and that his task is to identify it. He may do so positively ("That's a dog"), even extra-positively ("Definitely it's a penguin"), or his identification may be more tentative ("Might be a dog," "Is it a dog?"), but his phrasing indicates that whether he thinks he is right or wrong the "answer" lies in the blot. Nearly always this identification is made with a form of the verb *to be,* but occasionally a child indicates his assumption of the reality of the concept by plunging in in midstream ("Those two doggies are falling down"; "What are those men doing?").

The use of *identifying* phrasing ranges only between 13 and 26 per cent of responses. It is highest between 3½ and 7 years, but a developmental trend in use is not marked. Within the general category, however, the more assertive form of identification ("That's a . . . .") clearly declines in usage, especially after age 7, while more tentatively expressed identifications ("Might be a . . . .") increase.

Comparing the concept to the blot involves variations on "looks like," "seems like," "reminds me of . . . " The phrasing indicates some recognition that the concept does not lie solely in the blot, though this recognition is only rarely made explicit in a "to-me" statement ("To me it looks like . . . ."). As the sophistication of this concept would suggest, it is barely present in the early preschool period but is increasingly used as the child develops. After age 8, more than half of all responses are phrased in this way.

Tentativeness or qualification of response can appear at both levels II and III. When all the more qualified responses are considered together —those starred in Table 32—a steady increase appears with age, from none at all to about 20 or 25 per cent of responses after age 7. Moderate amounts of qualification of response appear to be a sign not of neurotic doubt but of mature tentativeness in giving associations to ambiguous stimuli.

Plurals

The symmetrical Rorschach blots frequently produce associations of pairs of things. How the child expresses plurality will reflect his language maturity. All concepts of twosomes were tabulated for our sample, and the frequencies of each form of expression are presented as a percentage of the total for each age in Table 33.

The phrasings are listed in order of increasing median age, and so form a rough developmental gradient. At every age the most common plural form is either the usual plural word or the usual plural with the specifying addition of "two." These forms together are least common in the early preschool period and increase with age.

TABLE 33. PLURALS

(Percentage occurrence of each wording at each age)

Wording	2	2½	3	3½	4	4½	5	5½	6	7	8	9	10
						Age in years							
One word meaning two	19	4	0	1	5	5	4	3	1	0	0	0	0
Doggie, doggie	19	7	14	3	3	4	2	3	1	0	0	0	0
Doggie, another doggie	3	15	14	3	4	2	4	3	1	0	0	0	0
Doggie, kitty	9	0	5	3	5	10	6	3	2	0	0	0	0
That's a dog and that's a dog—two dogs	0	0	0	2	0	0	1	0	0	0	0	0	0
Doggie, two doggies	0	2	1	0	3	6	4	3	4	0	0	0	0
Incorrect plural	3	11	0	3	1	1	0	0	0	2	2	1	1
Usual plural	32	48	49	63	57	47	42	41	45	46	39	48	28
Two doggies	16	13	17	23	22	25	37	46	46	51	59*†	51*	71*‡

* Adjective very frequently intervenes: "Two little dogs."
† A few say "Doggies, two."
‡ Several say "A couple of," "Those two look like dogs," "Those look like two dogs," "Dog, two of them."

The first six phrasings listed in Table 33 are clearly preschool constructions and rarely occur after age 5. A single word meant to include both of a pair (shown by pointing, etc.) and a single word repeated, alone or with "another" inserted ("Doggie, doggie"; "Doggie, another doggie") are found mainly in the earliest phrasings. "Doggie, two doggies" and incorrect plurals occur somewhat later. The usual plural form of the noun is the most frequent single category of phrasing at all ages up to 5½. From 5 to 7 years, this usual plural is about equal in frequency to responses with the specification of "two." After 7, "two dogs" is increasingly the standard form for expressing plurality.

Part Two

Part Two of this volume is made up of a series of chapters which depict the nature of the Rorschach response at each half-yearly age level from 2 to 6 years and at each yearly age level from 6 to 10 years. Each chapter presents a qualitative description of the individuality of the age in question both as determined by earlier investigations and as seen in the Rorschach response.

It also presents for ready reference a summary of the extent to which each of the common individual Rorschach determinants occurs. This is followed by a brief section on sex differences at the age in question, and by a tabular comparison of the Rorschach and developmental findings.

Several actual case records are then presented for each age level, one or more each for boys and for girls. Each case presented has been selected as typical of the age in question, and the actual protocol is in each instance supplemented by a comment as to the manner in which the response brings out not only the age but the individuality factors of the child giving the response.

CHAPTER NINE

Two Years

R = 9.6	90%F	4.8A = 50%A
	54%F+	.3H = 3%H
		1.3 plant
53%W	.1M .1FM .1m	1.3 object
42%D	.1FC .1CF .4C	.6 nature
4%Dd	.2F(C) .1Clob	
	.1M : .7ΣC	1.0P = 10%P

Qualitative Description

Of our fifty 2-year-old subjects, four-fifths, or forty children, gave at least one response to the cards. The average number of responses, for the forty children who could name what they saw in the blots, was, however, rather high—9.6—the range being from 1 to 18 responses per child.

At this age, the response is almost completely colored by what Klopfer has called "magic repetition," that is perseveration of the same response on three or more cards. The child gives a first response, for instance "doggie," to Card I or II, and then continues calling all or several of the other cards "doggie" even though such a designation may be completely inappropriate. Magic repetition characterizes the majority of responses at this age, 14 out of the 18 girls who respond, and 17 out of the 22 boys, giving this form of response. Thus 31 children out of 40, or 77 per cent, give responses which consist largely of this inappropriate repetition of a concept which may or may not have been appropriate the first time it was given.

Doggie, kitty, and *tree* are the words on which the child most frequently perseverates. A complete list of the perseverations found in our group, with an indication of the number of different children who use the term perseveratively, follows:

Girls: birdie 1; block 1; flower 2; house 1; kitty 3; lamb 1; lion 1; lollypop 1; owl 1; paint 1; pumpkin 1; sheeps 1; *tree* 4; turtle 1.

Boys: bird 2; butterfly 1; car 1; dog 3; flower 1; ghost 1; monkey 1; mountain 1; paint 1; smoke 1; snow 1; *tree* 4; turtle 1; umbrella 1.

Only three girls and four boys out of the whole group of fifty cases give more than three answers without including magic repetition. On the other hand, five boys and three girls perseverate on more than one concept.

In spite of this magic repetition which occurs so extensively that we must consider the giving of a Rorschach to a 2-year-old to be more of scientific than of practical value, it should be noted that out of this group of fifty children, forty do give some response; and the average number of refusals among those who do respond is surprisingly low—only an average of 2.4 per child.

The response at this age often appears to be the child's general impression. The card seems to call to the child's mind the general idea of doggie, kitty, tree, and the like, rather than specifically resembling the concept. Any effort on the part of the Examiner to clarify the response by getting the child to indicate exactly where he sees something or to point out which part of the blot is the doggie or kitty, usually only confuses matters. The 2-year-old appears to be very suggestible, and at the same time quite unclear as to what he has seen or where he has seen it. If asked where he has seen something, he will point to some part of the card, apparently at random, to satisfy the Examiner; and if the Examiner departs from proper procedure to the extent of making a specific suggestion, the child is almost certain to accept it. The most accurate response at this age can be obtained by going quickly through the whole series of cards and noting the child's initial responses.

There is, in spite of magic repetition, some variety of responses. Thirteen girls and 19 boys give more than one concept in their answers. Ten different content categories appear in all, the four most prevalent categories being animals, plants (mostly trees), objects, and nature responses other than plants. Of the 384 responses given in all by children of this age group, 146 occur in merely five categories, as follows. There are 38 tree responses, 32 dog, 27 bird, 27 cat, and 22 large wild animals. Several children who see nothing else see "doggie" plainly on one or more cards. Also the number of different items used in perseveration shows considerable variety. However the simple one-word response "doggie," "kitty," "birdie," "tree" definitely predominates and colors the picture at this age.

Movement responses are very scarce—perhaps it is surprising that they occur at all. There are three M responses, three FM and two m. Color responses are more numerous: two FC in all, five CF and fifteen C. This is the only age at which pure C responses predominate over the other two types of color. All but one of the C responses are "paint." One is "water."

With such a small number of both color and movement responses, it is inevitable that the F% is very high, the highest of any age. The average experience balance in this group is .1M : .7ΣC, but 16 of the 22 boys who respond and 12 of the 18 girls have an experience balance of 0M : 0ΣC.

F + % is only 54%, the lowest of any age except 2½ years, suggesting that only about half of the concepts given describe the blots accurately. Not only are the majority of the perseverative responses inappropriate as descriptions of the blot, but some of the nonperseverative concepts are also extremely inappropriate—for instance the response "moon" for all of Card III; "cow" for Card V; "kitty" for the white center of Card II; "car" for the man on III.

However there are a few rather advanced concepts: "Two doggies eating a bone" on Card III; "Bug climbing up on Christmas tree," or "Dere's da thing some bears climbing on" on Card VIII. Also we get "house" as a response to the tiny detail on Card VII in three children.

Single word responses predominate, but a few children use adjectives to describe their concepts. Most frequent is the adjective "broken" which occurs eleven times in all and is given by four different children. "Little" or "tiny" is given by three children. Other adjectives are: "pretty," "funny," "another," and "big bad." Inappropriate adjectives approach contamination: "foot snow," "turkey mountain."

There is some manipulation of cards, though this can usually be kept at a minimum by skillful procedure. There are in our group only fifteen instances of card turning. A few children try to open cards. A few look on the back (twelve instances of this in all) and one verbalizes as he does so, "Goodnight nobody," probably having gotten the idea from the picture book *Goodnight Moon* which includes a blank page entitled "Goodnight nobody." One child gives the response "mountain" to Card I and then pretends to grab the picture of the mountain and throw it away. This, however, appears to be more in fun than in earnest. Another child, however, gives the response "paint," then touches the paint with his finger and obviously expects it to come off onto his finger. Several, when they have finished with a card say "Put down," or "Throw away."

Two-year-olds in this, as in other situations, have a tendency to repeat exactly, word for word, what is said to them instead of making an appropriate answer. Thus TWO may say, "What do you see, Susan?" instead of telling what she sees.

Individual Determinants

Number: At this age the average child who gives any verbal responses to the cards, gives an average of 9.6 responses.

Area: Whole responses definitely lead with an average of 53% per child. D% is 42%; Dd% only 4%, the lowest of any age.

Form: F% is 90%, higher than at any subsequent age. Thus obviously nearly all of the child's responses at this age are determined by form alone. F + %, however, is only 54%, lower than at any other age except 2½ years. Only about half of the responses given are good form.

M, FM, m: These responses scarcely occur at 2 years. The averages per child are .1M, .1FM, .1m. M responses are: *people, daddy* (making a fist), and *man run.* FM is more active: *eating* and *climbing.* Water and fire in movement make up the m responses but there are several tendencies to m as seen in things breaking or being broken.

Color: There are considerably more color than movement responses, an average of .7, with pure C responses definitely leading—the only age at which this is true. The average C response is .4, average CF .1, FC only .1. C responses are all *paint;* CF, *flower.*

Shading: Shading responses occur only on the average of .24 per child at this age, being almost nonexistent. Nearly all are instances of diffusion—as *clouds* or *smoke.*

Clob: Is virtually nonexistent at this age.

Content: Ten different content categories appear at this age with an average of 2.6 per child. Animals, plants, objects, and nature are the outstanding content categories, in that order. A% is high, 50%; H% at an all-time low, only 3%. Domestic animals are the leading animal responses with butterfly-bird coming second. *Dog* occurs more than any other type of animal, with *cat* and *bird* next.

Length: Records at this age are shorter than at any subsequent age. A typical record, of either sex, may run to about twenty words.

Timing: The average timing for total response is the lowest of any age—4 minutes.

Semantics: The chief method of identification at 2 years is simply naming the blot: "Doggie," "Kitty." A few children identify the blot by saying, "That's a doggie."

Plurals: As at every age through 5 years, twoness is most often expressed by the correct plural form, but at this age one word, such as *doggie,* may mean, however, two doggies; or the repetition of the noun, as *doggie, doggie,* is frequent.

Best and Worst: Card II is most preferred by both sexes. Card II is also most disliked by boys. Girls dislike Card X most.

Sex Differences

Boys and girls give approximately an equal number of responses—an average of 9.9 in girls, of 9.3 in boys. Eighteen girls respond positively to the cards; twenty-two boys.

As to area, D% is higher in girls, W% in boys. Averages are: Girls: 48%W, 49%D, 2%Dd; Boys: 57%W, 36%D, 6%Dd.

M, FM, and m are very low, with slightly more M and FM in girls. Color occurs to about an equal extent in both, but color naming occurs six times in girls, once in boys.

Shading responses occur almost exclusively in boys—twelve times in boys, only once in girls. Clob occurs most in girls as the response *paint* to the black cards.

There are more animal responses in girls, more human responses in boys. Thus girls give more animal and more detail responses; boys more human and more global.

Content differences are small, but there are more food, architecture, and paint responses in girls; more nature, plant, and flower responses in boys.

Characteristics of Two Years as Shown by the Rorschach

At this age the Rorschach is not a useful tool for measuring the child's intellectual and emotional status or for revealing his characteristic individuality patterns, or characteristic individuality patterns of the age.

Sample Record of 2-Year-Old Girl J.O.

RESPONSE	INQUIRY			
			SCORING	
I. Turtle. Dat. Turtle	(Points to top right and left. Sees two turtles.)	W_2	F+	A
II. Dat turtle.	(Right hand figure.)	D	F−	A
Zat? Sock.	(Points to red.)	D	F+	obj
Dat's a hole.	(Center white.)	S	F+	obj
III. Dat? Turtle.	(Points to bow.)	D	F−	A
IV. Dat? (Pushes card away.) Turtle.	(Points to center top as head of turtle.)	W_0	F±	A
V. Turtle.	(Indicates top center as head.)	W_0	F−	A
VI. Turtle.	(W)	W_0	F−	A
Block.	(Top D)	D	F−	obj
VII. Getting anudder book. Dat turtle.	(Each card is a "book" to her.)	W_0	F−	A
Blocks.	(Each tier is evidently a "block.")	W_x	F±	obj
VIII. Dat. Block.	(Top gray.)	D	F−	obj
Dat. Block.	(Center blue.)	D	F−	obj
IX. Anudder book. Dat. Want to read it. Dat. Turtle.	(This time indicates green and pink as "book.")	D	F−	obj
(She turns card over and looks on back.)	(W, position inverted.)	W_0	F−	A

X. Dat. (She looks on back of card.)　(W)
Want to read it. Turtle.

　　　　　　　　　　　　　　　　　W₀　　F−　　A

R = 16　　　　　　　　　Time: 5 minutes

6W₀
1W₂
1Wₓ = 50%W　　　16F = 100%F　　　　　　　　　9A = 60%A
7D = 44%D　　　　3F+, 2F±, 11F− = 25%F+　　7 objects
1S = 6%Dd

0M : 0ΣC　　　　　　　　　　　　　　　　　0P

COMMENT　This is a typical Rorschach protocol for the age, and the simplicity and sparseness of the results are quite evident. The outstanding characteristic is magic repetition of the response "turtle," though at VII "block" also becomes repetitive. A glance at the totals will show that perception resembles that of most of the 2-year-olds in our group in being more global than detailed. The F+%, however, is lower than might be expected. This is due for the most part to the strong perseveration of response.

In the entire protocol there are five different responses, namely: "turtle," "sock," "hole," "block," "book." It is here that we may look for possible interpretive evidence of indi-vidual differences at this age. Individuality stands out more clearly if we compare this list of responses with those of the 2-year-old boy whose sample record follows. If "turtle" can be given any affective connotation, we have the impression that this child protects herself by limiting and confining her environment. Such an impression is confirmed by the other responses, which are all things well known, familiar objects close to home. The space interpretation on Card II is probably another evidence of the resistance offered by this child when a new stimulus is introduced. She appears to be of a determined nature and quite definite in her desire to be in control of the situation.

Sample Record of a 2-Year-Old Boy R. J.

RESPONSE	INQUIRY	SCORING			
I. A tree.	(Indicates W.)	W₁	F+	plant	P
II. A tree.	(Indicates W.)	W₁	F+	plant	
III. Dat's a tree.	Right dere (W.) He leaves the table and walks around the room. Ex. takes him on her knee.	W₀	F±	plant	
IV. Dat's a tree.	(W)	W₀	F+	plant	P
V. Tree.	Right dere (W).	W₀	F+	plant	
Big long tail.	Mr. Johnson's. (? the janitor.)	D	F+	Ad	
VI. Butterfly.	(W) Read this. He tries to open card.	W₁	F+	A	
VII. Bears.	(Two top tiers.)	D	F+	A	
VIII. Dat's a tree.	(Bottom pink and orange.) He claps his hands.	D	F±	plant	
IX. Shoes.	He seems to be referring to Ex's shoes.	D	CF	plant	
Dat a tree.	(Green)		Repetition		
Those are trees.	(Again the green.)	D	F±	A	
But those are bears.	(Indicates orange.)				
I get down.	Gets off Ex's lap.				
X. The brushoz. Dat's a brushoz.	Ex. is unable to interpret this even after several trials.		?		

Card most liked: VI
Card least liked: II

R = 11

Time: 4 minutes

$3W_0$
$3W_1 = 54\% W$

$10F = 90\% F$
$7F+, 3F\pm = 85\% F+$

3A
$1Ad = 36\% A$
7 plant

$5D = 46\% D$

1CF

$0M : 1\Sigma C$

2P = 18%P

COMMENT Here we see again how strong the age characteristics are at 2 years, with magic repetition, restricted content, and high F% the most outstanding items. But nonetheless, we can see the individuality in the responses themselves. Even at this age the subject reveals himself through his interpretations by indicating the kinds of things to which he reacts, the things which are meaningful to him. Certainly "tree," "butterfly," "bears," and "big long tail" reveals a different response to environment and a different organism (even organization) from "turtle," "butterfly," "block," "book," "sock," and "hole," as seen in the subject just preceding. This boy is not as self-protective in his reactions as the girl seems to be. He is willing to project further into his environment. A response such as "tree" is more diffuse, more pervasive than "turtle."

It is more elementary and fundamental, while "turtle" is more sophisticated.

"Butterfly" and "bears" are more dynamic concepts than "block," "sock," and "book," but they may indicate less predictability of behavior. This boy is probably more emotional and more instinctive in his reactions, while the girl is more intellectual. And there is more imagination in such a response as "big long tail" (of Mr. Johnson). Of course we must remember that there is a sex difference here which these responses may also typify.

From the configuration of totals and ratios of a 2-year-old protocol, one realizes the limited scope of the Rorschach for this age. However, individuality is to some extent revealed even within these narrow limits.

CHAPTER TEN

Two and a Half Years

R = 10.8	83%F	4.4A = 41%A
	54%F+	.5H = 4%H
50%W		1.8 plant
44%D	.1M .1FM .1m	1.0 nature
6%Dd	.1FC .5CF .2C	1.2 object
	.3F(C) .2Clob	
	.1M : .9ΣC	1.5P = 13%P

Qualitative Description

The response of the 2½-year-old is in many ways not strikingly different from that of the 2-year-old. The one-word answer and "magic repetition" of often inappropriate concepts prevail. There is little color or movement, and form—frequently poor form—largely determines responses.

At 2½ years, 48 out of 50 children give at least one response. The average number of responses is 10.8, and the range from 1 to 26. Thus more children respond than at 2 years of age and those who do respond give slightly more answers than at 2 years.

Magic repetition (the same response three or more times) is still very strong. Fifteen girls and 20 boys out of 48 responders (72%) have magic repetition. There are 21 instances of it in 15 girls, 6 girls perseverating on more than one word. There are 29 instances of it in 20 boys, 9 having more than one word perseverated.

Tree is the main response at this age, 16 out of 48 children perseverating on it. Different perseverations are:

Girls: bird 3; bow-wow 2; butterfly 1; elephant 1; flowers 2; flying horses 1; leaf 1; mask 1; mosquito 1; paint 1; painting 1; water 1.
Boys: bee 1; birdie 1; butterfly 2; castle 1; dog 1; fire 1; flower 2; lion 1; mountain 1; mouse 1; paint 1; *tree 11;* water 1.

Thus 15 out of 24 girls perseverate. Only 7 give more than three answers without perseveration. Twenty out of 24 boys perseverate. Only three have more than three answers without perseveration.

At this age, as at 2 years, the card seems to call up to the child more the general impression of some object or thing rather than a specific identifiable image. It is a very poor technique, after the child has pointed out even roughly where something is, for the Examiner to point out other portions of the card and to ask if this is a part, or if it is any special part, because the child will almost invariably say "Yes" to any such question.

Perseveration at this age is static, not dynamic; that is, no part of the concept changes.

There are numerous refusals, even in those who give "good" answers, though fewer than at two, the number having dropped from an average of 2.4 per child to an average of 1.8. This number of refusals drops again sharply after 2½ years to less than one per child.

There are now twelve different content categories occurring, with an average of 2.9 different categories being used per child. The four leading categories are as at 2 years: animals, plants (mostly trees), objects, and nature. As to types of animal response there is a shift since 2 years. Now butterfly-bird leads, with domestic animals second. There are 74 butterfly-bird responses, only 61 domestic animals. Elephant occurs 13 times and wolf 11. Some apparently unusual responses occur at this age: Christmas tree 9 times; merry-go-round 4 times; sailboat 4 times. A% is only 41%, much lower than at 2 years, in fact lower than at any other age until 5½ years. H% has increased to 4%. There are half again as many popular responses as at 2 years.

The simple one word response "tree" or "doggie" or "birdie" or "paint" definitely dominates at this age, and while it may be considered a "good" response at this age as at 2 years, it is not otherwise particularly revealing.

Adjectives modify the noun occasionally, the chief adjectives which occur being as follows. The adjective "big" occurs 23 times. Some color name occurs as a modifying adjective 16 times. "More" occurs 11 times, "another" 9 times. "Dirty" is used 7 times, "little" 5 times, "baby" meaning little, twice.

Movement responses, though more frequent than at 2 years, are still extremely few in number. The average number at this age is .1M, .1FM, .1m. M consists merely of two people just existing. FM is more active and includes running, sitting, fighting, climbing, flying, washing. m includes things cracked or broken or spinning in place.

There is a shift in color responses. At 2 years, pure C led; now CF leads, with pure C coming second. FC scarcely occurs—the child shows very little adaptivity at this age. Pure C responses are "paint"; CF "flower" or "butterfly." Color adjectives, as noted, are conspicuous and color naming reaches an all-time high, the average per child having increased from .1 to .5. Several also see color in the black cards, as green leaf on IV, blue paint on V, blue picture on VII. There is also an average of .2 Clob which occurs mostly as mention of blackness.

Form % is now only 83%, since there occur a few more color and movement responses than at 2 years; but F+% remains low, only 54%, suggesting the rather inaccurate form perception of this age.

Whole responses here decrease while detail responses increase. W% is only 50%; D% has risen to 44%.

Both card turning and looking on the back of the card have increased slightly since 2 years. Now there are 25 instances of card turning and 17 instances of looking on the back. Turning cards to look on the back, in our population, only occurs conspicuously at 2 and 2½ years. A few try to "open" the cards.

Several give excuses for getting out of the situation: "I can't see," or "I gotta go home." An occasional child personifies the card, as "Bite you" to Card V; or seems to think that the "paint" from the card will come off on his fingers.

The average experience balance is .1M : .9ΣC, but there are still 28 subjects whose experience balance is 0M : 0ΣC.

An occasional child makes conversational remarks, related to the blots, as the child who calls VI "A Christmas tree" and then remarks, "I got a Christmas tree home. We burned it"; but this is fairly unusual.

Individual Determinants

Number: Has increased slightly since 2 years. The average number of responses is now 10.8.

Area: Number of wholes has decreased slightly, now being only 50%; and the number of details has increased, now being 44%. Dd has increased slightly, to 6%.

Form: Number of responses determined by form alone has decreased from 90% to 83%. Accurate form remains low. Only 54% of answers are good form.

M, FM, m: Though each of these determinants has increased slightly since 2 years, there are still virtually no M, FM, or m responses. The average occurrence of these determinants is only .1M, .1FM, .1m. M consists only of two people, just existing. FM is more active and includes running, sitting, fighting, climbing, flying, washing. m includes things cracked or broken, water in movement, things spinning in place, flames moving upward.

Color: ΣC has increased from .7 at 2 years to .9. There is a shift here from a predominance of C responses to a predominance of CF, and FC though still very low has doubled since 2 years. Values now are FC .1, CF .5, C .2.

Of the pure C responses, paint still leads as at 2 years. Of CF responses, flower still leads, but butterfly has now come in strongly.

Shading: Shading responses have increased slighty since 2 years and now occur on the average of .3 per child. Diffusion still occurs conspicuously but the leading type of shading responses is now water forms.

Clob: Has increased to an average of .2 per child, occurring mostly as mention of blackness of the cards.

Content: There are now in all 12 different content categories which occur, and the average child gives responses in 2.9 different content categories. Animals, plants (mostly trees), objects, and nature responses are the leading content categories. A% has decreased to an extreme low of 41% and H responses have increased to 4%.

Butterfly-bird responses are the leading animal responses with domestic animals second. However, though there are slightly more domestic than wild animals, large wild animals is the leading single category.

Length: The average record, in both sexes, has increased slightly in length from an average of about 20 words per child to around 35 words per child.

Timing: The average number of minutes for the total response has increased from 4.0 to 5.3.

Semantics: Simply naming the blot continues to be the chief method of identification, with "That is a———" coming second.

Plurals: Though—as at all ages through 5 years—the correct plural form leads as a method of expressing twoness, "Doggie, another doggie" occurs here conspicuously.

Best and Worst: Card X is liked best by girls; Card I by boys. Card II is least liked by both sexes.

Sex Differences

Sex differences are minimal at this age. Boys make more responses than do girls—an average of 11.7, whereas girls give only an average of 10.

As to area, boys give more responses in every area than do girls. However, differences are very small as to percentage of responses in each area.

There are more M in boys than in girls; more FM in girls than in boys. FM is more active in both than M. As to color responses, there are few sex differences.

There are many more shading responses in boys than in girls—three in girls, thirteen in boys. As to content, girls use many more different content categories in all, and give more domestic animal and flying animal responses than do boys. Boys give more wild animal answers.

Boys give the adjective "big" twenty-two times, girls only once. "Christmas tree" occurs eight times in boys, only once in girls.

Characteristics of 2½ Years as Shown by the Rorschach

At 2½ years as at 2 years, it does not seem that the Rorschach is a uniquely useful tool for determining intellectual and emotional characteristics of the child or for revealing the characteristic individuality of the child *or* of the age.

However, even at this very early age, the Rorschach does yield a picture which—so far as it goes—describes accurately the individuality of the 2½-year-old as we know it.

We have the picture of an organism whose emotions are primarily egocentric and unmodulated, and who is to some extent at the mercy of these emotions, quite lacking the ability to adapt, emotionally, to the demands of the outside world.

This individual has only a minimal interest in other people as well as little ability to adapt to their demands. His stubbornness and rigidity are indicated in the Rorschach by the pervasive tendency toward perseveration which so markedly colors his responses.

His psychic life is extremely restricted; he has very slight endowments on either the introversive or the extratensive side of life. Simple form alone for the most part determines his perceptions. The content of his psychic life also is limited. His perceptions are not too accurate. His psychic drives are more at the instinctual than at the conscious level.

Comparison of Rorschach and Developmental Findings

Developmental	Rorschach
Child is egocentric and emotions are unmodulated. He is unable to adapt emotionally to the demands of others.	CF and C predominate definitely over FC. FC is on the average only .1 per child.
Little interest in other people.	H% only 4% on the average.
Stubborn and rigid.	A% is 41%. Marked perseveration.
Psychic life extremely restricted; its content limited.	Very limited variety of content. Basic equation is .1M : 9ΣC.
Perceptions are not extremely accurate.	F+% only 54%.
Psychic drives more at an instinctual than at a conscious level.	FM slightly exceeds M though both are extremely small.

Sample Record of 2½-Year-Old Girl N.A.

RESPONSE	INQUIRY	SCORING			P
I. A leaf.	(Whole)	W₁	F+	plant	
II. A boot.	(Points to top red.) *Else?* Nope.	D	F+	obj	
III. Ducks.	(Points to the usual black figures, each side.) *Else?* Nope.	W̸₂	F+	A	P
IV. A green leaf.	(Whole.) She turns card over and places it with others.	W₁	F±	plant	
V. That's green leaf too.	(Whole.) Again turns card over and places it with others.	W₀	F+	plant	
VI. Hanger toat [coat].	*Coat hanger?* She nods and stands up. *Where?* Just up there. (Top D only.) *Where's my coat? Coat tree?* Yes, little one. We go downstairs. Sits on request.	D	F+	obj	
VII. Green leaf too.	(Whole)	W₀	F−	plant	
VIII. A flower.	*Where?* She indicates whole, and then gets up.	W₁	CF	flower	
IX. That's a flower.	(Whole.) Turns card over and places it with others on table top.	W₀	CF	flower	
X. That's a flower.	(Whole.)	W₀	CF	flower	

Card most liked: X
Card least liked: III

Sample Record of 2½-Year-Old Girl N.A. (Continued)

RESPONSE	INQUIRY	SCORING
R = 10		
	7F = 70% F	1A = 10% A
4W$_0$	5F+, 1F±, 1F− = 78% F+	2 objects
3W$_1$	3CF	4 plants
1W$_2$ = 80% W		3 flowers
2D = 20% D		
	0M : 3ΣC	1P = 10% P

COMMENT In this 2½-year-old protocol there is still characteristic perseveration, this time on "leaf" and "flower," but this girl's F% is lower and W% higher than for most of her age group. Perhaps the outstanding individual response here is the projection of color onto the black and white cards (Cards IV, V, and VII are seen as "green leaf"). This is a characteristic which is rare at any age. When it is encountered in an adult protocol, it is thought to be indicative of a person who is extremely anxious, one with a rather depressed and hopeless attitude, but one who wishes to give an impression of being euphoric in order to cover up his real feelings. Whether such an interpretation is valid for a child of this age is questionable, though actually this child's history and environ-ment would lend credence to such a finding. This may be an unfavorable reaction to the blackness, which she translates into terms which she likes better; or it may be that she has always heard "leaf" spoken of in this way. This last is discounted, however, by the fact that she gives the response "a leaf" to Card I. That she may be disturbed by the blackness of the cards is supported by the fact that at both Cards IV and V she turns the cards over and places them on the pile herself, and that after Card VI she wants to go downstairs.

From her response to the color cards, one might say that her reaction to external stimuli is immediate and pleasant, if not too well controlled at present.

Sample Record of 2½-Year-Old Boy F.D.F.

RESPONSE	INQUIRY		SCORING	
I. Wolf. What he doing? He's washing.	(Top R profile is wolf's head.)	D	FM	A
II. A wolf. Go downstairs. (Tries to open card.)	(Black only, R side.)	D	F±	A (P)
III. A wolf.	(Man's figure, R.)	D	F–	A
IV. A man.	(*Head?* Points to top center. *Feet?* Points to usual feet.)	W_1	F+	H
V. A wolf.	(Indicates whole.)	W_0	F–	A
A Peter Rabbit.	(*Head?* Points to center top.)	D	F+	A
VI. A Christmas tree. I got a Christmas tree home. We burned it.	(Indicates whole.)	W_1	F+	plant
VII. A wolf.	(Top two tiers, R.)	D	F–	A
VIII. A Christmas tree. To stand up the Christmas tree.	(Indicates top gray and blue as tree. Red and orange as stand.)	W_2	F+ FC?	plant
A wolf.	(Usual animals.)	D	F+	A P
IX. Christmas tree (Looks on back of card.)	(Green)	D	CF	plant
X. Another Christmas tree. Bottom. Who's working in dere? (Indicates screened observation alcove.)	(Indicates bottom green.)	D	C	plant
Wolf.	(Indicates pink.)	D	F–	A

Sample Record of 2½-Year-Old Boy F.D.F. (Continued)

RESPONSE	INQUIRY	SCORING
Card most liked: I		
Card least liked: I. "Don't like dis."		
	Time: 7 minutes	
R = 13		
$1W_0$	$10F = 77\%F$	$8A = 61\%A$
$2W_1$	$5F+, 1F\pm, 4F- = 42\%F+$	$1H = 7\%H$
$1W_2 = 31\%W$		4 plants
	$1FM$	
$9D = 69\%D$	$1CF$	
	$1C$	
	1 tend. FC?	
	$0M : 2\Sigma C$	$2P = 15\%P$

COMMENT   This boy reverses the usual perceptive type for these early years, and he prefers details to global interpretations. This is an individual pattern which in this boy is stronger than the age characteristics. He perseverates on "wolf," giving this response seven times in all. This magic repetition is broken at Card IV by "man" and at Cards VI and IX by "Christmas tree."

This boy may be subject to strong fears, and he is quite responsive to external stimuli. He is probably quite responsive to cultural symbols, which appear to make a deep impression on him.

CHAPTER ELEVEN

Three Years

R = 12.9		84%F	6.0A = 47%A
		60%F+	.9H = 7%H
55%W			2.1 object
39%D	.2M .3FM .1m		1.8 plant
6%Dd	.3FC .4CF .1C		.9 nature
	.6F(C) .1Clob		
	.2M : .8ΣC		1.9P = 15%P

Qualitative Description

There are many changes in the Rorschach response which take place between 2½ and 3 years of age. At 2½ it is only an exceptional child who gives a Rorschach response full enough to reveal his unique individuality. Furthermore, most Rorschach responses are not revealing of what we consider to be the outstanding characteristics of the age level. By 3 years, however, we find that the Rorschach not only frequently gives us good clues as to the status of the individual child but that responses of a group of children are full enough and similar enough from child to child to be also revealing of the individuality of the age.

To begin with, there is a sharp increase in the number of responses, from an average of 10.8 to an average of 12.9 per child. This number is relatively high if compared with the 10-year-old average which is only 16.3. The average length of record is just about twice what it was at 2½ years, now being around 75 words per child. The response, however, in spite of this expansion, is still quite straightforward, easy to understand and easy to score. Not only does the average child give more responses than at an earlier age, but the number of refusals has dropped considerably, from an average of 1.8 per child to .8 per child, only 30 per cent of the children refusing any blots.

There is also a sharp increase in the number of whole responses to

113

55% of the total number, and a sharp decrease of D to 39%. The W% of 55% found at this age is exceeded at only a few ages. The F+% of 60% means that not only does the child produce many whole responses but that more than half of his responses are accurate perceptions.

Probably the greatest change at this age, and the one which most accurately highlights the personality characteristics of the age, is the change in color responses. ΣC is slightly lower than formerly, and for the first time FC responses hold one of the two leading color places, being only slightly less than CF responses. Pure C responses are third in order of importance. FC is higher than at any other age in the first 5½ years, pure C lower than at any other age. Thus emotions at this age are much more modulated than at earlier ages. Color naming, however, is still prevalent, occurring on an average of .4 per child.

Increased interest in people is reflected in the fact that for the first time *humans* is one of the four leading content categories.

Shading responses, which suggest an ability to make fine discriminations, occur on the average of .6 per child, more than at any surrounding age. Texture responses are now the leading type of shading response, suggesting possible wish for contact. Clob, however, is lower than at 2½.

M and FM have more than doubled since 2½ years and have become slightly more active. People talk, fight, touch hands; animals climb, eat, run. The average experience balance at this age is .2M : .8ΣC, but more than half of the subjects (twenty-nine) still have an equation of 0M : 0ΣC.

P% has increased from 13% to 15%. That is, 15% of any record is made up of responses so common that they occur in one out of every three records.

Magic repetition is still prevalent, occurring in 34 children or 68 per cent of the group, a slightly smaller percentage than at 2½ years. However, only one girl perseverates on more than one word and only four boys do so. Furthermore 13 children or 26 per cent of the entire group are able to give more than three answers without perseveration. Different perseverations which occur are:

Girls: butterfly 2; elephant 1; fox 1; fur 1; *leaf 3;* puppy 1; rainbow 1; smoke 1; stones 1; *tree 4*

Boys: bear 2; *bird 4*; butterfly 2; chimney 1; couch 1; elephant 1; flower 1; fox 1; horse 1; light 1; pig 1; *tree 6*

Since 68 per cent of the children still do use magic repetition, this definitely colors the picture, but the number of words perseverated on is less than formerly and, as indicated, 26 per cent of children give more than three answers without it. Thus the stereotypedness of response is at this age diminishing.

As to content, not only does the category *humans* now appear as one of the four leading categories, but *object* now surpasses *plant*, being second only to animal. Also *wild animals* for the first time are the predominant animals, domestic animals coming second. At this age only, *butterfly-bird* is not one of the two leading types of animals.

There is a much greater tendency to think about, weigh, and evaluate and even question responses than at 2½ years. Children say, "I think it is —————," "It's supposed to be —————," "Probably a —————." Or they give their response in the form of a question: "Is it a doggie?" or ask, "What is it?" and then answer themselves. " 'At one looks like a—what does that look like? I think it looks like another fly. Here it is." Some give an answer and then ask a skeptical question: "Kangaroo. Could a kangaroo fly?" The personal "It looks to me like" is beginning to come in. A few are especially definite, stressing the verb "is." "Dat *is* a butterfly." Others are so indefinite that they change their concept while they are in the process of giving it. Thus, "Dere's some leaves. Look like leaves but they aren't. They are ducks," or "A doggie. No it isn't. I guess it's a rat."

Instead of merely consisting of silence or physical rejection of the card, refusals may frequently be worded: "I don't know," a characteristic 3-year-old phrase.

Some children embellish their answers with extremely lucid explanations: "Looks like a turtle. Dat's how they walk" (Card V). "Dis part of a bird. He mouth. So he can peep peep peep" (Card II).

At 3 years we see the beginning of several behaviors which will come in more conspicuously later. One of these is the use of silly language. Examples of this are: (Card IX) "A gumba. A gunga. I don't know." Or, Card VII, "A broken bee bee bla." Also, strange combinations which become more prominent later first appear here as in "A furniture leg house." Another forerunner of more mature behavior is that a child may be giving a series of plant or simple animal responses and will suddenly and almost fortuitously give a good movement response.

Another somewhat mature behavior is the beginning of mention of sex or elimination parts, as on Card IV: "An eagle. His piddler," or "A cow, his body." In both these instances it is the center bottom projection which is described, and the child speaks with some apparent embarrassment.

There is some interest in how the blots came to be. "A boy came and he painted with a finger," or "Who painted this yellow?" An occasional child seems to feel that the paint will come off on his finger: "That's black too. Look! I got paint all over my hand."

A few children are already mature enough to give excuses or alibis for poor performance, or to give reasons for leaving the test situation: "Too hard to see," "I'm too tired," or "I can't stay too long cause my teacher wants me and then my mommy wants me to be there." There is also a little extraneous though related conversation. The child names an object and then adds such comments as, "I got a white pocket book at home," "We had a Christmas tree," "I saw a fire engine last night."

Thus by 3 years the Rorschach responses have become complex and varied enough in character that they offer several criteria for judging whether the child's performance is at, above, or below his age level. We can, for example, note whether or not perseveration has, as is characteristic of the typical child at this age level, been cut down to the repetition of only some one word. We can determine whether or not the more adaptive FC color responses are making their appearance, as is characteristic at this age, or whether such pure C responses as "paint" are still prevalent. Has F+% risen above 50% as it should have normally? Do shading and tiny detail responses occur?

Have refusals been reduced to less than one card per child? Is the subject advanced enough to be giving human and animal movement responses?

Does he give more than ten responses? Have these responses advanced beyond the simple one-word "doggie" and "tree" responses?

All of these and other points can be checked to determine whether or not any given 3-year-old is performing at his age level or below.

Individual Determinants

Number: The average number of responses is definitely more than at 2½. Now the average subject gives 12.9 responses.

Area: W% is on the average 55%, the largest amount to date. D%, conversely, is the lowest of any age to date, only 39% on the average. Dd% is barely larger than at the preceding age—6%.

Combinatory whole responses have increased since 2½ years. WS also is twice what it was formerly, now being .1. S and Do also are slightly larger than at 2½ years.

Form: Form determines 84% of responses, approximately the same as at 2½ years. F+%, however, has increased sharply from 54% to 60%.

M, FM, m: M and FM have both doubled since 2½ years. There is now an average of .2M and .3FM. m remains at an average of .1, virtually non-existent.

For the first time, M responses are moderately extensor in character—shaking, touching, or posturing of hands being the leading activities. As to FM, strong extensor movements tie with static movements for first place, climbing and vocalizing being the two leading types of activity. m responses are very few but if we include tendencies to m, we find that cracked or broken things predominate.

Color: There is a marked change here. Though CF responses still predominate, for the first time FC responses hold second place and pure C drops to third.

Of the CF responses, flower, butterfly and design or painting occur equally. Of pure C responses, nature responses predominate.

Shading: Number of shading responses has nearly doubled since 2½ years, there now being an average of .6 such responses per child. Diffusion responses are still conspicuous, but for the first time texture responses lead slightly among different types of shading responses.

Clob: Has decreased slightly, to an average of .1 per child.

Content: The number of content categories used in all by the group is now 13, one more than at 2½ years. The average child uses 3.9 different categories. The four leading categories are now animals, plants, objects, and humans. Thus *humans* replaces nature other than plants, and is for the first time one of the leading categories. A%, 47%, is slightly higher than at 2½ years; H%, 7%, is also higher than at 2½ years.

Wild animal responses are for the first time the leading type of animal responses, with domestic animals coming second. Large wild animals predominate over small.

Length: Length has doubled since 2½ years; the average record in both sexes now contains approximately 75 words.

Timing: The average record now is approximately 5.8 minutes in duration.

Semantics: Naming the blot still definitely leads as a method of identification, occurring 427 times. Identifying the blot with the positive "That is" comes second, occurring 74 times. The phrase "looks like" for the first time occurs conspicuously, 57 times.

Plurals: The usual correct plural is used most to suggest plurality, but such phrases as "Doggie, doggie" or "Doggie, another doggie" are frequent.

Best and Worst: Card X is liked best by both girls and boys. Card VI is disliked most by girls; Card II by boys.

Sex Differences

Sex differences at this age are minimal. Girls give more whole and more tiny detail responses than boys; boys more detail responses than girls.

M is about the same in both sexes, but there are many more FM in boys than in girls though about equally active. There are more m in girls than in boys.

As to color—many more girls than boys give FC responses, and there are more FC responses given by girls than by boys. There is also slightly more CF and more C in girls than in boys.

Slightly more girls than boys give shading responses, and more shading responses are given by girls.

There are few conspicuous differences in content. Girls give more domestic animal responses, especially dogs, than do boys. Boys have more flying animals and more wild animals.

Girls take slightly longer in their total answering than do boys. There is slightly more perseveration in boys than in girls, fifteen girls perseverating and nineteen boys.

Comparison of Rorschach and Developmental Findings

Developmental	*Rorschach*
Listens to adults, and listens to learn. Improved personal-social relations.	Humans now one of the four leading content categories.
Distinguishes between the personal and the physical in the outside world.	Texture now leads in shading.
Tries to please and conform. Likes to please and is pleased when he pleases others. Emotionally less turned in on himself.	FC now the second leading color category.
Thoughtful. Considerate and considering.	Semantic expression: "I think it is," "Probably is."
More self-control.	Increased FC.
Capable of sympathy.	Empathy increased. M higher than at any age to date. Shading responses increase.
Increased emotionality.	More children use all color determinants except C.
Interest in telling extraneous stories of his adventures, to teacher or other adult.	Extraneous but related comments in addition to naming blots.
Enjoys language, and some use of silly language.	Silly language beginning.
Routines now easy for the child.	Perseveration. A% is 47%, higher than at 2½ years.

Sample Record of 3-Year-Old Girl M.K.

RESPONSE	INQUIRY	SCORING			
I. A tree.	(Whole)	W_1	F+	plant	P
II. A doggie.	(Points to both blacks. Each is a doggie. Puts her finger on the reds, but does not interpret.)	D	F+	A	P
III. Turkeys.	(The two men.)	W_2	F+	A	
Chop up woods.	(Points to usual legs. Evidently means sticks.)	Dd	F+	obj	
IV. May I take it home? What's that? A leaf.	(Whole)	W_1	F+	plant	
V. A leaf.	(Whole)	W_1	F±	plant	
VI. What's this? A turkey.	(Whole)	W_1	F−	A	
VII. What's that? Doggie.	(Whole. Cannot define parts.)	W_1	F−	A	
VIII. Leaf. Pink leaf and blue.	(Shows pink as one leaf, blue as another.)	D	FC	plant	
		D	FC	plant	
IX. Anudder. Anudder pink leaf.	(Pink only.)	D	FC	plant	
X. Leaf.	(Whole)	W_0	F±	plant	

Card most liked: X
Card least liked: VII

Sample Record of 3-Year-Old Girl M.K. (Continued)

RESPONSE	INQUIRY	SCORING
R = 12	Time: 3 minutes	
1W$_0$	9F = 75%F	4A = 33%A
5W$_1$	5F+, 2F±, 2F— = 66%F+	7 plant
1W$_2$ = 58%W		1 object
	3FC	
4D = 33%D	0M : 1½ΣC	2P = 17%P
1Dd = 8%Dd		

COMMENT M.K. still shows perseveration, but with greater variety than in some children. "Leaf" occurs 4 times, "turkey" twice, and "doggie" twice. The second occurrence of both "turkey" and "doggie" indicate a magic repetition with little regard to form, but this does not continue indefinitely. The perseveration on "leaf" is stronger, but again there is some suggestion of the more dynamic perseveration seen at a later age, when with a new stimulus this girl defines quite well "a pink leaf and blue" in reaction to the color.

She probably adapts quite well to environmental stimuli, but very likely needs a frequent change of stimulus in order to prevent a deterioration of her behavior.

One feels that in this child at 3 years, the age characteristics express themselves much more strongly than do individuality characteristics.

Sample Record of 3-Year-Old Boy G.C.

RESPONSE	INQUIRY	SCORING			
I. (Picks up card and turns it all around.) A tree. Dis is a point.	(Whole) (Points to bottom center projection. But this has no context. Not scored.)	W₁	F+	plant	P
Anudder one?					
II. (Spins card around, flat on table.) A tree too. All finished with it.	(Points to different parts of whole. "Dose are trees, one two three four five." Includes whole as tree, but sees it in parts too.)	Wₓ	F−	plant	
Dose are points.	(Points to top red, but again there is no context though Ex. tries to find out if he is relating it to "pointer" and various other things. There is a sense of direction, but it is not related to anything specific.)				
Anudder one?					
III. Kangaroo. What's in dere? Balls? All dose wed things.	(Usual figure, R) He indicates cabinet in the room. (Points to red spots on card. Look like? "Look like points.") Starts to mouth card.	D	F±	A	
		Color remark			

Sample Record of 3-Year-Old Boy G.C. (Continued)

RESPONSE	INQUIRY		SCORING		
IV. (Spins card on table.) It's a man. (Puts face down to card.) He has funny curls. You can't see his face because he has a hat on. His feet. (Spins card.) His tummy.	(Whole. Indicates parts such as head, feet, tummy.)	W₁	F+ / F(C)	H	P
V. A tree too. (Gets up, climbs on table and chair, goes to all parts of the room.) Guess I want to go now.	(Whole)	W₀	F+	plant	
VI. A tree. (Becomes more and more active. Nearly falls off chair.)	(Whole)	W₀	F+	plant	P
VII. All finished. Doggies. (Gets down onto floor.) Tree.	(Indicates top tier.) (Indicates bottom tier.)	D / D	F+ / F−	A / plant	P
VIII. Trees. (Now is kneeling on chair.)	Now sees each part as "tree"	W₀	F±	plant	
IX. I see li'l pink things, animals. These are bunnies. Have to go down now.	(Usual) (Orange)	D / D	F+ / F+	A / A	
X. Tree. Lots of trees. Now we have to go down.	This is the same process as at Card II. He sees the whole tree, and then the parts separate and he calls each part "tree."	W₀	F−	plant	

Card most liked: "I don't like
all these." Finally indicates
III as best.
Card least liked: VI

R = 12

$4W_0$
$2W_1$
$1W_x = 57\%W$

$5D = 43\%D$

Time: 5 minutes

$12F = 100\%F$
$7F+, 2F\pm, 3F— = 66\%F+$

1 tend. F(C)

$0M : 0\Sigma C$

$4A = 33\%A$
$1H = 8\%H$
7 plant

$5P = 43\%P$

COMMENT Here we have perseveration on "tree" seven times, which shows how strong perseveration can be at this age. There is an interesting variation here, however, in that this boy responds to the whole blot as "tree," and then sees the parts, even though the perseveration continues and he calls all the details "trees" also. This is a new development in the perceptive process.

There is a variety of animals including "doggies," "bunnies," "kangaroo," indicating a more expansive reaction to the environment. His description of the man at IV indicates a much greater refinement of description than we have seen thus far, and there is also some perception of the shading. Except for the variety of animals and the perception at IV, however, age characteristics are more outstanding than individual traits. This is an extremely active and highly intelligent boy and though his emotional behavior may not be as well integrated as the rest of his development appears to be, there already are indications of more mature projections. This is one instance in which we should consider that another type of projective technique such as the Kaleido blocks might give us more insight into individuality and potentials than the Rorschach.

CHAPTER TWELVE

Three and a Half Years

R = 13.5	80%F	6.5A = 48%A
	67%F+	1.4H = 10%H
60%W		1.8 object
34%D	.3M .7FM .2m	1.0 plant
6%Dd	.2FC .6CF .3C	1.0 architecture
	.4F(C) .1Clob	.8 nature
	.3M : 1.1ΣC	2.1P = 15%P

Qualitative Description

By 3½ years of age the Rorschach response has become in many respects quite mature. Now every child in our group gives at least one response and the average number of responses has risen to 13.5 with a range of 3 to 27. Refusals have dropped to an average of only .3, lowest of any age studied, only 14 per cent of the children refusing.

Magic repetition, though still prevalent, has decreased in frequency. Only 52 per cent of the subjects now perseverate and 48 per cent of subjects now give more than three responses without perseverating. Perseveration, even when it does occur, is less stereotyped, and other responses often intervene between the perseverated answers so that the behavior seems less like magic repetition than formerly. Thus at this age even more than at 3 years it seems that the response to the Rorschach is discriminating, and that the Rorschach constitutes a "good" test for the child of this age.

Though 52 per cent of the subjects do perseverate, no child perseverates on more than one word. Perseverations which occur are:

Girls: baby 1; butterfly 2; castle 1; dog 1; flower 2; house 2.
Boys: alligator 1; bear 1; bleeding 1; bumblebee 1; dog 1; birdie 2; flower 2; leaf 1; monkey 1; painting 1; tree 4.

The number of responses determined by form alone has decreased to 80%, and both movement and color responses have increased markedly.

124

Human movement responses have increased in number since 3 years and are slightly more passive in nature than at 3, while animal movement has doubled in number since 3 years and has become even more active than it was. Inanimate movement has increased even more, being four times what it was at 3 years—in fact it is higher than at any other time in the first five years, suggesting considerable suppressed aggressivity on the part of the 3½-year-old.

In relation to all types of movement, considerable purposefulness is indicated as witness the following verbalizations:—

Card VIII: "A bear coming up dere and take a wide."
Card VIII: "He's trying to climb up the Christmas tree. Trying to get some candy canes."
Card IX: "Looks like the edge of a bar. This is what you stand on." (Stand on it?) "To watch ducks."
Card X: "Stick, has some sand there. Know why this is there? So the 'piders can't walk up them."

Such comments imply considerable ability to realize and to predict the results of actions.

Responsiveness to external stimuli, and general emotionality, as measured by ΣC, has increased sharply, to an average of 1.1. This is made up chiefly of CF responses. FC has dropped from second to third place and C has almost doubled since 3 years. This means that the 3½-year-old is definitely nonadaptive in his emotions, in contrast to 3; and that emotions are egocentric or even completely uncontrolled.

One aspect of color response which we find here resembles color naming yet represents a marked step forward in that it combines the color name with an actual object, even though perseveratively. Examples of this occur especially on Card X as follows: "Lots of instruments. Blue instruments and red ones and white ones and dark ones." Or, "It's powder. Blue powder and pink powder and yellow powder."

Whole responses predominate even more than at earlier ages, and many more children give W_2 and W_3 responses. Four per cent of the 3-year-olds produce a W_3; 38 per cent of the 3½-year-olds do so. This indicates a marked increase in the ability to generalize and to combine concepts into larger wholes even though this may not always be done accurately. It implies a considerably advanced maturity of thinking over 3 years.

Drive to combine parts into total wholes is in many instances considerably greater than the ability to do so accurately. We know from other measures that the 3½-year-old has difficulty in correlating his visual patterns (Gesell, 29), and this is reflected in such strange and confused responses as the following, which appear to be quite typical of the sometimes muddled thinking of the child of this age:

Card III: "Butterfly: What are dese? The eyes. [Center dark.] Somebody seeing a butterfly. Hands [top red]. These must be a feet be a hands.
These must be hands [the usual heads]. Funny seeing hands be a
feet."

Card II: "What is it? [red]. These are red spots. Little cross. Little spot. You
paint it over like Jack Frost does. They are talking over the radio
and then they're standing up, they're kitty kats. [Red tops.] On the
roof sitting down listening to the telephone. [White part.] Roof.
And little crosses."

Card X: "Eek! Hey! [Peers at card.] Let's see. These are all cross and they
all little things that don't have to go cross the lines you don't have
to get the other ones up. These are part of it. And everything is part
of it. Things that don't belong to you. I don't see anything more."

In everyday life the child of this age frequently complains, with no
apparent physical justification for such complaint, "I can't see," "I can't
hear." Such complaints also are voiced in the Rorschach situation, usually
followed by good descriptions of the card in question.

A further example of the immaturity of thinking and the confused
perceptions and conceptions of the child of this age is the fact that he
frequently confuses the animate with the inanimate. Inanimate objects
abruptly sprout arms, legs and even tails—as witness the following typical
responses:

Card　II: "Another grocery store. The front. The chimney. Another chimney.
Feet of the grocery store."

Card　IV: "A fireplace. Feets dat hold it up. Hands of the fireplace."

Card　VI: "Fireplace with hands and hands and feet and tail and other tail.
Dis one has tails on it."

Card VIII: "Dat's a sailboat. Udder arm and udder arm."

Independence of the usual spatial orientation is seen by the fact that
some children apparently see forms upside down but give their answers
without disturbance, without turning the cards, and without mentioning the
fact that they see the objects upside down.

A further confusing factor is that the child seems to feel perfect
freedom to introduce objects and animals which do not actually exist in the
blot. Thus we get descriptions such as:

Card V: "A big horsie. Horsie's neck and foots and then de horse doesn't have
them in now; went home to get his supper and came back and went
to soldiers."

Card X: "Moo cow walks on" [center blue]. "I can't see moo cow."

An additional indication that the child of this age is having difficulty
in correlating all his perceptions into a whole which resembles the actual
reality is indicated by the frequency of Do responses, which occur here on
the average of .4 per child, the highest to date:

Card III: "That looks like a duck. That's a ribbon. That's a pointed nose [man's face]. Feet. There's another feet [center black]. They're playing with the ribbon. Ribbons [top red]." (Is satisfied to stop here. Asked by Ex. who is playing with the ribbons says "Men with sharp noses.")

Card VI: "Wow! Such big wings! Two arms, two arms [top]. All arms. Jus some mouse's arms or somebody's arms or cat's feet. Big cat. [Feet are usual arms and top]. Fur [at very top]. Big cat sticking up. Her body. Her whiskers [top]; that holds her whiskers."

There seems to be some confusion between reality and pictured items. Thus one boy brings the cards to life very vividly with the serious comment on VIII: "Bears. Ouch! They bit me!" snatching his finger away. Another on VII says, "That's snow. You could make snowballs." Others name the blot and then go on to give attributes of the real thing. "Mosquito. Makes blood on the wall" (telling a long story about a mosquito at home). Or, "that looks like an Indian. I know what an Indian looks like. They scalp him and pull off your hair"—pulling at own hair. One child comments to Card X: "Here's some kind of a rabbit standing up on its hind legs like I do. I don't have four legs like he does." It may be that the difference between himself and other animate forms is new enough at this age to be noteworthy.

Others, especially boys, identify their concepts positively as follows:

Card   I: "Looks like a face. It *is* a face."
Card III: "Whole big thing is a rocking cradle. I bet it is!"
Card V: "Hey! It looks like a cricket. It *is* a cricket."
Card VI: "A church. Really *is* a church."

Still others, slightly less vehement, are nevertheless certain of their accuracy: "A lamb. That really looks like a lamb," or "That really looks like an animal."

All of these signs of confusion and of inaccurate perception and of inability to assemble accurate total wholes are indicative of a type of perceptivity which, though certainly less mature than that found in the 5-year-old for example, must be recognized as a marked step in maturity over the simpler and more "accurate" response of the 3-year-old. It reflects chiefly a drive toward organization of wholes which is greater than the child's ability, at the moment, to perceive accurately and to coordinate piecemeal perceptions into an "accurate" total.

Though the 3½-year-old, as indicated, quite frequently expresses himself with great positiveness, "That looks like a face. It *is* a face," nevertheless we know the child of this age to be quite characteristically unsure of himself, uncertain and insecure. This uncertainty is reflected in aspects of the Rorschach response. Unsure of himself, he gives his answer and then seeks confirmation. "Dat looks like a fox. It is a fox too, isn't it?" "Looks like a bear to me? Is it a bear?" "Looks like a star. Might be, you never know." Or, the child asks, "What could it be?" or makes an initial query, "What is dat?" and then without further encouragement, gives a good answer. Or, he gives his answer and then criticizes or denies his own response. "Dat's snakes. . . . Spider. Looks like a snake but it isn't." "Mouse. No no. Bow tie." "Bat. No, moo moo. At first it looked like a bat." "Froggie. No not a froggie, a cat. *No*, it is a froggie." "That's a splash. Hey! No! That's the bear went over the mountain."

Though shading responses at this age are slightly less than at 3 years (only .4 per child), the chief kind of shading responses is now diffusion, suggesting the vagueness of the perceptions of the child at this age.

Some slight disturbance if not shock is indicated by such initial exclamations as "Eeh!" "Hey!" "Wow!" used by four different children and occurring thirteen times. Criticism of the blots is implied by the use of such adjectives as "funny," "silly." Six children described objects as "cracked," or "broken."

A trend started at 3 years and increasing at 3½ is the mention of sex or elimination parts. At this age five children mention "His poopoo," "To make grunt with," "Tinkle part," or "An this must be his thing where he toidies. Why didn't he put his pants on? Funny without pants on." Such remarks almost without exception occur in response to Card IV.

Silly language, first appearing at 3 years, increases slightly at 3½. We find such examples as: "That's a silly old moo coose." "It's a dog with do do do," "It's a parade bee bee bee," "Dat's a forest. Bee bee go."

The majority of children at this age cannot verbalize their reasons for preferring or disliking cards beyond such statements as "Cause I like it," or "Cause I don't like it."

The high H% (10%, the highest of any age in the first five years), reflects the interest in adults and in adult-child relations which is characteristic of this age.

Individual Determinants

Number: Average number of responses is now 13.5 per child, as compared with 12.9 at the preceding age.

Area: Whole responses still predominate, in fact by a larger margin than ever before. W% is 60%; D%, 34%; Dd%, 6%. W% is the highest to date and D% the lowest. The ability to produce combinatory wholes has increased. S has dropped to .1 per child but Do is the highest to date—.4 per child.

Form: The number of responses determined by form alone is decreased steadily. Here F% is 80%. Correct form is steadily increasing—here it is 67%.

M, FM, m: M has increased since 3 years, an average of .3 per child. FM has more than doubled—occurring now on an average of .7 per child. m occurs more than at any other age in the first five years.

Static M definitely leads with moderate extension coming second. Just two people existing is the most common type of human "movement." FM is much more active than M. Strong extension leads, with climbing the predominant single item. As to m, fire and light forms occur most, with downward activity most frequent.

Color: ΣC is by far the highest to date—an average of 1.1. CF responses occur most, on an average of .6, with C next at .3; and FC falls to third place with an average of .2 per child.

Responses to red parts of cards are more frequent than at any other age to date. Flower responses are the most frequent CF responses; paint, the most frequent C response.

Shading: Shading responses fall off slightly to .4 per child, diffusion responses such as cloud and smoke definitely leading.

Clob: Clob is very low, .1 per child.

Content: There is a great range of content—there being now 16 different content categories as opposed to 13 at 3 years. The average child uses 4.2 different categories as opposed to 3.5 at 3 years. This is a wider range than at either the preceding or following ages. Leading content categories are as at 3 years, animals, objects, humans and plants. H% has risen from 7% at 3 years to 10% at 3½. A% remains about the same as before, 48%.

Flowers are prominent, average of .3 per child. Architecture reaches an all-time high, 1.0 per child, occurring about as much as plants. Blood also is a frequent response.

Wild animals occur more than any other kind of animals; butterfly-bird coming next. For the first time and from now on "domestic animals" does not constitute one of the two leading animal categories.

Length: The response tends to be slightly longer at this age than at 3 years, being on the average from 80 to 90 words.

Timing: The total response takes an increasingly long time as the child grows older—at this age on the average of 6.6 minutes per child in contrast to only 5.8 minutes at 3 years.

Semantics: Simply naming the blot is the chief method of identification. As at 3 years, identifying the blot with a positive "that is" comes second.

Plurals: The customary grammatically correct plural still predominates, but the phrase "Two ———" now and for the first time comes second in frequency.

Best and Worst: Card X is liked best by both sexes; and Card VI is liked least by both. Most children are not able to give reasons for their preferences beyond, "Cause I like it" and "Cause I don't like it."

Popular Responses: Popular responses, as at 3 years, occur to the extent of 15% per child.

Refusals and Denials: Refusals are somewhat less than at 3 years, only .3 per child. Denials of own response, however, are relatively high—.2 per child.

Sex Differences

Sex differences are rather marked at this age. Differences occur in regard to many factors and in nearly all things boys exceed girls. Thus boys give on the average one more response than do girls, and boys' records are longer not only in number of words and in number of scorable responses but in actual duration—5.9 minutes per girl, 7.3 per boy.

More boys than girls give W and Dd responses; girls and boys are about equal on D. Boys give many more DW responses than girls, but girls give more S than do boys. Boys give many more Do than do girls.

Boys give many more FM responses than do girls and FM is a little more active in boys than in girls. Boys, also, give more m than do girls.

Initial shock to the cards as indicated by such exclamations as "Wow!" "Eek!" "Hey!" occurs almost exclusively in boys. Positive identification of the card, "That looks like a face. It *is* a face," or describing the cards as if they were real, "Ouch! He bit me!" occurs much more frequently in boys than in girls.

Mention of sex parts or of elimination functions also occurs almost exclusively in boys; only one girl mentions such features.

ΣC is higher in boys than in girls and C especially is higher in boys. Shading responses occur slightly more in boys than in girls and more boys than girls use shading.

As to content, there are more different kinds of animals and many more animals, in boys than in girls—especially wild and flying animals.

Comparison of Rorschach and Developmental Findings

Developmental	Rorschach
Highly imaginative; seems to confuse real and unreal in his play with imaginary companions. Impersonation of animals, and animation of inanimate objects.	Describes inanimate objects as possessing arms, legs, hands, tails. Seems to think objects seen in cards are real. Says of bears on VIII: "Ouch, he bit me!"
Has difficulty in correlating visual perceptions.	Gives strange and confused responses in which various parts he describes do not add up to a clear-cut accurate whole.
	Gives Do responses which add up to a whole figure but has difficulty in naming the whole figure.
Visual difficulty—child complains that he cannot see.	Child complains that he "can't see" the blots; then gives a good response.
Child has difficulty with spatial relations.	Sees object upside down and gives no indication that he differentiates between upside down and right side up.
Child seems often to feel insecure, vulnerable, unsure of himself.	Answers and then seeks confirmation: "Dat looks like a fox. It is a fox, isn't it?"
	Or gives response and then criticizes

Comparison of Rorschach and Developmental Findings

Developmental   *Rorschach*

or changes his own concept: "Mouse. No, no, bow tie."

Child is considerably more emotional than at 3 years.

Initial exclamation of "Wow!" "Eek!" ΣC has increased from an average of .8 to an average of 1.1.

Emotional in his relation with adults, often tearful, demanding, hard to get along with.

CF predominates strongly over FC. m higher than at any other age in first five years.

Strong interest in people and considerable demand for adult attention.

Marked increase in H% from 7% to 10%, highest of any age in first five years.

Behavior in some children becomes rounded, better organized, in spite of emotional disequilibrium.

Greater drive toward seeing wholes.

Interest in sex and elimination.

Mention of elimination on Card IV.

Use of silly language.

Silly language in describing the blots.

Sample Record of 3½-Year-Old Girl A.D.

RESPONSE	INQUIRY	SCORING			
I. ∨ It's a tree.	(Whole)	W_1	F+	plant	P
II. Cat.	(Black only.) How many? "Only two."	D	F+	A	
III. These are rats.	(Usual men.)	W_2	F±	A	P
That's a mouse.	(Center red.)	D	F−	A	
IV. Puppy dog.	(Whole)	W_1	F+	A	P
That's a bell.	(One boot.)	D	F±	obj	
Puppy's foot.	(Points to other boot.)				
V. Dat's a bumblebee.	(Whole)	W_1	F+	A	
VI. That's a fly.	(Whole)	W_1	F+	A	
VII. Dat's a dog.	(Top tier.)	D	F+	A	
VIII. Dat's a cat.	(Usual animal.)	D	F+	A	P
IX. Dat's a lion.	(Orange)	D	F−	A	
X. That's flowers.	(Whole)	W_0	CF	flowers	

Card most liked: V
Card least liked: VI

R = 12

1W_0
4W_1
1W_2 = 50%W

6D = 50%D

Time: 3 minutes

11F = 91%F
7F+, 2F±, 2F− = 72%F+

1CF

0M : 1ΣC

9A = 75%A
1 plant
1 flower
1 object

5P = 42%P

COMMENT   This girl is receptive to many of the stimuli in her environment both large and small, and her reaction is usually very specific and in general of good form. Her poorest forms occur when she associates from "rat" to "mouse," at III, and when she calls the orange portion of IX "lion" without being able to specify further.

This record is in marked contrast to that of the 3½-year-old boy, and yet it is just as typical of the age. This girl is probably quite realistic, little given to imagination. She has a widening intellectual horizon, seen in this instance more in the variety of animals than in the number of categories used. She is probably quite self-sufficient, with no great effort toward interpersonal relationships, though with adequate acceptance and adjustment to environmental demands when they occur. There is probably as yet no great consciousness of self nor realization of self, for there is no response with which she might be identified in any way.

Sample Record of 3½-Year-Old Boy G.M.

RESPONSE	INQUIRY	SCORING			
I. Mask. Eyes, nose, ears, the masker's ears. (Now turns the card upside down, but gives no response.)	(Indicates the top white spaces as eyes.)	WS,	F+	obj	
II. Another grocery store. The front, the chimney, another chimney. Don't know what that is [bottom red]. Feet of the grocery store.	(Whole including center space as grocery store, top reds are chimneys, bottom red becomes feet of store.) This shows mixture of human and inanimate elements.	WS$_x$	F—	arch	
III. Animals. Seals. Their feet. Screaming on the tree. The tree is so little. All broken up.	(Usual men. Tree is center red.)	W$_x$	FM m	A	P
That? Two animals with big ears. Seals.	(Side red)	D	F—	A	
IV. Bats. No, moo moo. At first it looked like a bat. (Turns card upside down to see head.) Horns. I think that's a cow. Hands, horns. Cows have to get horns. Don't know what that is [top center]. One leg, two feet.	(From center head, he includes whole blot as cow.) Denies first response of "bat."	W$_x$	F±	A	

W₁	FM	A	P	(Whole)	V. Another bat. Buzzy. Just like an umbrella. Feet and horns, ears. Flying.
D	F(C)	obj		(Top detail only. Indicates rays of the light.)	VI. Light. And there's the light shining. (Looks on back of the card and mentions writing.)
D	F+	A	P	(Indicates top two tiers.)	VII. Quite a job. I don't like that noise. (Refers to noise outside.) I think these are bow-wows, puppies. Ear, tail, feet.
S	F±	plant		(Center white detail in bottom tier.)	Tree.
D	F±	scene		(Bottom tier is house. Ocean is white of card below the third tier. Sandpile is tiny fleck on margin of card. This is his own home which he is describing.)	House. Way down to Woodmont. Ocean. I don't know where the sandpile is. That's it.
W₃	FM	A	P	(Usual animals. Tree is center.)	VIII. Animals climbing up on the tree. That's a leopard and that is a leopard climbing up on the tree.
D	FM	A		(Orange)	IX. Seals fighting. Through with that one.
Wₓ	FM	A(scene)		(Side blues are mama seals. Side green is baby seal. Side brown is papa seal. Tree is center pink and top gray. Remarks about flat top of gray	X. These are seals getting ahold of a tree. That's a baby seal. Kind of funny. Papa one and two mama ones. He has to

Sample Record of 3½-Year-Old Boy G.M. (Continued)

RESPONSES	INQUIRY	SCORING
get a great big man. He has strong hands. He [papa seal] is getting ahold of the tree. The tree hurts his teeth. Lookut, that's where he hurt his teeth. That's where they cut off so the animals can eat it. But not him [baby seal]. It hurts his teeth. I'm Mike.	"where they cut it off." Expression "He has to get a great big man" means "he has to become a big man." This is in reference to the baby seal.)	

Card most liked: VII
Card least liked: X

$R = 13$

Time: 15 minutes

$2W_1$		$8A = 61\%A$
$1W_8$	$7F = 54\%F$	2 objects
$4W_x = 54\%W$	$2F+, 3F\pm, 2F- = 50\%F+$	1 architecture
$5D = 38\%D$	$5FM, 1$ tend. m	1 plant
$1S = 8\%Dd$	$1F(C)$	1 scene
	$0M : 0\Sigma C$	$4P = 31\%P$

COMMENT   In this boy's record we see a transitional stage, both from an individual and an age standpoint. There is a widening of the intellectual and emotional horizons which is typical of the age. Perseveration continues but in this case there is some projection toward the 5-year-old stage when dynamic perseveration is stronger. There is a free mixture of animate and inanimate characteristics, and the animal movements and characters are beginning to assume human qualities.

This boy has a high sense of the dramatic in such expressions as "screaming on the tree," and in the conception of the family group as seen in Card X. The "mask" response at I may also be expressive of his dramatic sense, although it is at the same time a resistant response in that it incorporates the space details. Such a response in an adult protocol would be interpreted as that of a person who wished to "mask" or hide his feelings. It is undoubtedly a sign of some restraint. This is a boy closely related to home and family, whose releases are highly imaginative. The easy intermingling of animate and inanimate characteristics shows the facility of the 3½-year-old in fluid and rapid change of meaning which apparently seems perfectly uncomplicated to him. This age, as we know, is the one when imaginary companions often appear, or the child assumes some character other than his own. This is noted in this boy on his last remark, "I'm Mike."

This boy has a drive toward completion of concepts as seen in the high number of W_s and W_x responses. This drive sometimes causes him to sacrifice clarity of form, so that the F+% is reduced, but this may also be a result of easy interchange of form, characteristic of this age. It is often necessary, in children's protocols, to revise our thinking as to good and bad form, for if a response appears often enough, we must presume that the child sees it clearly, if differently from our idea of good form.

This boy surpasses most of his contemporaries in the amount of animal movement expressed—all active and dynamic if sometimes conflictual, as the "seals fighting" at IX. There is some projection to the 5½-year-old stage in the little tree "all broken up" at III. He is also dissimilar from most of the 3½-year-old group in his lack of color response. There are high maturity potentials here, but the environmental stimuli are probably being handled in terms of inner absorption and no direct approach is as yet revealed. One might suppose that this boy will be much more responsive to inner than to outer stimuli. It will be interesting to follow this child longitudinally in order to chart his development.

CHAPTER THIRTEEN

Four Years

R = 14.7	75%F	8.3A = 56%A
	67%F+	1.4H = 9%H
52%W		1.5 object
38%D	.5M 1.2FM .2m	1.4 plant
10%Dd	.2FC .6CF .2C	1.0 nature
	.5F(C) .1Clob	.9 architecture
	.5M : 1.0ΣC	2.3P = 15%P

Qualitative Description

The 4-year-old lacks modulation. He tends to be excessively exact and certain. He knows his own mind and is not quick to accept suggestions from others. A semantic analysis of his manner of describing the Rorschach cards reveals this definiteness and exactness. There is an almost complete lack of qualifying statements. Simply naming the blot leads as a method of identification; use of the phrase "looks like" comes second in frequency. Further the child tends to make positive statements about the identity of the blots. I. "It looks like a black cloud. And it *is* a black cloud." III. "Ah! I know what these are *with no doubt*. Butterfly. Penguin. *With no doubt at all!*" IV. "Ah! that's a butterfly again. I did that with no doubt."

A further example of FOUR'S lack of modulation and of relative values is his apparent belief in the reality of things seen on the cards. VIII. "He bit me!" X. "A broken leaf. Who tore the leaf?" III. "Old bad men. What are they going like that for?" VIII. "Crab. Is that a real crab?"

Or, as does the very old person, the 4-year-old gives an answer and then reassures himself as to its accuracy: IX. "A tree. Yuh! And here's the bottom of it."

Though the response at 4 years is much more clear-cut than at 3½, there is still considerable confabulation, as might be expected when we consider the high unbridled imagination of the 4-year-old. However at this age confabulation is more clear-cut and not merely the confusion of the earlier age. We know that the 4-year-old goes "out of bounds" in much of his everyday behavior. His confabulations are an example of his "out of bounds" behavior. Thus we get such confabulations as the following:

Card VII. ∨ "Looks like a stone. These are two stones [tier 3] and dust [tiers 1 and 2] coming up to stones. Little boy moving inside stone but you can't see him cause stones are hard to open. He's got a little bed and table inside the stone and the dust hears him moving. Moving about playing with his toys."

Card VII. "That's the natives and they're fighting around the other natives. Elephant but the natives are fighting around to catch the elephant and eat him up. I heard the natives out in the woods. I was picking flowers for my mummy's birthday. They had spears but I had even sharper spears, I poked my spears right into the natives. (Who told you about the natives?) My grandsons told me about the natives.

Card III. "What's that? That's the wolf who came down from the roof. Two of them. See look what happened to the end of the wolf. His tail (leg) fell off in the hot water. Roof [top red]. Three little pigs put hot water" . . . etc.

A further source of confusion is that plants and objects are frequently described as having arms and legs, suggesting that the child has not entirely cleared up in his own mind even at this age the difference between animate and inanimate, human and sub-human. Examples of this type of confusion are:

VI. "Big big big building. Don't know what part that is [top]. Hands [top side projections]. Buildings don't have hands."

VII. "Fireplace. With feet."

V. "A bridge. How come the cars go? It's bumpy. Why does it have feet?"

Some give evidence of trying to clear things up in their own minds, as for example the child who gave the following response:

VII. "That looks like a bunny's ear and tail and nose, ears and tails. What he standing on? Rocks. That's the only way to stand up or you could stand up on a ladder. Not bunnies, just grownups."

Other evidences of trying to achieve clarity appear when the child describes something and then objects to his own answer:

II. "That looks like a kitty cat. Never heard of a kitty cat having red ears. I had a kitty cat but he moved away."

VI. ∨ "Turtle. A turtle with 1, 2, 3, 4 wings. Never seen a turtle that flies but that's the kind of a turtle that flies if he has wings. Ooh I wonder what that line is in the middle. Just something but nothing."

The 4-year-old is an endless questioner. His Rorschach response is not immune to his questioning. He frequently questions the adult instead of giving an answer. "What's those?" "Nothing. What is it?" Or, "A funny gun do you think it is?" He may merely question and then give the answer himself without waiting for a reply from the adult.

VIII. "That looks like a tree. What's climbing on the tree? Lizards. What they climbing on it for? To get something to eat. What do they like to eat? Tree."

IX. "What does that look like? Bunnies. Where are the bunnies? Under the tree. Can't see them under the tree."

These are characteristic examples of 4-year-old verbalization. FOUR also questions a good deal about who made the cards and where the cards come from. Not only does he ask "Why" but he likes to go into endless detail. The Rorschach confirms this tendency with a marked increase in both D and Dd.

Though a constant questioner himself, the 4-year-old is not as a rule able to give clear-cut answers to questions of "Why?" from the adult. Asked why Card II looks like "clouds," one child answered, characteristically, "Cause they are." Another sees "Mountain" on IV and when asked why he thinks it is a mountain, replies, "Cause it is."

The 4-year-old expresses his maturity and his new-found independence by resisting adult commands and suggestions. We see some evidences of this resistance in the Rorschach when the child makes such comments as:

III. "I don't want to tell"; IV. "Gun." (Show me) "No!"; VII. "I don't want to do all of these"; VIII. "I don't want these"; IX. "Well I don't feel like talking any more."

One child even went so far as to mutter, when Card VI was presented, "Oh dry up! Oh dry up!" Refusals are highest of any age after 2½ years (1.1).

Or resistance may not go beyond an initial refusal followed by a good answer:

I. "Nothing. What is it? Mountain"; I. "I forget now. A tree"; I. "Doesn't look like anything. What is it? What is it? I don't know. Looks like a lobster."

Four is an age of expansion. We see evidence of this in the Rorschach response in the fact that there are more responses to the cards (an average of 14.72) at this age than at any other age in the first five and a half years. Also we find that total records are considerably longer than at the preceding age.

We think of Four as an age of violence. This is borne out in the Rorschach not only by the fact that M and FM responses have nearly doubled in number, but in the fact that for the first time strong to violent M predominates, and that in FM also, strong extension prevails.

Not only the nature of the movement but the total quality of the response frequently expresses violence, as the following examples will indicate:

IV. "I think that's a skeleton. An lookit at it. Its things it fights with [arms], cause skeletons fight. Eyes, nose, and spikes on his nose [center]. An' these hurt everybody. He's killed."

VIII. "Looks like a fire. Where you get all of these? Pigs catching on fire. Knocking down Christmas tree."

III. "Two men, but their legs are off. Everything is cut off, one leg. Two babies [top red] have one leg sawed off and one arm cut off. Two babies [center black] but they didn't notice a robber who can steal some money, at night, carrying money. [Butterfly.] Robbers. The robbers [top red] only lost two pennies. They were as sharp as a knife."

Very young children seem often to perceive things in a manner somewhat different from that of the normal adult. Between the ages of 3 and 5, many children seem to see things not as immediate wholes but as a succession of parts which eventually lead up to some whole. In many instances this eventual whole is never actually named, though enough parts are mentioned to make a whole. The 4-year-old thus gives such answers as:

IV. "Big flower? Arm, leg, hand. His steam part where he goes to the toilet. Funniest flower I ever saw." (Concept of man approached but not reached.)

IV. "Shoes. Feet. Hand. Faces. Neck. No mouth." (Whose?) "His face."

V. "Stick. Legs. Stomach. Arms. Hat. All fru."

Another oddity of perception at this age is the seeing of things upside down without any apparent need or wish to turn the cards. Thus:

IX. ∧ "Dat looks like two babies looking down from a tower." [Pink is babies; green is tower.]

VI. "A tree that's all I see." (When asked to show parts of tree points out top projection as trunk. When asked if tree is right side up or upside down says—"Upside down.")

X. ∧ "Old tree that's upside down."

In other cases, position alone appears to determine responses. This type of response is considered suspect in the adult, but is probably not atypical at this age.

The 4-year-old tends toward symmetry of posture and movement. Four is one of the high points in the Rorschach for giving "balanced" answers. Thus he names a part of the blot "doggy" and its counterpart on the other side of the blot "kitty"; or "This is a man and this is a girl." Often the two parts are named alike. "This is a duck and this is a duck," "This is a pig and this is a pig," "This is a sea horse and this is a sea horse."

The 4-year-old, for all his expansiveness, tends to behave much of the time in rather a predictable and stereotyped fashion. This tendency is suggested in the Rorschach by an exceedingly high A%, 56%—higher than at any other age in the range.

Sex, or at least elimination, is a matter of considerable interest to the 4-year-old. His tensional outlets often lie in the genital region and frequently in drawing a man he adds sex parts. In the Rorschach this age is one of the high points for responses mentioning sex or elimination parts. Four children give in all seven such responses.

Four represents an interesting stage with regard to the formation of plurals. The usual plural predominates, with "Two ———" coming second as a way of expressing twoness. However we find a number of children who at this age say as they point out two corresponding parts of a blot —"Stockings—stocking," "Legs—leg," "Wings—wing." Earlier they stated, "Stocking—stocking," "Leg—leg," etc., and later they will merely say, "Stockings," "Legs."

40% of the subjects (44% of the girls, 36% of the boys) still perseverate. Different perseverations at this age are:

airplane, bear, bird, bridge, butterfly (3), crab, flower (2), house, leaf (3), monkey, rock, sun, tree (3), Xmas tree.

There is at this age one case of dynamic perseveration—that is, the same basic response repeated but in a changing context. Thus:

I. "Wolf"; II. "Pigs climbing house to see if wolf is coming down"; III. "The wolf who came down the roof, two of them"; IV. "The part of the wolf running home, puffing the house down"; V. "Wolf"; VI. "Wolf"; VII. "That's the wolf fell into the water." And so on, throughout all ten cards.

As to color responses, the child is definitely extratensive at this age. Egocentric and unmodulated CF response predominate, with C coming second; and the child is strongly drawn at this age to the red portions of the cards.

There is considerable use of the adjectives "silly," "funny," "foolish" and some use of silly language as "That looks like a krozokus," "A pink and a pock."

Individual Determinants

Number: There is a definite increase in average number of responses here, from 13.5 to 14.7. This is the highest average number for any age in the first five and a half years.

Area: There is here a slight change in type of apperception. Average percentage of wholes drops to 52%; average percentage of large details increases to 38%. The greatest change occurs in regard to small details which increase sharply, to 10% per child.

Do responses occur conspicuously, on an average of .5 per child, more than at any other age except 9 years. S is low, an average of .1 per child.

Form: The number of responses determined by form alone is decreasing steadily. At 4 years, 75% of responses are determined by form alone. F+% is only 67%, exactly as at the preceding age.

M, FM, m: M has nearly doubled since the preceding age, now occurring to the appreciable extent of .5 per child. FM also has increased markedly, from .7 to 1.2 per child. m has decreased slightly.

Among the M responses extensor movements predominate, and for the first time strong to violent movements exceed moderate extension. This is one of the most active ages for M. In FM responses also strong extensor movements lead. Climbing is the most frequent single FM response.

As to m, upward activity especially of flames and smoke predominates. Things being torn or breaking apart also appear conspicuously.

Color: ΣC is slightly lower than at the preceding age—1.0 per child. As at preceding ages, CF responses predominate, now occurring on the average of .6 per child. C and FC responses each have means of .2. The outstanding CF response is flower; the outstanding C response is paint. Responses to the red portions of the blot have increased markedly, there now being a mean of 2.9 responses per child.

Shading: Amount of shading remains about the same as at the preceding age, an average of .5 per child. The outstanding type of shading responses is diffusion—clouds and smoke.

Clob: Clob responses are few, only an average of .1 per child.

Content: The leading content categories are animals, plants, objects and humans, as at 3½ years. Two other conspicuous categories are nature and architecture. There are no anatomy responses, and blood and paint responses are few. Of animal responses, wild animals predominate with the butterfly-bird category coming second.

Length: Records are somewhat longer at this age than at 3½ years. Girls' responses average around 140 words; boys' around 100.

Timing: Duration of total response increases steadily. Girls' records now average 6.7 minutes per child; boys' average 7.6 minutes.

Semantics: As at the preceding age the most common method of identifying the blot is simple identification. However, comparing the blot to the concept with the phrase "looks like" comes second. The positive, "That is a ———" now comes third. Qualified concepts expressing some uncertainty on the part of the subject are virtually nonexistent.

Plurals: The usual plural is used most, with "Two ———" coming second.

Best and Worst: Card II is liked best by girls; Cards II, III, IV least; Card X is best liked by boys; Card I least.

Popular Responses: The average number of popular responses has increased to 2.3 per child, but the average percentage is 15% as at the preceding age.

Sex Differences

Boys' responses are shorter and are given more quickly than are girls'. Thus boys' total responses average in length 97 words and take on the average 7.6 minutes for a total record. Girls' responses average in length

141 words and take 6.7 minutes. However, though less verbal, boys give more responses than do girls.

As to area, girls exceed very slightly in number of W responses; boys in D and Dd.

There are a few more M responses in girls than in boys; *many* more FM in boys than in girls. FM is more active in boys than in girls. There is more violence expressed by boys and more confabulation in the records of boys.

As to color, there are more color responses of every type in boys than in girls. There are more shading responses (especially diffusion responses) in girls than in boys.

There are more different content categories in boys than in girls— 46 in boys and only 34 in girls. Total number of animals given by boys is also higher—218 in boys and 160 in girls.

Comparison of Rorschach and Developmental Findings

DEVELOPMENTAL	RORSCHACH
Exact. Definite. Lacks modulation.	Positive identification of concepts, and absence of qualifying concepts. "Penguin, with no doubt." "It *is* a black cloud." Apparently believes that objects seen on cards are real.
Out of bounds; high unbridled imagination.	Confabulated responses.
Expansive.	More responses than at any other age in the first 5½ years—an average of 14.7 responses per child. Total record considerably longer than at the preceding age.
An age of violence.	M has doubled and FM nearly doubled. For the first time, strong to violent human movements predominate; and in FM strong extension leads.
	General violence expressed in responses.
Does not distinguish thoroughly between animate and inanimate.	Plants and objects are described as having arms and legs.
Endless questions, "Why? Why? Why?" Or goes into endless detail.	Questions Ex. instead of replying. Or may question, and then answer self several times in response to one card. Marked increase in D and Dd.
Resistant to adult commands.	Direct refusal to respond. Or may refuse, then may give a good answer.

Comparison of Rorschach and Developmental Findings

DEVELOPMENTAL	RORSCHACH
Symmetric; likes to balance things.	Balances things on two sides of card: "Doggie-kitty." "This is a pig and this is a pig."
Predictable and stereotyped.	Highest A% (56%) of any age in this range.
Interest in sex and elimination.	A high point for mention of sex or elimination parts, though actually only seven such responses are given.
Draws and writes in "upside down" orientation.	Sees images "upside down."

Sample Record of 4-Year-Old Girl A.B.

RESPONSE	INQUIRY		SCORING		
I. What is it? I don't know. (Rubs finger on blot.) I can't figure out what it is. (Laughs.) Dese look like leaves.	(Top central extensions.)	D	F+	plant	
Dese look like piles of sand. Whole big pile of sand. Isn't that all on this picture?	(Indicates small rounded top center extensions, and then includes whole.)	W_x	F±	nat	
II. Dese are splatters of paint. Dese are splatters of paint too.	(Top and bottom red.)	D	C	paint	
Dis is a church steeple. Dis a church.	(Center hands are steeple and then whole blot becomes church.)	W_x	F±	arch	
III. Monkeys playing with something, ball I think.	(Usual men.)	$W̸_s$	FM	A	P
Monkey turning upside down.	(Right side red.)	D	FM	A	
Horse.	(Left side red.)	D	F±	A	
Butterfly he's chasing. Monkeys are chasing butterflies. I wish I could make a picture like that.	(Center red.)	D	F+	A	P

Response	Inquiry	Location	Determinant	Content
IV. Big flower isn't it? What's this on the flower? Arm. Head. His steam part, where he goes to the toilet. Just a certain kind of a flower. Funniest flower I've ever seen!	(Whole. Designates usual foot as "arm." Head is top center. "Steam part" is bottom center. Again we see an easy mixture of animate and inanimate characteristics.)	W_x	F±	flower
V. Another flower. What parts are those? Wings. He can fly. Never saw a flower fly. Nothing else. Top of flower.	(Whole, with again a mixture of concepts.)	W_x	F±	flower
VI. Big big big building. Don't know what part [indicates top D]. Hands. Buildings don't have hands. Church building.	(Whole. Hands are side projections of lower D.)	W_x	F±	arch
VII. I wonder. I don't know. Just looks like a weentzy lamb. Funny one. Who made these? His arms.	(Top two tiers.) Remind you? "The shape."	D	F+	A
Looks like a piece of meat.	(Bottom tier.)	D	F(C)	food
VIII. This is a Christmas tree.	(Center gray.)	D	F+	plant
Frog. Pink one. I never saw pink.	(Usual animals.)	D	F± color remark	A
IX. Another Christmas tree.	(Whole) Why? "Because it's the shape of a Christmas tree."	W_o	F+	plant
X. Another Christmas tree looks like.	(Indicates whole blot, but does not see whole tree.)	W_o	CF	plant

Sample Record of 4-Year-Old Girl A.B. (Continued)

RESPONSE	INQUIRY	SCORING			
		D	F+	A	P
		color	remark		
Spiders. Blue spiders. I've never seen blue.	(Side blue.)				
Parts of Christmas tree, just parts.	(Here she is reacting to the colors.)				
Card most liked: II				7A = 39%A	
Card least liked: IV				4 plant	
R = 18				2 flower	
	13F = 72%F			1 food	
$2W_0$	6F+, 7F± = 73%F+			2 architecture	
$1W_3$	2FM			1 nature	
$5W_x$ = 44%W	1CF 1C			1 paint	
10D = 56%D	1F(C)				
	0M : 2½ΣC			3P = 17%P	

COMMENT: This girl shows what might be termed "initial shock." She forestalls response, and then chooses one of the smallest details on the card, which she calls "leaves." Another very small detail follows and is then used as the basis for a confabulatory type of response as she generalizes to a "whole big pile of sand." Initial shock is felt to be an indication of resistance to or conflict with authority, usually paternal authority or its symbol.

At Card II, she responds immediately to the red as "paint." She then interprets the center hands as "church steeple," but generalizes from this into "church" for the whole blot. This type of confabulation is strong with this girl. She is probably easily disoriented and when emotionally disturbed, her perceptions and her intellectual efficiency are easily upset. ... impulsive and probably tends to react somewhat er-

ratically in a new situation. Equilibrium is probably reestablished through inner control as shown by the good organization and the active animal movement response at III.

Her reaction to both inner and external stimuli is rather widespread. Her perceptions are more detailed and less global than those of many 4-year-olds, and thought content is quite extensive. There is little or no perseveration until the color cards when "Christmas tree" becomes the stereotyped response, though this is interspersed with other interpretations, indicating a step forward in the intellectual and emotional development. In a new environmental situation, or with added stimulus, her initial response tends to be immature and regressive. When in doubt she reverts to a safe and familiar formula. But with this as a base, she makes a good response and adjustment.

Sample Record of 4-Year-Old Boy J.D.

	RESPONSE	INQUIRY		SCORING	
I.	(Tries to open card.) Clay.	(Whole)	W_0	F(C)	nat
	Airplane. Looks like an airplane cause it's wings.	(Whole)	W_1	F+	obj
	Popovers.	(Small projections top center.)	D	F+	food
II.	That looks like a kitty cat. Never heard of a kitty cat having red ears. I had a kitty cat but he moved away. Tummy.	(Center S and blacks are the body of the cat, center hands are cat's nose and top red are ears.)	WS_1	F–	A
III.	(Smiles) Donkeys. Ears. What are those? Feet. (How many?) Two.	(Donkeys are usual men. But then side red become ears, and center red become hands. Feet are usual legs. This is a good original concept but with a strong drive to completion he includes the other parts and reduces the clarity of the form.)	W_2	F–	A
IV.	That looks like a doggie. There's his feet and there's the doggie. Poodle. I have a poodle at my grandmother's. Standing on his head. Ears (top side projections). I haven't heard of a doggie having ears there.	(Whole. Head is lower center, feet are usual, ears are top side projections.)	W_1	FM	A P

Sample Record of 4-Year-Old Boy J.D. (Continued)

RESPONSE	INQUIRY		SCORING		
V. That looks like a dragon fly. Feet, ears. What are these? Feet. These? Stingers. Look like stingers.	(Whole, with ears at top, feet at bottom and stingers side projections on wings, which he has also termed "feet.")	W₁	F+	A	
VI. That looks like a bear. Hands, tummy, head.	Why? "Cause he has a big nose" (top projection). "Pretty long." (Hands are bottom side projection, tummy is in the center, head at top.)	W₁	F+	A	
VII. That looks like bunny's ear and tail and nose, ears and tails. What's he standing on? Rocks. That's the only way to stand up or you could stand up on a ladder. Not bunnies, just grown-ups.	(Points to details of bunny on each side, top two tiers, rocks are bottom tier.)	W₃	FM	A	P
VIII. That looks like a tree. What's climbing on the tree? Lizards. What they climbing on it for? To get something to eat. What do they like to eat? (Else?) Tree. Standing on a I don't know, and rest of it is a root.	(Center blue and gray is tree, orange and pink is root, and usual animals are lizards.)	W₃	FM	A	P
IX. What does that look like? Bunnies. Where are the bunnies? Under the tree. Can't see them, they're under the tree.	(The bunnies are the pink, tree is the green. The bunnies are hidden behind the tree.)	D	F+	A	
		D	CF	plant	

X. Another tree. What's on it? All kinds of things. Birds.
Who is that? A woodpecker.
What is this? Bunny. Ears like a bunny.

Tree. It needs to stand up some way. Put stem in a hole and it stands up.

(Top gray is stem and pink is tree, rest is birds and "things" on it.)
(Side brown.)
(Usual bottom green.)

(This indicates again that it is seen inversely even though the card is not turned.)

W_x	F+	plant
	CF	
D	F+	A
D	F+	Ad

Elaboration

Card most liked: II
Card least liked: III

Time: 10 minutes

R = 15

$1W_0$
$5W_1$
$1W_2$
$2W_3$
$1W_x$ = 67% W

5D = 33%D

10F = 67%F
8F+, 2F− = 80%F+

3FM
1CF, 1 tend. CF
1F(C)

0M : 1ΣC

9A
1Ad = 67%A
1 nature
1 object
1 food
2 plant

3P = 20%P

COMMENT At four we see a growing consciousness of the situation itself, as expressed by the qualifying words "looks like." This marks a definite forward step in development. This boy's first response starts at an immature level, but at the second response the card "looks like an airplane," and he can also give a spontaneous reason, "cause it's wings." This boy is cautious and probably needs the familiar and the enjoyable for protection in any situation which makes him feel insecure. But from there he can project and respond in a thoroughly mature manner (for four!)

There is a strong drive to complete concepts and he likes things well organized and integrated, though his own abstract organizational ability is poor and he probably needs outside help to organize adequately. There is a good deal of identifiable animal movement ranging from passive ("standing") to humorous ("standing on his head"), to active ("climbing"). These variations in activity may be indicative of some unpredictability of behavior. He has an easy and fluid association process though he is quite realistic and practical. There is some projection here in his reference to "grown-ups" at VII, but he seems in general to be related to the things at hand and to the past.

CHAPTER FOURTEEN

Four and a Half Years

R = 14.2	72%F	6.3A = 44%A
	75%F+	1.2H = 8%H
56%W		1.9 object
33%D	.3M .7FM .1m	1.3 plant
11%Dd	.3FC 1.3CF .3C	1.0 nature
	.6F(C) .2Clob	.7 architecture
	.3M : 1.9ΣC	.6 flower
		2.6P = 19%P

Qualitative Description

Four and a half is an age level which has not, up till now, been described in the literature. By comparing behavior trends in the first five years with those expressed in the second five years, we might surmise, however, that 4½ may resemble 9 years of age. If this is the case, it can be described as an age of some disequilibrium lying between an expansive age (4 years) and an age of focalized equilibrium (5 years). Naturalistic but as yet unsystematized observations bear out this supposition. Information about this age yielded by the Rorschach protocols may, in this instance, help clarify our view of the age rather than, as at other ages, confirming an already familiar picture.

Several factors in the Rorschach response suggest at least traces of confusion, instability, strong but uncontrolled emotionality, and marked unpredictability and variability from child to child.

Most conspicuous perhaps is the marked increase in color responses. ΣC has nearly doubled, increasing from 1.0 per child to 1.9 per child. Also many more children now use color as a determinant than at the preceding age. Thus the child is both more emotional and more extratensive than at 4 years. All types of emotional response increase, but CF responses definitely lead. This is the first age at which well over half the children give one or more CF responses. C responses come second, "blood" leading and "fire" occurring more than at any other age to date. Conversely, M,

FM, and m all decrease, M and FM not only decreasing in number but becoming less active in nature. m movements are now predominantly downward instead of upward as at 4 years.

Shading and Clob responses, often considered indicators of disturbance, both increase slightly at this age.

The most clear-cut example of color shock seen in our entire group of cases occurs at this age, in a boy who gives perfectly usual responses to the first seven cards. On Card VIII he regards the card for a long time, picks it up, fingers it, turns it repeatedly, looks away and around the room, tries to leave the table and when restrained says, "That's a flower." Presented with Card IX he says, "I don't want it," looks at Examiner, and falls off his chair. "I won't look at it." Presented with Card X he leaves the table and pounds on the window sill.

Many examples of uncertainty and insecurity appear. Many children, for example, give an initial refusal but then do answer. Or they respond with an initial "I don't know" and then answer. Thus:

"I don't know. I think it's a silly old animal."
"I don't know what it is. Nothing. Looks like a bear or something."
"I can't tell. I don't know. I think it looks like a pumpkin."

Many criticize their own response having given it; and others give a response and then ask confirmation of its accuracy from the Examiner. Thus:

"I don't know. Looks like a little house to me. Funny house. Is it really a house?"

Some, in their uncertainty, tell about things they *would* be able to identify. Thus:

V. "Uh! I know what these are but I can't think of the name. If you had a house I could tell that easily because if it had a chimney and smoke I could tell it's a house."

Complete refusals are fewer than at 4 years. Many children who are unable to answer, alibi: "I think it looks like something. I did know but I forgot." One child who called Card II a pumpkin was asked what gave him the idea. He replied, "I thought of it all by myself." Another saw a cat on Card VI. Asked how much was the cat, answered, "Eight dollars."

Many seem to be trying to confirm the accuracy of their identification by assuring themselves and the Examiner that the real object looks like what they see in the cards:

III. "Tie. 'Cause ties have these 'cause they go right up here."
VI. "A snake. Just the straight part." [Top projection.] "I don't know what this is" [main part of card]. "Maybe snakes have these. I don't know. I never saw a snake."

VI. "A tree. Because I could tell because trees have this kind of long thing to hold the branches on, like a great big stick."

In contrast to those who express themselves "I can tell because ———" are those who say they "can't tell" what the cards are. The phrase "I think it is ———" occurs more here than at any other age to date. More children question the identity of the figure now than at any other age. "Is it a deer?" "Is it a pool?" "Is it another butterfly?" More qualified concepts are given than at any other age to date. This seemingly increasing indecisiveness may be due to increasing critical abilities. The child may now be less satisfied than formerly with inaccurate or generalized answers.

There is some stressing of the reality of the cards, though less than at 3½ and 4 years:

Card IV. "That's a *real* man."
Card II. "That's the sun. Head and eyes. Bright shining sun. . . . Looks like a forehead. It *is* a forehead."

Marked variability and lack of stereotypy in response is indicated by the relatively low A%, which has decreased in six months from 56% to 44%.

There is less confabulation than at 4 years, but nevertheless confabulation does occur. An example is:

Card X. "These are two big shoots. This thing that shoots way up in the sky. It's pointing at this. Just a picture so it can't shooting. They put poles and then they shoot and kill the birds very badly. And then they fall down on the ground and then some people buried them so nobody could step on their dead foots and everything."

Though there is less confabulation, this is the high point for the giving of extremely confused or unrelated concepts. We get typically, "animal with two noses," "fish with two heads," "dog with head at both ends," "bug with two tails," "bear with two heads," "person with two pairs of arms."

Further confusion is caused by the fact that some children appear to be striving for a full WS response, more characteristic of later ages—as for example a human or animal face on Cards II or III—but still see separate human or animal figures at the sides. They seem to see both types of percepts simultaneously and their resulting description of what they see is extremely confused. There is also a marked increase in the expression of oppositional tendencies. WS increases from an average of .2 per child to an average here of .6, the highest point to date. S also rises from .1 to .4, its highest point to date.

Also there occur several responses which *approach* the full contamination seen at 5 years: "A cabbage—nose, eyes, cheeks"; "A bridge—its legs."

Card III. "That looks like fire burning. This is the fireplace. This is the hands, these are the feet that they are putting them in so that they can have the fish for dinner."

Card III. "The sun. Another sun. Here's a tie. Another forehead." (Whose?) "The sun's. His eyes." (Whose?) "The sun's."

Card IV. "A tree. The branches. The climbing part. The arms." (Whose?) "The tree's. And the tree's foots."

As suggested, the perceptions of many children at 4½ years appear to be confused, to say the least. The following responses, which cannot be classified, but which may loosely be described as "strange" are characteristic of this age level:

Card VIII. "Here a butterfly flying up [bottom pink and orange] and he has to keep this thing right on a straight line [center]. He can't put anything in that it's a snap thing, you can put a paper there to hold it."

Card   II. "Red men and lady. Live up in a garden."

Card   I. "It looks like some I don't know but oh I know I think it might be a wolf. A Masonic wolf. A very good wolf that won't bite you. When you come near it all it'll do is rub against your back. His white fur and black fur. His crocks, places he gives out milk."

Card   VI. "A wolf. Real. Look at his mouth, oh I'm a scared to touch him! No that's a nice wolf but he'll put sores on you but they go off in one day."

Card   X. "What did the other children say? A rage for me. A thing that you skip about. All kinds of songs about lullabies. (How tell?) (She shows small "seed pod" in top center.) Cause like a lullaby song. A music player."

Four and a half year olds not only tend to give rather strange and unusual answers but many behave in rather a strange manner while they are responding. Thus, among quite "normal" children we get the following:

Card IX. "That looks like nothing. Gloop. Gloop." (Puts face right down on the card. Taps card. Acts a little peculiar, rather "flighty.") "An antelope with horns."

Card IV. "I don't know." (Peers closely at card, looking worried.) "I can't see what it is." (Looks as though he might cry.) "I can't think about that one."

Card II. "A fish." (Stares at card in a strange, rather glassy-eyed manner.) (Else?) "Yes." (She twists her fingers.) (Show me.) "Doggie."

Many at this age reinforce their answers with comments about things at home:

Card II. "What that? Another bird? Why all birds? We have real birds at home, out in my back yard."

Card VI. "A tree. We have a big tree. Where squirrels climb up."

Earlier, children described objects which they apparently were seeing upside down, without mentioning that they were upside down. Now they may mention this upside-down-ness.

Card VI. ∧"Ugh! Eeh! A kitty [top]. Just been made a kitten.
Dear God has to put whiskers on. Just inside, needs other part. Has to make sure that he's all right.
∨ Same, only upside down."

Now only 30 per cent of the subjects, seven girls and eight boys, perseverate. Concepts perseverated are: blood, bone, bug, butterfly (3), clouds, design, dog, flower (3), tree (2), Xmas tree (2). Such perseverations are especially common on Cards VIII, IX, and X, the child calling all three cards the same thing, as "butterfly" or "flower." There is no dynamic perseveration.

Though the percentages on area of card used do not bring this out clearly, we note that many children at this age select a small part of the card, name it, and seem perfectly satisfied to have ignored the main part of the card.

"Do" responses are becoming fewer in number, having dwindled from .5 per child at 4 years to .2 here. The earlier observed tendency of naming separate parts which eventually may or may not be correlated into a total whole still persists, but decreasingly.

Initial exclamations of surprise do occur, but not frequently: "Ooh!" "Yikes!" "Brr!"

There is a marked tendency, especially among the boys, to describe things seen as silly, funny or crazy. Thus: "A silly one!"; "A silly old mouse"; "Wow! It looks funny."

Of these several behavior characteristics just described, those which are probably most significantly characteristic of the 4½-year-old age level are the following:

The very marked extratensivity and emotionality indicated by an average ΣC per child of 1.9. Insecurity and uncertainty, as indicated by initial refusals voiced even when the child is capable of giving a good answer; criticism of own response; alibiing, as "I did know but I forgot." Many children also give their response in the form of a question: "Is it a butterfly?"

There is marked variability and lack of stereotypy, indicated by the low A%. There is confabulation, near-contamination, and there are many strange and confused responses. Animals may have two heads or two tails; and, as earlier, plants and objects have human appendages—legs, arms, hands. Oppositional tendencies express themselves strongly.

The entire response at this age stands in marked contrast to the clarity of the 5-year-old response.

Individual Determinants

Number: There are slightly fewer responses per child here than at the preceding age—14.2 here; 14.7 at 4 years.

Area: Dd% remains about the same as at the preceding age—11%. But there is a shift in W and D. W% increases to 56%, D falling to an all-time low of only 33%.

S and WS both increase markedly at this age: .6 WS per child; .4 S per child, higher than at any preceding age. Do is only .2 per child, half what it was at 4 years.

Form: As at preceding ages, F% decreases—to 72%. F+% increases, to 75%.

M, FM, m: There is a definite decrease here in M, FM, m, all three. The average number of M per child is .3; FM is .7 per child; m is .1 per child.

M not only occurs less extensively but is less active in nature. Static M leads here with "standing" the largest single item. FM remains active as at 4 years—strong extension, especially climbing, leading. Water forms and downward activity predominate in m.

Color: Average ΣC has doubled since 4 years, FC, CF, and C all increasing. Averages per child are .3FC, 1.3CF, .3C.

"Blood" responses predominate among C responses; "flower" among CF. Red portions of blots attract fewer responses than at 4 years.

Shading: Shading responses increase slightly, from .5 to .6 per child. As at the preceding age, diffusion responses lead.

Clob: Clob too increases slightly, from an average of .1 per child to an average of .2 per child. "Blackness" responses lead, but "monster," "ghost," or "threatening animal" occur conspicuously.

Content: Major content categories, as at 4 years, are animals, objects, plants, humans and nature in that order. A% is very low, only 44%. H% is 8%. Other conspicuous categories are: flowers, architecture, scenes, blood, and anatomy.

Leading type of animal response has shifted again to the butterfly-bird category. Total number of animals is less than at 4 years, but there are as many different kinds as at four.

Length: Total records are considerably longer in number of words—an average of about 175 words per girl, 136 per boy.

Timing: Total duration of records has increased to an average of 7.8 minutes per girl; 6.7 per boy.

Semantics: Simply naming the blot still leads, as at preceding ages, as a method of identification. Comparing the blot to the concept with the phrase "looks like" comes second. Concepts are not as a rule qualified; child makes definite statements.

Plurals: The usual plural predominates; "two———" comes next.

Best-Worst: Card X is liked best by girls, here and from here on. Card VI is least liked by girls. VIII is liked best by boys; Card I liked least.

Sex Differences

Sex differences are neither conspicuous nor striking at this age. The only conspicuous sex differences in area are that girls give many more Dd responses than do boys.

Boys give more FM responses than do girls, and their FM responses are slightly more active than are those of girls.

ΣC is much larger in girls than in boys—1.5 on the average in boys; 2.3 in girls. Boys give more FC responses than do girls but girls definitely exceed in CF and C.

Girls give more shading responses than do boys. Boys give more wild animal responses than do girls.

Comparison of Rorschach and Developmental Findings

Due to the fact that developmental characteristics of the 4½-year-old age level have not as yet been determined, no comparative table will be given for this age.

Sample Record of 4½-Year-Old Girl M.B.

RESPONSE	INQUIRY	SCORING		
I. (Whirls card around.) I've played this game before. (Long delay.) Boats. All the water. Ferries. (Looks on back of card.)	(White spots are the boats, all the black is water.)	WS$_x$	F+	scene
II. Fire.	(Reds)	D	C	fire
House.	(The black.) Idea? "Cause it looks like one."	D	F+	arch
III. That looks like a car on fire.	(Fire is red, car is all the black.)	W$_x$	CF	scene
Back of the car.	(Center red.)	D	F+	obj P
Looks like a ribbon.	(Usual) Whose? "Giant's."	Do	F+	Hd
IV. Ooh! What that looks like! Feet.				
That looks like the hand.	(Lower center proj.)	D	F–	Hd
What is this? (She puts her finger on top side proj.) I don't know. (Traces the edge of the blot with her finger.)				
V. Rat. (Whispers) Ears and mouth and feet.	(Center detail only.)	D	F+	A
And this is water.	(Usual wings.)	D	F±	nat
Legs. (Whose?) I don't know.	(Usual side proj. on wings.)	Dd	F+	Hd
Cept it looks like a butterfly.	(Whole)	W$_1$	F+	A P

Sample Record of 4½-Year-Old Girl M.B. (Continued)

RESPONSE	INQUIRY		SCORING	
VI. Mm! Doesn't look like anything! (Looks around room.) Think it looks like a snake. Grass or else dirt. Wouldn't have to be grass cause grass is green.	(Snake is midline and top proj. All the rest is dirt.)	W_x	F± F(C)	A
VII. Back of an apron. Back of the straps. Shaped like a dress.	(Apron is the blot with straps the top proj. The center white is the dress.)	WS_1	F+	obj
Buffaloes. Just this part, his head.	(Tiny nose of figure on first tier is head of buffalo.)	Dd	F+	Ad
(Else?) No, cept that button.	(Girl's mouth at right.)	Dd	F±	obj
VIII. That looks like a flower garden. Here are all the pretty pink flowers.	(Whole, with delineation of parts. Tree and blanket are part of the garden. Tree is center gray, and blanket is lower orange and pink.)	W_3	CF	scene
Here's the tree. (Else?) No, 'cept flowers. Blanket they put underneath the flowers.				
IX. Don't know what that looks like! Just like some shoe house burning down. House, house and fire. (She recites "Old woman who lived in a shoe.")	(Pink and green are house; fire is orange.)	W_x	CF m	arch
X. Like all the flowers going away to die.	Why? "Cause it's spring. Spring is my birthday." (Shows all the parts as flowers.)	W_x	CF m	flowers abstr

Card most liked: VIII (Long regard.) Why? "Cause it looks so nice."
Card least liked: VII. (Why?) "Cause it looks so funny."

R = 18   Time: 11 minutes

$2W_1$ $13F = 72\%F$
$1W_3$ $9F+, 3F\pm, 1F- = 80\% F+$
$5W_x = 44\% W$

$6D = 33\%D$ 2 tend. m
                          4CF   1C
3Dd   1 tend. F(C)
$1Do = 22\%Dd$

                          $0M : 5\tfrac{1}{2}\Sigma C$

3A, 1Ad = 22%A
3Hd = 16%H
3 scene
1 fire
2 architecture
3 objects
1 nature
1 flower

2P = 11%P

COMMENT Here we see widespread intellectual activity as well as a rather volatile and impulsive emotional reaction which is immediate and expressive. This girl is aggressive and self-assertive (WS response at Card I plus extratensivity). She has initial impulses which are somewhat uncontrolled, but she immediately tries to incorporate her response into a more acceptable pattern. (See progression of response on Cards II and III from "fire" to "car on fire.")

Her intellectual process is erratic and proceeds in a progressive-regressive pattern which probably makes things quite difficult for her as well as for those around her. (See progression of response on IV, V, VI, and VII.) Her reactions are often poorly integrated, and then suddenly the behavior appears well organized and mature, followed by just as sudden a reversal to less well organized performance. Her most imaginative and best integrated responses come with the color cards, though at IX she interjects "shoe house burning down."

This child's perception is quite different from that of most of her contemporaries since she sees more detail and small detail than wholes. There may be some sign of anxiety in the high number of Dd and the number of Hd. This latter may also indicate that her approach to others is peripheral and as yet only partial. Her attention span is short for any one activity or process and she is easily distracted, mostly by her own impulses. Her response to external stimuli is positive and active as well as "warm" and impulsive. She shows productive imagination and good originality. She probably enjoys herself and her activities immensely though she may create some chaos in the environment—chaos in which she herself eventually becomes involved.

Sample Record of 4½-Year-Old Boy D.G.

RESPONSE	INQUIRY		SCORING		
I. I don't know. A pumpkin to me.	(Whole, white as eyes and mouth.)	WS₁	F+	obj	P
II. I can't guess what that is. I can't find out. It doesn't look like anything much. I can't guess.			Refusal		
III. Dogs.	(Usual men.)	W₂	F+	A	
A bone.	(Center red.)	D	F±	obj	
I don't know what these are.	(Side reds.)				
IV. A fireplace. Hearth. Chimney, mantelpiece.	(Whole. Usual foot is hearth, chimney is bottom center, mantelpiece is usual arms.)	Wₓ	F± ? tend. to Clob F	obj	
V. Is it a deer? Head, legs.	(Whole, legs are usual wings.)	W₁	F±	A	
VI. Butterfly.	(Whole)	W₁	F+	A	
VII. (Sighs) Is it a pool? Water, some cement and stones.	(Cement is center S, stones are bottom tier, water is two top tiers.)	WSₓ	F±	nat	
VIII. Is that another butterfly? Two butterflies.	(Pink and orange.)	D	FC	A	
	(Other butterfly is blue and gray.)	D	FC	A	
Nothing else. This is something. A animal. Can't guess what kind it is.	(Usual animal.)	D	F+	A	P
IX. A butterfly. All butterfly, not two butterflies.	(Whole)	W₁	CF	A	
X. Flowers. Stem.	(Whole, with top gray as stem.)	Wₓ	CF	flower	P

Card most liked: VIII
Card least liked: IV

R = 12

4W₁
1W₂
3Wₓ = 67%W

4D = 33%D

Time: 5 minutes

8F = 67%F
4F+, 4F± = 75%F+

2FC 2CF
1 tend. ClobF?

0M : 3ΣC

7A = 58%A
3 objects
1 flower
1 nature

3P = 25%P

COMMENT The uncertainty and insecurity of this age is here expressed in the questions directed to the examiner: "Is it a ——?" The 4½-year-old needs confirmation even for his own most adequate responses. He is also capable of refusing politely with, "I don't know," or "I can't guess" when there is no real inner or environmental assurance about his reactions.

Initial resistance is seen here in the perception of the white spaces on Card I. The other space response occurs at VII, and although this space is not perceived precisely, it is a definite part of the response. In contrast, this child is also quite conscious of the darkness of the card when at IV he interprets "fireplace." Refusal at II is a possible indication of red shock.

This boy appears to be somewhat resistant to authority, finds it difficult to express his feelings, probably has a strong conscience and sensitive reactions to the judgment of others (red shock is interpreted in adults as a sign of guilt feelings), may tend to have vague anxiety feelings about problems of birth and death, and has a good deal of inner emotional vulnerability. He makes a good adaptation to external stimuli. There is much going on here in the inner emotional field which is indicative of advanced maturity.

CHAPTER FIFTEEN

Five Years

R = 13.9	70%F	6.2A = 44%A
	78%F+	1.3H = 9%H
58%W		2.0 object
34%D	.6M 1.1FM .2m	1.2 nature
8%Dd	.2FC 1.2CF .2C	1.0 plant
	.4F(C) .2Clob	
		3.0P = 22%P
	.6M : 1.6ΣC	

Qualitative Description

FIVE approaches the Rorschach task willingly, though often without the intense expectation shown at some later ages. He settles himself firmly in his chair and regards the first card as Examiner holds it out to him, but often does not take it in his hands until the Examiner says, "You may hold it." Characteristically he peers at the blot, frowns slightly, and as often as not says, "Well, I don't know what it is." After only a little encouragement, however, nearly all are able to give a good, scorable response. In the majority of cases the first card receives a single interpretation, which is an immediate whole response—most characteristically *map, face,* or *bird.*

After his slow beginning, the 5-year-old usually proceeds competently, giving one or at most two responses to a card. No child gives fewer than six responses in all. There is little perseveration (only 28 per cent of the cases), and when it does occur the concept is nearly always adapted somewhat to the actual appearance of the blot. Perseverations which occur are:

Girls: cloud, design (2), leaf, map (2), rabbits.
Boys: bird, grasshopper, fire, heart, insides, owl, smoke, rock.

Dynamic perseveration, that is perseveration on one concept but with slight change of detail with succeeding cards, now occurs in four children. An example is:

Card II: "A fire and this is the smoke." III: "A fire just getting up and this is all the smoke." IV: "Just smoke coming up—all of it." V: "The smoke." VI:

164

"The fire just starting up and the smoke." VII: "This is a fire just getting out cause there's no more fire and this is just the smoke I think."

The response of the 5-year-old is primarily global; he attempts to encompass the whole of the blot in his interpretation. He responds focally, often picking out an area at the center of the card, then relating the sides to it, with nice bilateral balance. When he gives a detail response he often chooses details in the center of the card, or if he points out a detail on one side of the card he balances it by mentioning its duplicate on the other side. Sometimes he names these two balanced parts alike, sometimes gives such comments as: Card X. "Here's the mother, here's the daddy," or X. "That looks like the sun and that looks like the moon," or III. "That looks like two birds. I think I could call it mummy and daddy." There is also much use of the phrase, "Two ———," in fact it is at this age that the transition from the expression of plurality by use of the customary plural word to its expression by use of the phrase "Two ———" is taking place.

The child frequently assumes that the two parts go together by pointing to only one but saying, "Two ———." He may even be able to take the outstanding parts of Cards II and III, and by bridging the white spaces, make the whole blot into a single face, front view, with the reds of either card as eyes or ears, the center as a nose, and the lower red or black as a mouth. For small and unusual details, FIVE has a fine disregard; barely half the group give any rare details.

Thus we find that FIVE has very high generalizing ability. Not only is W very high—58%, but use of all the more complex W forms—W_2, W_3 W_x—has increased. Note also on Card X the frequent use of such grouping phrases as "A bunch of ———," "A lot of ———," "All kinds of ———."

Sometimes the 5-year-old's refusal to give more than one interpretation to one "picture" leads him into confusion, as when he sees elements of two concepts in the card but tries to include both in a single response. He may then give a contaminated response. At 4½ years one or two children gave responses and then added spare parts to a main concept: "A bridge, its feet"; "A cabbage, its eyes." Many more of these responses are found at 5: "A star, it has extra hands"; "Leaf, its arms up here"; "Bunny with wings." Now, however, there is also some full contamination or mixing of two equally important concepts: "Butterfly-map," "Dog-map." Or, on VIII, "Insides of a bear"; on IV, "Horsefly—because of horse's head and wings." Virtually all of these contaminations are given by girls. However, even this amount of contamination is less than will occur at 5½ years, and frequently, as in horsefly, it is not completely implausible.

Approximately two-thirds of the 5-year-old's responses are based on shape alone. The average accuracy of form is 78% good forms per record. Girls give a higher percentage of good forms than do boys.

Human movement responses, though still few at this age, are double what they were at 4½ and more than at 5½. Less than half the children, however, give any M. Average M is .6. For each child there is an average of one animal movement and virtually no minor movement. Now we find static M leading, but with moderate extensor movements coming next. Just two people existing definitely leads. FM is much more active than M— strong extensor movements predominating. Climbing and flying occur most, with standing also prominent. There is notably a lightness to the movement, and responses are often given with a light, humorous touch: two elephants boasting; elephants dancing on one foot with a watermelon on their heads sticking out tongues, or dancing so much that smoke is coming out of their heads; fish flying in the water; little pink bears climbing; butterflies eating flowers; girls with high heels and pocketbooks going for a walk; little black men tipping their hats. There also appears a theme of uncertainty in M: trying to hide, trying to get away, trying to get through. As to m, water forms predominate. Upward activity of water or of flames occurs most.

ΣC has dropped since 4½ years to 1.6, the lowest of any age from 4½ through 9 years. This drop is caused equally by drops in FC, CF, and C. FC is now very low (.2) and is used by only 16 per cent of the children. Although the mean for pure C drops somewhat, the percentage of children using it has increased. Compared with 4½, only half as many girls now use C but twice as many boys use it. This pure C is mainly fire and blood. Of the CF responses, nearly half are anatomy: lungs, heart, insides. This is by far the outstanding age for use of CF as anatomy. For girls, rainbows and sunsets are prominent. Nearly all the rest of the CF responses are flowers. Color naming is nearly absent.

At 5 years, most of the boys and nearly half the girls are extratensive; a few are introversive and a very few are ambiequal. The average experience balance is .6M : 1.6ΣC. Six girls and no boys still have equations of 0M : 0ΣC.

The main content categories are now animals, objects, nature and humans. All but animals occur more extensively than at 4½ years. Wild animals, especially large wild animals, are the leading type of animal response.

The aspect of content response most characteristic of the age, however, is that objects seen are for the most part close to home, simple and familiar objects. Clothes of some type—chiefly bow or hair-ribbon, shoes, socks, are the leading object response. Articles of furniture come next, then boat and puzzle. Both food and map responses occur here more than at any other age.

Anatomic responses also occur more than at any age to date, in fact to the extent of nearly one half a response per child, on the average. "Insides" of things are the chief responses in this category. Nearly half the CF responses, as indicated above, are anatomic.

In his choice of forms, the 5-year-old is factual, close to home and close to his own body. His emphasis on concreteness often makes inquiry difficult or useless, for he refers to his own experience or to the actual object rather than to the blot, in answering questions. When asked how he could tell that Card IV was a bear, one boy refused indignantly, "I never saw a bear in my whole life." Other children when asked how they could tell about certain other responses, answered, "Looks like a wall because we go home by that wall"; "A body because it tells in my encyclopedia"; "Camels —I could tell because my mother makes them out of cookies"; "A butterfly because I painted one today." Or, "Can tell it's a map by looking at it. My poppy has a map"; "Clouds cause some clouds are like that"; "Because I know what lions look like." The question "What reminded you?" brings the answer, "I just reminded myself," or "I just thinked of it."

FIVE is also factual and matter of fact in his manner of responding. Both his tone and his manner are extremely reasonable. He gives his answer —"A tree. Just a plain tree"; "Just plain teeth"; "Looks like a face. Just a plain face"; "Looks like a table. A real table."

In his wish for complete accuracy the 5-year-old often shows a marked hesitancy to speak out, take a chance, or run the risk of giving a wrong response. Thus at this age we get a great many refusals, "I don't know"— and then without further prompting, an adequate response. "I don't see anysing in zis. Looks like two men." "I don't know what this looks like. Kind of hard. There's some bears." "I don't know what it looks like. I think so hard but I don't know. They look like fishes." "Well I don't know exactly. Myself it looks like a rock with some holes in it." "I can't recognize it. What is it? The earth."

Or the child protects himself with the phrase "to me," implying that it may not be this but to him it looks as if it were. Thus he says, "It looks to me like ————." This phrase occurs here more than at any other age.

Or he may qualify his concept with such phrasing as "It looks something like," or may suggest changes in the structure of the blot to make it fit his concept, "If you cut this off." Qualifying concepts of one type or another occur here more than at any other age except 7 years. Another self-protective device is to turn the question back to the examiner, "What do *you* think it is?" "What do they look like *to you*?" Or, "What did the other kids say it was?" The child may complain that the task of naming the cards is "hard"—"Well this is going to be hard," or "The hardest one that ever was." Or conversely he may boast that it is "Easy!"

Denial of own response, having given it, or complete refusal of difficult blots are further methods of self-protection. One girl and three boys (8 per cent of the children) now deny responses having given them. This is the first age at which more than one child denies a response.

One further evidence of a wish to be accurate and to give a satisfactory performance is FIVE's criticism of his own concepts. He may say, "That is a butterfly. Too long a ear though. Never saw feet on a butterfly."

We consider the 5-year-old to be a thoughtful creature. His very speech reflects this attribute. He says as he looks at the blots, "I think it's pigs." "I sink I see a face." "I think this looks like a stove, *to me*." The phrase "I think" or its companion phrase "I guess" occurs more often here than at any other age except 8 years.

There are few signs of disturbance at this age. Shading responses occur only on an average of .4 per child, less than at any succeeding age. Clob also is less frequent than at any succeeding age until 10 years.

However an awareness of darkness or blackness of the cards is frequently expressed when the child is asked why he likes certain cards and dislikes others. Card X, the almost universal favorite, is chosen chiefly because "It's more prettier," "Cause it's all different colors." Cards I, II, and VI are disliked most because "It's all black," "It's so black," "All the dark ones they don't look so good," or "Cause it doesn't look so pretty." A few express dislike of the red on Card II and there is at this age a definite decrease in the number of responses to all red portions of blots, though the avoidance of red is not yet as marked as it will be at 5½.

S is moderately high—.4 per child. This and a rather high WS (average of .9) suggests at least some oppositional tendencies.

Individual Determinants

Number: Average number of responses is 13.9, slightly less than at the two preceding ages.

Area: W% is very high, an average of 58%. D% is conversely very low, only 34%. Dd% is 8%. WS is high, exceeded at only one age, 7 years. The average occurrence is .9 per child. S also is high, .4 per child.

Form: F% is the lowest of any age to date, though higher than at succeeding ages, an average of 70% per child. F+%, conversely, is the highest of any age to date though lower than at succeeding ages—an average of 78%F+.

M, FM, m: M is double that at the preceding age and higher than at the succeeding age, an average of .6 per child. FM also is approximately double that of the preceding age—1.1 per child. m is low—.2 per child.

Static M leads with moderate extensor movements coming second. Just two people existing definitely leads. FM is much more active, strong extensor movements leading. Climbing and flying lead, with standing also prominent. As to m, water forms predominate. Upward activity of water, or upward activity of flames occurs most.

Color: ΣC is lower at this age than at surrounding ages and lower than at *any* following ages except 10 years. ΣC at this age is only 1.6. CF leads with an average of 1.2. C and FC each average .2. Flower and anatomy responses lead among the CF responses; fire among the C responses.

Shading: Shading responses are very few at this age, lower than at the preceding age and lower than at any following age—an average of .4 per child. Diffusion responses (clouds and smoke) are the outstanding types.

Clob: Average number of Clob is .2 as at the preceding age, but much lower than at any following age till 10 years.

Content: Leading content categories shift again here, to a more mature group which is maintained for several years: animals, objects, nature other than plants, and humans. For the first age plants including trees is not one of the outstanding categories. Of animals, wild animals, especially large wild animals, lead; the butterfly-bird category comes second. Food responses though occurring only on the average of .2 per child, nevertheless here reach an all-time high. The same for map responses.

Length: Total records have again increased in length and now are about 200 words in length, in both sexes.

Timing: This is about half a minute longer on the average than at the preceding age. The average record now takes 7.8 minutes.

Semantics: Simply naming the blot still leads as a method of identification but at this age it occurs only slightly more often than comparing the blot to the concept by use of "looks like." "Looks like" is particularly frequent at this age, and qualifying remarks such as "It looks something like" or suggestions for change in the blot, are more frequent here than at any other age till 7 years.

Plurals: At this age the change from the customary plural to the phrase "Two ——" is taking place. The two types of plurals are virtually equal in occurrence.

Best and Worst: From here on, Card X is liked best by both girls and boys. Card II is liked least by girls; Cards I or VI by boys.

Popular Responses: The average number of populars has risen to three per child and the average P% has also risen, to 22%, definitely the highest to date.

Sex Differences

Sex differences are not marked at this age. As to area, boys give more W and D than girls; girls give more Dd. There are slightly more M and more FM in boys than in girls, but they are about equally active. Girls give slightly more m than boys.

ΣC is higher in boys than in girls—1.8 in boys to 1.4 in girls. Girls have slightly more FC and CF; boys more C. More girls than boys give FC and CF responses and more boys give C responses.

Shading responses occur more in girls than in boys. An equal number of boys and girls give shading responses.

The total number of animals is more in boys than in girls.

All boys have at least one color or movement response, but six girls still have an experience balance of 0M : 0ΣC. Girls give more contaminations. But girls have better form and their records tend to be neater, more popular and more conforming than those of the boys.

Comparison of Rorschach and Developmental Findings

Developmental	Rorschach
Matter of fact and self-controlled. Not over-emotional.	ΣC lower than at the preceding age. FC, CF, and C *all* lower than at surrounding ages.
Calm, collected, well-adjusted. Self-contained. In good equilibrium.	F(C) and Clob less than at any succeeding age until 10 years.
Compliant and conforming. Interpersonal relations are important. Child wishes to please.	An increase in FC would have been expected here but did not occur. FC like all other color responses is less than at surrounding ages. But the child turns questions back to Ex: "What do they look like to you?" None of the resistance to Ex. seen at later ages. Manner and tone are friendly and reasonable.
Capable of self-criticism.	Criticizes own concepts after giving them. Denies response if it does not suit him.
Not adventurous or daring. Likes to do what he can do well. Likes to be certain, accurate. Does not respond unless sure.	Refusals and denials and criticism of own response fairly high. Temporizes with "I don't know" even when he can give a scorable response. "It looks *to me*," or "It looks something like." Complains that pictures are too hard.
Here and now. Factual and concrete. Matter of fact.	Objects seen are simple, familiar, and close to home: clothes, furniture. Describes blots as "Just a *plain* tree," "Just a *plain* face."
Little fantasy and imagination. Not expansive.	Many blots are refused (for lack of imagination?) when first presented, even though answered after initial refusal. N is low here; only an average of 13.9.
Thoughtful.	Generalizes easily, very high W%. The phrase "I think" occurs more than at any other age but one.
Interest in self strong.	The phrase "It looks *to me*" used here more than at any other age. Anatomic responses higher than at any other age to date. Boasts that things are "easy" for him.
Focal.	Responses primarily global. Often picks out central area then relates the sides of it.

Sample Record of 5-Year-Old Girl M.E.

RESPONSE	INQUIRY	SCORING			
I. A butterfly.	Reminded you? "His wings." (Whole)	W_1	F+	A	P
II. I don't know that. A bee?	Remind you? "The wings." (Points to top red.) "I don't know what this is." (Black) "Part of the bee, but not the wings. I don't know what."	W_1	F—	A	
III. (Pause) This doesn't look like anything to me. Looks like to me a duck—two ducks—all I can think of.	Feet? (Points to men's feet and hands.) "Know why I think it's a duck? Cause ducks have a mouth like that." (Points to beak.)	W_2	F+	A	P
IV. You know what I think it is? A bear with no head—cause —a bear has feet like that. I don't know what that is [lower center head]. Doesn't look like anything.	"Bear's body" (upper center): "These." (Small side projections.) "I don't know—part of the bear. This (lower center) not part of the bear. That's not part."	W_1	F+	A	P
V. (There is no response. Ex. asks what it looks like or reminds her of. She shakes her head.) Can't tell. Another bee, is it? These are—uh [top projections] I know bees and I see these on them, but I can't tell what they are. These are wings here.	(Whole)	W_1	F+	A	

Sample Record of 5-Year-Old Girl M.E. (Continued)

RESPONSE	INQUIRY		SCORING	
VI. That looks like a violin.	(Whole) Remind you? "Cause the handle there." (Points to top detail and midline.)	W₁	F+	obj
VII. (She shakes her head) Two bears with one ear.	"Their paw's back here, their little nose here. They're on the rocking horse (third tier). I think they're not real bears. Maybe part of the rocker." "What did the other kids say that was?"	W₃	F+ FM	(A)
VIII. I don't know what *this* is. Another butterfly.	(Whole) "Cause of this—the wings." (Whole blot right and left of midline.)	W₁	F± CF	A
Or a piece of candy.	"Just the pink. Cause it's pink candy."	D	CF	food
IX. That looks like a cow or a horse—up here.	(Orange only.) "Cause these things." (Points to orange spikes toward center.) "Those?" "I don't know—what, but they have them."	D	F—	A
X. They look like flowers.	"No, not the whole thing, just these." (Side blues.)	D	CF	flower
This is another butterfly here. The butterfly is eating the flowers.	(Top gray with pink as wings.)	D	FM	A
Those look like chickies.	(Center yellow.)	Dd	CF	A

Card most liked: VI. "I think the violin is."
Card least liked: VIII. "It's all different colors."

R = 13

6W$_1$		
1W$_2$		
1W$_3$ = 61% W	9F = 69% F	9A, 1(A) = 77% A
	6F+, 1F±, 2F— = 72% F+	1 object
4D = 31% D		1 food
	1FM, 1 tend. FM	1 flower
1Dd = 8% Dd	3CF, 1 tend. CF	
		4P = 31% P
	0M : 3ΣC	

COMMENT This is probably an over-conscientious child (probable red shock, 4 popular responses, 77% A) who is reflecting the conformity and the amenability of the age as well as of her own individuality. The age is a conforming one, but her personality probably tends to exaggerate this characteristic. Her extratensivity is more marked than for most children of her age, as is the degree of stereotypy. The stimuli of the environment tend to make her more expansive, but at the same time less efficient (F— at Cards II and IX, more responses on color cards, no P responses on color cards). When the stimulus originates from within, she is much better organized though less original.

The only movement response occurs at Card X, "butter-fly is eating the flowers." This may indicate some aggressive feelings, though they have probably not reached any overt stage.

Sample Record of 5-Year-Old Boy T.K.

RESPONSE	INQUIRY	SCORING			
I. >V Looks like an old brick house. Whole house, all except the windows.	(Windows are the S details. Whole blot is house.)	WS₁	F+	arch	
II. I sink I see a face.	"Nose" (center white). "Eyes" (top white either side of center hands). "Mouth" (bottom red). Else? "No."	WS₁	F+	Hd	
III. I don't see anysing in zis. V Looks like two men this way.	"Feet" (usual heads). "Head" (center heads). "Arm" (usual leg). Anything else? "No."	W₂	F±	H	
IV. A bear sitting on a hollow log.	(Whole)	W₂	FM	A	P
V. (Narrows eyes) Looks like a spider.	"Cause it had these" (legs). "That spider looks like a bat."	W₁	F+	A	P
VI. \\ I can't tell anysing from this thing. That's nussing to me. If this was going like this, I would sink it was a caterpillar.	(Midline, top D.) (Indicates that the details are not as they should be, but it does remind him of a caterpillar.)	D	F±	A	
VII. \\V I bet that's supposed to be an old stone tunnel.	"Tunnel hole right here." (Center S)	WS₀	F+	arch	
VIII. Let's see. V This looks like a bunch of colored stones, in the shape of a sailboat.	(Whole)	Wₓ	CF	obj	

	W_s	FM	A	P
∧ This way it looks like two animals going around two rocks. (Usual animals, includes whole.)	W_s	FM	A	
IX. ∨∧ These look like lungs. ∨ Can't see anysing else in here. (Pink) "My father was teaching biology and he showed me in his book."	D	CF	anat	
X. >∨ This looks like a bunch of insects. "At first when I saw it I thought it was insects. Now I don't know. Just some." (Indicates side brown only as insect.)	D	F+	A	
Zis is like a man: arms, leg, head, body. (Center green.)	D	F+	H	
These look like trees. (Side blues.)	D	F±	plant	
This looks like a tree. (Top gray.)	D	F+	plant	
These look like just strips of brick. (Pink)	D	CF	obj	

Card most liked: I like these (VIII, IX, X). Chooses X.
Card least liked: II.

Time: 10 minutes

$R = 15$

$1W_0$
$3W_1$
$2W_2$
$1W_3$
$1W_x = 53\%W$

$7D = 47\%D$

$10F = 67\%F$
$7F+, 3F\pm = 85\%F+$

$2FM$
$3CF$

$0M : 3\Sigma C$

$5A = 33\%A$
$2H, 1Hd = 20\%H$
2 architecture
2 objects
1 anatomy
2 plants

$3P = 20\%P$

COMMENT This is a boy of rather superior intellectual and emotional endowment who is constantly disciplining his mental and emotional faculties to more acceptable ends. His response anticipates a later age (6–7 years) when initial interpretations are often discarded for better ones and when the subject makes a demand for precision in any response.

This boy shows a rather synthetic and structural quality to his thinking, though he is perfectly willing to use only the details if the whole is not acceptable to him. His drive is somewhat ambivalent, varying between passivity ("bear sitting on a hollow log" at IV) and adaptive dynamism ("Two animals going around two rocks," at VIII).

He reacts rather expansively to external stimuli, and though he has some aggressive tendencies (WS at I, II, and VII), he probably most characteristically tries to adapt rather than attack. Resistance and opposition are further expressed in the eight responses given with the card in the inverse position.

There is strong orientation toward others, though this may not be a completely heterosexual one (all H responses are "men"). He shows good initiative and though he probably can adapt to routines and regulations, they are not always easy for him.

CHAPTER SIXTEEN

Five and a Half Years

R = 13.6	62%F	5.7A = 41%A
	84%F+	1.5H = 11%H
55%W		1.8 object
33%D	.4M 1.3FM .5m	1.3 plant
12%Dd	.2FC 1.4CF .5C	1.3 nature
	.6F(C) .5Clob	
	.4M : 2.3ΣC	3.0P = 25%P

Qualitative Interpretation

Although a neglected age in the literature, 5½ years can be characterized clearly both in terms of Rorschach performance and general behavior. Many kinds of behavior occur here which are uncharacteristic of the ages directly preceding and directly following.

Briefly, the equilibrium of 5 years of age is breaking up, resulting in marked disequilibrium and in variability and unpredictability of behavior. Behavior is not only unpredictable but decidedly unmodulated. The child is unduly sensitive and vulnerable, and emotions are notably uncontrolled. In many respects the Rorschach response foreshadows that of the 7-year-old in its morbidity and unpleasantness.

At this age probably more than at any other to date, the age characteristics can be determined directly from the table of determinants, without recourse to more "qualitative" considerations. There are at this age significant changes with regard to nearly every major determinant, which set off the 5½-year-old response clearly from responses characteristically given at surrounding ages.

Most significant is the drop in A%. A% at this age is only 41%, as low as at any age in this entire range, indicating that responses are here neither stereotyped nor predictable.

177

That the child is now experiencing more outwardly, and less inwardly, and is more responsive to factors in the environment, less motivated by inner drives, is suggested by a drop in M and a marked rise in ΣC. The average M at this age is only .4, less than at surrounding ages, and far fewer children give M responses than at 5 and 6 years. By six years, twice as many children give M responses, and the mean M is two and a half times as great as at 5½. M ranges from fairly static—sitting, looking—to violent —boxing, pushing each other. The more instinctual FM responses occur three times as frequently as M. FM is the largest here of any age to date.

Both aggressivity and explosiveness are suggested by the larger number of m responses, an average of .5, the largest of any age to date, and triple the amount seen at 5 years. The number of m is higher even than the number of M, and is made up largely of fires and explosions. Activity is chiefly upward, and violence prevails.

Greater externalization of experiencing is suggested by the sharp rise in ΣC, which is on the average 2.3, the highest of any age to date. Not only is ΣC unusually high, but the unadaptive CF responses lead, with uncontrolled pure C responses second. Adaptive FC responses occur least of any color responses. Pure C responses have doubled in number since 5 years, and occur not only more than at any age to date but more than at any succeeding age except the somewhat troubled ages of 7 and 9 years. Leading CF responses are flowers and flame. C responses are chiefly fire, rainbow, sunset. Fire alone accounts for one-third of the total CF and C responses in boys, and for half of their total pure C. Furthermore color naming is higher than at any age since 3½ years. The total color picture, therefore, is one of predominance of egocentric, unmodulated and uncontrolled emotion and almost no ability to adapt to demands of the outer world.

Various "trouble" indicators are high. Shading responses, for example, occur more than at any other age to date, on an average of .6 per child. Clob, too, is extremely prevalent—occurring more than at any other age except 7 years. It is almost entirely made up of large, threatening figures— giants, ghosts, monsters. Also, this is the highest age in the entire series for emphasis on the blackness of the blots. Boys, especially, are much concerned with the black, responding to it as a determinant and also commenting on it, especially in relation to the card liked least. (There is a similarly contradictory response to the red. Red parts of blots are avoided—the 5½- year-old giving a mean of only 1.7 responses to red areas of the blots while the 6-year-old gives 2.7 and the 7-year-old 3.5. Nevertheless, more fire responses are given here than at any other age to date.)

A further possible indicator of difficulty, over-concern with the tiny portions of the blots, is reflected in the fact that Dd% is 12%, the highest of any age to date and higher than any succeeding age in our range except 6 years.

There is considerable emphasis on broken and crooked things, or on things with holes in them. In fact, the cards almost appear to shatter before the very eyes of the 5½-year-old. Thus: "Looks like part of a sidewalk broken," "Part of a leaf. I saw one like this. It broke all in pieces. We set it on fire," "A big piece of stone that was part broken," "That one's broken— a rabbit," "This hat, breaking to pieces," "Stones breaking up." Or, "Two doggies, crooked doggies, look at their ears," "Legs of a tree, all crooked."

Overt discomfort caused by the blots is expressed directly in initial exclamations, such as "Yiii!" "Kriki!" "Golly!" Dissatisfaction with cards is also expressed by use of such adjectives as "funny," "crazy," "goofy." Five-and-a-half's initial reaction to the test situation tends to be somewhat ambivalent. He may wriggle with delight as he goes to the examining room, or he may hang back. Once in the examining room he squirms in his chair, scratches, fingers his face. Almost no children reject the first card.

At this age 26 per cent of the children perseverate, but a large number of the perseverations are dynamic. In such cases, once the child has picked his concept, he cannot seem to let go of it, and it may, so to speak, pull him along through the series, through wholes, details, through good form and bad, into combination, contamination, and confabulation. An example of this dynamic perseveration is the following: "I. Rock; II. Rock on fire; IV. A French rock; VI. Butterfly on a rock"; or the entire record of Child W.M., which follows, in which more than one concept is dynamically perseverated.

Outstanding in the record of the 5½-year-old is the range from good, plain, popular forms to vague, unclear mixtures. The child's greater drive to combinatory activity sometimes introduces much confusion into the record at this age. Contamination is stronger than at Five, especially in a perseverating record where the child first recognizes good, new responses in the blots but is unable to give up earlier decisions about the cards. One girl called the first four cards "maps," then called Card V a "butterfly-map" and VII a "dog-map." One boy called the first three cards "stones," then to Card IV he responded: "The rock is all black and his hands are there and his feet are there." This boy insisted that Cards IV, V, and VI were stones though he referred to them as "he," and by VII he had changed his concept entirely to a person. Mixing of parts also leads to confused responses. Card II was seen by one child as a "rail-man," Card VI as a "rail-fly." Card VI was seen by another child as a "leaf-fish." A typical response to Card VI gives an example of the 5½-year-old's difficulty with combinations:

"Telephone pole. [Center, top to bottom.] And it's night time. Because it's black and trees are usually black in the night." (Trees?) "Telephone poles. It's a silly one—it has head, eyes, and mouth and whiskers." (What has?) "Telephone pole . . . [pause] . . . Ah you get me all mixed up."

W_x and W_s have increased and are highest of any age to date. Wholes tend to be broken up and recombined—e.g., on VI—instead of seeing a whole animal it is a butterfly on a leaf, kitten on a rock. This is the strongest age for splitting I vertically and seeing two birds, a girl with leaves, or three bears dancing. This is also the strongest age for W_s on VIII—animals climbing something.

FIVE-AND-A-HALF is rigid and exact in his responses. Modification and qualification are difficult for him. To him the blot seems to be less a picture and more of a puzzle than to the 5-year-old. He asks, "Is that right?" or questions, "Ducks, ain't it?" Answers are to him potentially "right" or "wrong." Semantically he expresses this rigidity of thinking by simply naming the blot. At this age and the age following, such qualifying phrases as "Looks like," or "Looks something like" are conspicuously infrequent. F+% is high—84%. The child of this age is exacting but also accurate. The high CF and low FC also bear out high egocentricity and lack of adaptivity and modulation.

FIVE-AND-A-HALF is not only unmodulated in his behavior, but strongly oppositional. S is very high at this age, an average of .6 per child, the highest of any age. Since this high S occurs in an extratensive setting, this suggests definite opposition to the environment. Refusals are more frequent than at any nearby age, a mean of .7.

This is an age when contradictory and opposed forces make themselves felt, with the result that the child has difficulty not only with the world around him but with himself as well. Such contradictory forces are seen in many facets of the Rorschach response. As already mentioned, the child gives an exceptionally high number of "blackness" responses yet expresses a dislike of blackness. Conversely he tends to avoid red portions of the blots and yet gives more fire and flame responses than at any age to date. There are an unusually low number of responses determined by form alone and yet F+% is extremely high.

Further contrasts occur in that many children see very tiny objects—"Eyelashes for the mouth" (VI), or "Clam's tongues" (VII)—while others see in the blots "The world." Map responses occur frequently and may be combined with the global world concept into "Map of the world." Contrasting to world, in a different dimension, is the response "Nothing." "It reminds me of nothing." Refusals, which are high at this age, in keeping with the child's somewhat rigid all or none attitude, are frequently given in these terms, one going so far as to say, "That reminds me of nothing. It certainly *does not*."

As to content—the percentage of the record made up of animal forms is lowest at 5½ of any age studied except 2½ years. The boys' animals are mainly harmless creatures. Butterflies and birds are the most frequent by far. A few dragons and bears creep into the picture. It is in the girls' records that spiders, crabs, bats, bad wolves, and fighting dogs appear. One or two human beings occur in most records, especially in the girls' records, and frequently the person is being burned or eaten up.

Objects are less popular now, and consist mainly of sticks and poles, socks and bows, and things that pinch (fly-pincers, nose-pincers, hand-clips, or just plain pincers). Natural forms are very frequently chosen at this age, especially Nature in its more spectacular aspects: grass on fire, sunsets, clouds and smoke, explosions. Rocks occur very frequently. Fire has a great attraction for the 5½-year-old. Explosions are more favored by the girls. Plants are chosen frequently at this age. Trees and leaves are prominent, flowers are given somewhat less frequently. A few anatomic responses are given, especially hearts or blood, and a very few children mention sex parts of humans or animals. Maps occur prominently.

As might be predicted from the foregoing description, interpersonal relations at this age are far from smooth. However, 5½ is markedly aware of the Examiner as a person, as the following characteristic comments will indicate. The child makes such remarks as "Bet you don't know what my last name is," "Why do you write?" "How many cards you got there?" "You have more pictures than anyone I ever saw," "You're just like my brother— all freckles," "My eyes are brown. Yours are brown too." Or in a characteristically unmodulated and often unsuccessful attempt to show himself in a good light before other people he boasts, "I'm smart!"

Though some subjects can explain their perceptions, inquiry is frequently rendered fruitless by the fact that many children answer the question, "How could you tell?" or "What reminded you?" with, simply, "Because," seeming to feel that this is a sufficient explanation. If pressed, they may elaborate—"Because it's easy to tell," or "I just look at them," or "Because I can tell by looking at it." Some give their "because" explanation spontaneously: "I think this is a cat because of these eyes."

Thus, to summarize, we see the 5½-year-old, as reflected in his responses to the Rorschach test, as an organism whose behavior patterns are breaking up and leaving him in a more or less constant state of emotional tension and ferment. His behavior is above all variable and unpredictable. He is at peace with neither himself nor the world. At one moment he is dawdling and hesitant, at the next over-demanding and explosive. He fluctuates from one extreme of behavior to another but in an unpatterned way. He is rigid and uncompromising, largely uninfluenced by outside forces. Behavior tends to be oppositional and aggressive. Interpersonal relations are, obviously, very poor. Though he cannot adapt to the environment he is over-sensitive to its demands, excitable, impetuous. The total picture thus stands out in complete contrast to the calm, smooth, untroubled and adaptive behavior which normally characterizes the 5-year-old.

Individual Determinants

Number: Approximately as many as at 5 years, an average of 13.6 per child.

Area: Whole responses definitely predominate—an average of 55%W. D% remains about the same as at 5 years—33%, though actual number of D's is slightly lower than at five. Dd%, however, is by far the largest to date with an average of 12%, as is also the actual number of Dd which is 1.9 per child.

W$_x$ is now the highest of any age to date, an average of 1.2 per child. WS is also relatively high with an average of .8 per child. S, like WS, is high at this age, in fact the highest of any age to date with an average of .6 per child.

Form: The percentage of responses determined by form alone is only 62%, much lower than at any preceding age. F+%, on the contrary, is 84%, much higher than at any preceding age.

M, FM, m: There is a drop in M from .6 at 5 years to .4 at 5½. The sharp decrease in F% therefore is entirely due to an increase in color, not in movement responses. FM, however, has increased, being 1.3 per child, the largest to date. m is double what it was at 5 years, and the largest to date, an average of .5. Thus, at this age as at 3½ years, m is larger than M.

Of the M responses, static or "strong to violent" extension leads. Like other responses at this age, however, M responses are very variable in nature, so that they are difficult to classify. Strong extension definitely leads in FM, climbing and flying being the outstanding animal movements. A slight exhibitionistic theme appears in FM. Animals perform, act in circus, do tricks, look at each other. There are nearly three times as many FM as M, and FM are definitely the more active though both are active.

In m, explosions, and fire and light forms predominate. The chief direction of activity is upward, and a definite violence prevails.

Color: ΣC is, on the average, 2.3, by far the highest to date, and higher than at the following age. Since 5 years there have been increases in number of FC, CF, and C responses. CF definitely leads with an average of 1.4 per child; C comes next with an average of .5. Both of these factors occur here more extensively than at any other age to date. Red portions of the blot, however, are avoided at this age.

CF responses consist chiefly of flower and nature responses; C responses outstandingly of fire. Color naming is stronger than at any age since 3½.

Shading: Shading responses occur here more than at any other age to date—an average of .6 per child. Diffusion responses predominate, but hard texture is coming in conspicuously.

Clob: Clob takes a tremendous jump here from an average of .2 Clob responses per child at 5 years to .5 per child at 5½ years—by far the largest amount to date and more than at any other age except 7 years. Monsters, ghosts, and threatening animals occur here more than at any other age.

Content: As we might expect from the general variability of this age, there are more different content categories used at this than at any preceding age, i.e. 16. Also the number of different categories used by the average subject is more than at any age to date, i.e. 4.9.

The leading content categories are: animals, plants, objects, nature, and humans. Plants and nature other than plants tie for fourth place. Architecture and fire are also strong.

As at 4½ years, butterflies and birds lead among animal responses. However it should be noted that A% at this age is lower than at any other age—only 41%.

Length: Average length is just over 260 words per record, about equal in girls and boys.

Semantics: At this age the chief method of designating the blots is as at earlier ages, simply naming the blot. Qualified concepts, so strong at 5 years, do not occur appreciably at this age.

Plurals: At this age for the first time the phrase "Two ————" predominates over the usual plural.

Best and Worst: As at the preceding age, Card X is the card preferred by both sexes. Girls most dislike VI; boys I and VI. Boys especially dislike blackness of cards.

Sex Differences

Boys give on the average about one more response per child than do girls. Marked sex differences occur as to area. There are more whole responses in boys—an average of 8.7 in boys, only 6.6 in girls. D predominates over W in both boys and girls—4.8 D per girl, 4.5 per boy. Total Dd is larger in boys than in girls as to actual number of responses; slightly larger in girls as to Dd%. Also, both WS and S are higher in boys than in girls.

There are more M and more FM responses in boys than in girls, and more boys than girls give M. FM is about equally active in the two sexes; M a little more active in girls.

Although the number of FC and C responses is the same for boys and girls, boys definitely have a higher ΣC than girls, and this is due to a much higher CF.

Sex differences in content are small.

Comparison of Rorschach and Developmental Findings

DEVELOPMENTAL	RORSCHACH
Breaking up of 5-year-old equilibrium, and resulting disequilibrium. Sensitive to environment. Highly vulnerable.	Many broken, crooked, mutilated objects. Very high m; m larger than M. Highest Clob to date. Highest F(C) to date. Very high ΣC. Contaminated responses.
Breaking up of 5-year-old patterns also results in temporary variability and unpredictability of behavior.	Low A%. Shading high, largely diffusion.

Comparison of Rorschach and Developmental Findings

DEVELOPMENTAL	RORSCHACH
Uncontrolled emotion.	C and CF both highest of any age to date. FC very low.
Temper tantrums.	
Excitable, impetuous.	Largest use of "fire" to date.
Contradictory tendencies: at peace with neither himself nor the world. Dawdling and hesitant, then over-demanding and explosive. Opposition and aggression shown.	Low F% but high F+%.
	Few responses to red parts of cards but greatest number of fire responses of any age.
	High use of black but dislike of it.
	Very high CF and C.
	Very high S—.6 per child, highest of any age.
	Very high m.
	Responses of "nothing" or some very tiny detail; or "the whole world."
Child is very unsure of himself, insecure.	High Dd%. High F(C). Many refusals.
Fearful. Concerned with the supernatural.	High Clob, mostly giants, ghosts, and monsters.
Rigid. Lack of modification and modulation.	Appears to think his answers are "right" or "wrong."
	High F+%.
	High CF.
	Semantically—does not use qualifying phrases.
	Refusals high.
	"Looks like nothing."
Poor interpersonal relations.	Low FC.
	Relatively high Hd and (H) as compared with H.
	High S in an extratensive setting.
Less focal and introversive than at 5 years. More extratensive. Less constricted than at 5 years.	Drop in M.
	Marked rise in ΣC.
	Very low F%.

Sample Record of 5½-Year-Old Girl A.P.

RESPONSE	INQUIRY		SCORING		
I. Looks like a bird to me. Wings, body, sides.	(Whole)	W₁	F+	A	P
II. Chicken. This is the little thing under here. This is the red part on top.	Remind you? "The red." (Only the top red is interpreted. Inner projection is wattle of chicken, and top of red is the comb. She sees only the head of the chicken.)	D	CF	Ad	
III. That looks like a bow. That's part of the bow.	(Center red, points to each side of the bow.)	D	F+	obj	P
IV. That looks like smoke.	(Whole) Remind you? "The black."	W₀	ClobF	nat	
V. That looks like a big butterfly. Two legs, ears, part of his head.	(Whole)	W₁	F+	A	P
VI. That looks like a kitten on a black rock.	"That part makes it look like a kitten—those legs." (Feathers on top D.) "All this is rock" (lower D). "It looks like a rock and it's big." (Kitten is top D, lower D is rock.)	W₂	FClob	A	
VII. ∨ If you turn it upside down it looks like a bridge. That looks like part of the bridge.	(Whole)	W₁	F+	arch	

RESPONSE	INQUIRY		SCORING		
(Side projection.) This is the top and the middle of the top. (Third tier with center clasp.) The rest is the bottom.					
VIII. Oh that looks like a little doggie climbing up a tree. And here's the stem, and here's the two doggies and here's the rocks.	(Rocks are pink and orange, tree is blue and gray, usual animals.)	W$_s$	FM	A	P
IX. This looks like it's porridge in a garden. And this is the rest of the porridge. (Points to orange.) And here's some more. (Pink)	Porridge? "Stuff you eat." (Points to green.) Remind you? "Cause this here." (Indicates whole blot.) "My mommy eats this stuff. That looks like salad, the green. This is the stem they're growing on [midline]. My father has two flower gardens and one porridge garden. It grows everything we eat." Kind of porridge? "This is the salad (green) and this (orange) looks like squash." (Ex.'s note: Family evidently defines porridge as anything that grows.)	W$_x$	CF	plant	
X. Looks like a green spider. These look like flowers. That there looks like a black stem. And they cut something off of it. And these are leaves.	(Lower center green) (Center yellow) (Top gray) (Side green)	D Dd D Dd	CF CF FClob CF	A flower plant plant	

Card most liked: IX. "Cause these pictures are pretty."
Card least liked: VII. "Cause it's black."

R = 13

1W$_0$	4F = 31%F
3W$_1$	4F+ = 100%F+
1W$_2$	
1W$_3$	1FM
1W$_x$ = 53%W	5CF
	2 FClob, 1ClobF
4D = 30%D	
2Dd = 15%Dd	0M : 5ΣC

5A, 1Ad = 47%A
3 plant
1 flower
1 architecture
1 nature
1 object

4P = 31%P

COMMENT   This is a child highly susceptible to new stimuli and easily affected by them. Most of her interpretations are influenced by factors other than the form of the blot. Although F+%, ΣC, and Clob responses customarily increase at this age, all of these factors appear unusually high in the totals of this girl. She is a highly intelligent child who demands a great deal of herself.

Both her peripheral and profound emotional responses are spontaneous and active but little nuanced. She responds to the red only at II and III and to the "black" at IV, VI, and X. This is one instance (at X, "a black stem") where our scoring FClob may be questioned, since this child appears to interpret any nuance of gray as "black" and is using it here as a color. The same might possibly hold at VI. But even so, she interprets the "black" a good deal more than most children of this age, and is probably deeply and easily disturbed in her profound emotional reactions. The "smoke" at IV is the type of response interpreted as indicative of free-floating anxiety.

She probably has more widespread intellectual activity than most children of her age, though there is no H response, which may indicate some under-development of interpersonal relations.

At VII, she turns the card upside down for the only time during the test, and interprets it as a "bridge." This may represent antagonism or resistance to the mother, but it also indicates a desire or a striving to resolve conflicts.

In summary, then, this is a highly intelligent child whose intellectual and emotional activities are expansive but exigent, spontaneous but little nuanced; interpersonal relations are probably quite low; free-floating anxiety is probably quite marked; and there are conflicts which she is striving to resolve. Many of these characteristics are determined by the age, but any tendency too greatly exaggerated is always a possible area of disturbance for any child.

Sample Record of 5½-Year-Old Boy W.M.

RESPONSE	INQUIRY	SCORING		
I. V Looks like a stone. There's hands on it and feet.	? "Cause it got holes in it and it got a tunnel." (S details are holes and S curve into top outline is tunnel.) (Hands are wing projections; feet are top projections.) "They walk and hold the hands out and people give them something to them, and they could put it in their pocket." ? "The hand's part of the stone."	WS$_x$	F$\pm$ M	nat
II. Stones getting on fire.	"Cause they got red things—got fire blowing up." (Whole) (Black and lower red)	W$_x$	m CF	expl
And someone's starting to burn up and his hand's already burnt up and his feet. Blood coming out of him down here.	Person? (Points to center hands as head, blood is lower red.) Hands? "They're burnt, they aren't here."	D	CF m	H blood
There's ears.	"Part of the fire." (Side projection, usual animal's ears.)	Do	F+	Ad
III. The rock is starting to burn all up. The fire is going right through it and it's falling off. All black the fire is. The ears are gone and the hands are over here. (Usual feet.) And	(Whole) (Points to usual men's heads.) "Part of the ears are gone and it should be up on top of his head. His feet isn't there because it's burned up. The hands are burned up. Should be here." (Points	W$_x$	m Clob C	nat

Response	Inquiry	Location	Determinant	Content
his part of his head is gone and his hands are chopped off. Part of the rock is all burned up. IV. The rock is all black. And his arms are there, just his arms, no hands. And his feet are there, on the bottom. Then his head is here. There's the fire. The fire goes through here and you could see the holes. His feet are all black and you can't see them very good. Can't tell his head very good, can't see the eyes and nose. Part of his feet is not down at the bottom, it's up a little bit. That's all, that one.	to men's necks, and draws hands off into white.) (Whole) (Usual arms.) (Top is head.) (Fire is lower center head.) (Usual feet.)	W_x	ClobF m	nat
V. His head is almost gone. His arm is almost gone. His feet are almost gone, and his arms are gone.	Head? "Almost starting to go away. Because the fire made it go away." What is this? "A rock." Arms and legs? "He looks like a man because sometimes they make a rock look like a man." (Whole)	W_x	F± FClob	nat
VI. His head is starting to burn up. His hands are starting to burn up. His hands are up cause	(Whole. Head is top projection. It is on fire, with feathers as fire. Two light gray spots at midline are bullet	W_x	m	H

Sample Record of 5½-Year-Old Boy W.M. (Continued)

RESPONSE	INQUIRY	SCORING	
somebody got a gun pointing at him. He got shot here. That's why the fire's starting to burn his neck up. One kid in school has a bullet and if you stick it hard, all blood comes out on your arm. He seen it in a movie." etc., etc. (Tells long scenario about movie he saw.)	holes. Hands up are top projections, lower D.)		
VII. His head is already burned up and his eyes are already burned up. And the arms are like this, and his feet are gone.	(Head is not there; eyes are S details between forehead and nose of women, arms are side projections on second tier. This is what remains of a person who has been "burned up." The arms are the only detail he sees clearly.)	WS$_x$	F— m Hd
VIII. A wolf is coming up in his head and going to eat him up. He's going to push him off and when he gets pushed off then the other one will climb up. He's going to bite his arms off and then he can't do nothing, and the wolf is eating him up. The feet are gone and the arms are gone.	(Usual animals. Central portion of blot is "him" minus legs and eventually arms.)	W$_x$	FM A P

IX. The wolf ate him up already, and the wolf fell down and got killed. (This is apparently a termination of the response to VIII.)

(See *here?*) The fire's starting to come all over him, and he's all chewed up, and shooting guns all over there, one shooting that way, one shooting that way.

(Orange. Two men are shooting at one another with fire surrounding them.) D M, C H

X. This is the last one. All these things are shooting guns. And a wishbone's falling off. (Whole) Wₓ m obj

This is the part of his head, and part of his legs and feet, and part of his hands and part of his tunnel.

(Center orange.) Dd m anat

(Lower center green. Usual rabbit's head. Legs, feet, and hands are side green projections, tunnel is white between projections.) D F— H

"There's more parts of it."

Card most liked: X.
Card least liked: II. "Cause it don't look good." (For amplification, Ex. asked: Ever see anything burning? "Yeah, I saw a house and all the woods burning, and it almost came near the house —near where we live.")

R = 14

9Wₓ = 64%W

3D = 21%D

1Dd

1Do = 14%Dd

5F = 35%F
1F+, 2F±, 2F— = 40%F+

1 M, 1 tend. M, 1 FM
5m, 4 tend. m
1 CF, 1 tend. CF, 2 tend. C
1 ClobF, 1 tend. FClob, 1 tend. Clob

1M : 1ΣC

1A, 1Ad = 15%A
4H, 1Hd = 36%H
4 nature
1 object
1 anatomy
1 explosion

1P = 7%P

COMMENT   As sample 5½-year-old records, we have chosen two children who exaggerate the characteristics of the age, in order to highlight kinds of responses which are encountered here and which might appear more disturbing at another age.

This boy is a perseverator. However, it is not the kind of magic repetition which we have seen earlier, but the more mature type which we term "dynamic perseveration." He is undoubtedly finding it difficult to make transitions, and he is probably one who holds on to many traces of his earlier behavior as he works toward maturity. He perseverates on "stone" and "rock" and on things "burning up," but each time he embroiders the concept somewhat to fit the blot, and he animates his more static concepts so that they are sometimes identifiable human and movement responses. This characteristic has usually disappeared by 4½ years.

He is reactive to the color and to the black in a very elemental and what appears to be an almost antisocial manner. He is quite susceptible to the stimuli of his environment and there is a good deal of compulsive verbalization of experience. The most disturbing elements here are the high number of m responses, which imply a good deal of unemployed energy and suppressed aggressivity, and the fact that there is low animal and popular response.

This boy is easily overstimulated in both peripheral and profound emotional reactions and since stereotypy is low and his participation in the cultural thinking is also low, he probably finds it necessary to establish his equilibrium through approaches that might be used by a younger child. His outlets for aggressivity and for unemployed energy now seem to be high verbalization combined with imagination which easily evolves into confabulation. This, however, seems to be the way that many children handle the emotional and developmental disturbance which occurs at this period—in a somewhat "stream-of-consciousness" verbalization.

This boy appears to be fascinated by and to take a rather morbid pleasure in things which appear to us unpleasant. This is a precursor of the morbid and gory details which characterize the response of the 7-year-old. The ambiequality of this boy's reactivity may be another indication of his ambivalence and difficulty with transitions. He is striving toward a more mature emotional and intellectual behavior, and at the same time he is bringing with him many characteristics of the less mature child. This boy exaggerates the characteristics which are indicative of the "normal" disturbance of the age itself.

This record indicates to us the kind of personality which finds it difficult to relinquish earlier behavior as it progresses toward more mature performance, and it gives us some insight as to the guidance and handling necessary if we are to help such a child make the transition successfully. Such a protocol appearing at 5½ years is certainly less a sign of a disturbed child than it would be if we should see the same characteristics at 8 or 9 years of age.

CHAPTER SEVENTEEN

Six Years

R = 15.8	60%F	7.5A = 48%A
	81%F+	1.7H = 11%H
51%W		2.5 object
34%D	1.0M 1.6FM .4m	.9 nature
15%Dd	.4FC 1.5CF .3C	.8 plant
	.7F(C) .3Clob	.6 anatomy
	1.0M : 2.2ΣC	3.6P = 23%P

Qualitative Description

The 6-year-old child is above all things egocentric. He is the center of his own world—wants to win, to be first, to be loved best. This egocentricity is expressed in the Rorschach by the predominance of CF among color responses, an average of 1.48 per child, higher than at any other age in our range. Anatomic responses also are prominent, occurring on the average of .60 per child, more than at any other age until 8 years.

SIX is not only egocentric, but extremely stubborn, domineering, unsubmissive, and generally opposed to the commands or suggestions of others. This strong oppositional tendency is borne out in the conspicuous occurrence of both S and WS responses in the Rorschach. S occurs here more than at any other age except 5½ years, and WS more than at any ages except 5½ and 7. This high use of oppositional responses in an extratensive setting indicates marked opposition to the environment.

SIX is expansive and also aggressive. He covers a good deal of ground and meets obstacles head on. His expansiveness is expressed in the Rorschach by a very full weighting of both color and movement responses. Only 60% of responses are determined by form alone, the least of any ages but two. Movement responses have doubled since 5½ years, now being 1.0 per child; and the average ΣC is 2.2, higher than at any but two other ages. Expansiveness is also suggested by a marked increase in number of responses, the average number now being 15.8, two more per

193

child than at 5½ years. Aggressivity is indicated by an average m of .4, most of any age but one to date. Among m responses explosions are the leading kind of activity.

SIX besides being egocentric and extraversive is extremely responsive emotionally to environmental factors, and his emotions tend to be violent. ΣC as indicated is higher than at any but two ages, CF responses definitely leading. Color naming is more frequent than at any age since 3½ years. Color is often mentioned and at least twenty children say that they prefer Card X because of its color. Conversely the most disliked cards are most frequently disliked because of their blackness. There are now more responses to the red parts of the blots than at any age to date except 4 years (2.7 per child as against only 1.7 per child at 5½ years). CF responses are chiefly *flower* and *flame;* C responses especially *fire.* This suggests the violent nature of SIX's emotions.

For all his brashness, SIX can on occasion be excessively sensitive and vulnerable. Clob responses occur less than at 5½ and 7 years, but nevertheless this is one of the three highest ages for Clob, which occurs to the extent of .3 per child; and shading responses occur more than at any other age to date. Blackness of blots is emphasized much less than at 5½ years and is mentioned mostly in relation to blot liked least: "Too much blackness in it—all this awful black here and awful light here," or "Got too much dark black and too much light in it." These two comments also serve to emphasize the fact that SIX operates at *opposite extremes.* That is, as here emphasized, he dislikes "dark black" but he also dislikes "too much light." There is also a somewhat contradictory interest in very large and in very small things so far as content is concerned.   Contrast is also shown by the fact that the child of this age is extremely egocentric but also tends to project far outward from himself in his concepts.

Vigor of drive is indicated by the fact that extensor movements predominate in both human and animal movement. Animal movement responses are particularly active—climbing and flying being the leading activities mentioned. The activity of animal movement on Card X is particularly noteworthy.

However in spite of his violent emotions, his egocentricity, his stubbornness and contrariness, one aspect of SIX's behavior which makes him easier to deal with than his 5½-year-old self is his predictability and the tendency to stereotypy in his behavior. Like the 2½-year-old, SIX protects himself with rigidities and rituals. He is stereotyped and ritualistic even though not conforming. The Rorschach reflects this tendency to stereotypy. A% is higher than at any ages except 2, 4, and 10 years. Objects occur here more than at any age except 7 years. But perhaps most expressive of the similarity in behavior from child to child is the fact that on Card I, 36 out of 50 children give responses falling in only three categories: 1) things with holes in them; 2) butterfly or bird; 3) face or mask. Also though

18 per cent of subjects perseverate, there is no dynamic perseveration as at preceding and succeeding ages. If the child perseverates, he perseverates statically.

SIX, for all his expansive violence, is in many respects quite matter-of-fact and realistic. His use of the word "real" is characteristic: "real birds," "a real baby," "this is real ink," "a real honest design." Or in expressing a preference, he may choose the card "that looks realest." Note his specificity, also, particularly in explaining why he dislikes certain cards: "Because it's a fox and they eat chickens," "Cause it has pointing wings," "Cause it has a lot of germs," "Hasn't got many things. All it has is a nose and two whiskers like that." Also though total responses still lead, tiny specific details are selected here more than at any other age in our range. Finally, shading responses are now used primarily for discrimination of details within the blot and for differentiating fine texture (grass, bushes) rather than for expressing diffusion as earlier.

Along with a marked rise in clarity and accuracy of perception at this age, comes a marked decrease in tendencies toward contamination and confabulation. There are only three instances of confabulation at this age and no instances of contamination.

SIX tends to be very definite and apparently sure of himself. Refusals and denials are both low at this age and almost no qualifying phrases or suggestions to change the blot to make it better fit the concept are given.

It is interesting to note that in respect to some factors, the Rorschach behavior of the 6-year-old is in sharp contrast to that of surrounding ages, whereas in others SIX is merely a halfway station between 5½ and 7 years in an eighteen-month period which emphasizes several types of behavior. Thus SIX is sharply contrasted to surrounding ages in such characteristics as the following: Dd rises very sharply at this age; pure C drops; there is little confabulation; Clob drops considerably and A% rises very sharply; there is more color naming. On the other hand, six years resembles its surrounding ages and to some extent differs from other ages in this range with regard to the following: ΣC is very high; CF is high; Clob and m though less than at 5½ and 7 occur conspicuously as compared to the rest of the age range.

Sex is a matter of considerable concern and interest to the child of this age. Reference to elimination does occur in the Rorschach, though infrequently: "A bear, where he goes to the bathroom, his heinie," "A bear and a place where he goes to the bathroom." Furthermore, we find that "flower," which especially in girls is found often to accompany a readiness for or an interest in sex, occurs more than at any other age except 4½ years. Also anatomic responses occur here more than at any other age in the first seven years. In a few instances confusion of sexes occurs—"It looks like a little boy—here's her hair and here's her hat."

We know as a matter of practical experience that the interpersonal relations of the 6-year-old are poor. Since his Rorschach responses show him to be egocentric, violently aggressive, oppositional, unmodulated and unyielding, this is not surprising. However in spite of this we frequently find SIX to be extremely alert to adult demands and apprehensive of what failure to comply may bring. Thus: "What if I don't know? Then what do you do?" "Am I bad about this?" Or he may make excessively conscientious comments such as "This is fun! Besides educational!"

Individual Determinants

Number: Average number of responses has increased sharply—from 13.6 to 15.8.

Area: Number of D responses remains about what it was at the preceding age—34%. Whole responses still lead (average of 51%), but they are less than at 5½ years, being to some extent reduced in favor of Dd responses which now occur to the extent of 15% per child, the most of any age.

Form: Form now determines a very small percentage of responses—only 60%. At only two ages, 7 and 8 years, does this percentage fall lower than this. F+% is 81%.

M, FM, m: M has doubled in frequency since the preceding age and now for the first time occurs on an average of 1 per child. FM also has increased, from an average of 1.3 at 5½ years to an average of 1.6. m is less than at immediately surrounding ages—average of .4 per child.

Extensor M leads, with moderate extension exceeding violent—sitting, walking, dancing, holding, or carrying leading. FM is more active, strong extension occurring most—climbing and flying being the leading activities mentioned. Among m responses, water forms predominate with downward activity occurring most. Explosions are the largest single type of activity.

Color: Color, though slightly less extensive than at the two surrounding ages, nevertheless occurs to the extent of 2.2ΣC, exceeded at only two ages. CF responses lead, occurring to the extent of 1.5, more than at any other age in this range. FC occurs next most, an average of .4; C coming third with an average of .3. Flower and fire are the leading CF responses; nature and fire are the leading C responses. There are more responses to the red parts of the cards than at any age to date except 4 years.

Shading: The highest of any age to date, .7 per child. Texture responses lead, but diffusion and differentiation of details within the blot are both still frequent.

Clob: Clob is less at this age than at surrounding ages, but is nevertheless fairly high, an average of .3, more than at any other age but one to date.

Content: Leading content categories are now animals, objects, nature, and humans. Plants do not from now on at any age hold one of the four leading places.

Most outstanding is the marked rise in animal responses, which have increased from an average of 41% at 5½ years to a high point of 48%. This percentage falls off at the next age to 42% and does not again in this age range rise so high. Number of objects has also increased sharply, from an average of 1.8 to 2.5 per child. Nature responses have dropped from 1.3 per child to .9. Actual number of humans has increased slightly, but H% is 11%, as at 5½. Among animals, the butterfly-bird category leads. As to human and animal details, human details make up 47% of all human responses; animal details are only 19% of animal responses, but compared to other ages this is relatively high.

Length: Records are just slightly longer in total number of words than at 5½ years, just under 300 words on an average.

Timing: Average timing of total records is longer than at 5½ years, an average (for those cases on whom we have timing recorded) of 8.9 minutes per record.

Semantics: Simply naming the blot still leads as a method of designation but by a smaller margin than earlier. Qualifying concepts scarcely appear.

Plurals: As at the preceding age, the phrase "Two ———" leads as a method of expressing plurality.

Best and Worst: Card X is preferred by both sexes. There is great variety in cards disliked. Girls dislike I, IV, and IX; boys I, IV, VI.

Popular Responses: P% is high, 23%. Number of P is 3.6 per child.

Sex Differences

Boys give one more response on the average than do girls (girls 15.2 per child, boys 16.4). Boys also have a higher percentage of global responses than do girls (55% W in boys, 48% in girls). Number of detail responses is about the same in the two sexes; Dd is higher in girls than in boys—17% in girls, 12% in boys.

Boys have a higher ΣC than do girls (2.3 in boys, 2.0 in girls) and CF and C occur slightly more in boys than in girls.

Many more boys than girls give shading responses; and many more boys than girls give Clob responses. Also more boys than girls give m responses.

However girls give more popular responses than do boys.

Boys name more different kinds of animals than do girls (girls, 37 different kinds, boys 44 kinds). Anatomic responses occur much more in boys than in girls (.2 in girls, 1.0 in boys).

Comparison of Rorschach and Developmental Findings

DEVELOPMENTAL	RORSCHACH
Egocentric.	Highest CF of any age, average of 1.5. Many anatomic responses.
Stubborn and oppositional.	S more than at any age except 5½. WS more than at any age except 5½ and 7.
Expansive.	Good variety of different content categories—15.8.
	Only 60% of responses determined by form alone. M twice what it was at preceding age; ΣC one of three highest ages.
Violent emotions: explosive and aggressive.	CF highest of any age, mostly fire and flame.
	C responses chiefly fire.
	Cn higher than since 3½.
	Colored cards preferred; black ones disliked.
	More response to red parts of cards than at any age since 4 years.
	m highest of any age but one to date, and leading m responses are explosions.
Contradictory tendencies.	Egocentric but projects far out from self.
	Dislikes "dark black" but also "awful light."
	Interest in the very large and the very small.
Sensitive and vulnerable in spite of egocentricity and boldness.	Clob high.
	F(C) highest to date.
	Strong avoidance of black.
Poor interpersonal relations.	Egocentric—very high CF.
	Aggressive—high m.
	Oppositional—S and WS both high.
	Sensitive and vulnerable—shading highest to date.
	Unyielding—few qualifying expressions.
Responses certain and definite.	Refusals and denials low.
Realistic and down to earth.	Very low point in use of qualifying phrases.
	Strong use of the word "real."

Comparison of Rorschach and Developmental Findings

DEVELOPMENTAL	RORSCHACH
Predictable, stereotyped behavior.	A% higher than at any ages except 2, 4, and 10 years. Very great increase here in A%.
	P% high—23%.
	36 out of 50 children give responses to Card I in only 3 classifications.
	Static perseveration.
Specific and detailed.	Highest number of Dd of any age.
	Specific reasons for disliking cards.
	F(C) used primarily for discrimination of details in the blot and less as diffusion.
Interest in sex.	Reference to eliminative functions.
	Highest use of anatomic concepts in first seven years.
	Highest use of "flower" of any age but 4½.

Sample Record of 6-Year-Old Girl M.W.

RESPONSE	INQUIRY		SCORING		
I. Owl?	(Whole. Points to wings and ears.) Remind you? "His—I guess horns." (Points to center top details.)	W₁	F+	A	P
II. These look like little birdies. Just their faces. They're chattering.	(Top red.)	D	FM	Ad	
III. This looks like a bow.	(Center red.)	D	F+	obj	
This looks like a face and a man and a coat around in back, and his hand. Maybe picking something up.	(Usual men.)	W₂	M	H	P
IV. This looks like some ears. Not on anybody, but an animal's.	(Usual hands.)	D	F+	Ad	
Looks like a lady bug, but this [lower center] is not part of it.	Remind you? "This face." (Top center.)	W₁	F±	A	
V. That looks like a bunny here. (Covers wings.) With his ears sticking up and his legs. Looks as though he's standing in a bush.	Bush? "It went out more than him." (Bunny is center detail with the remainder as bush.)	W₂	FM	A	
VI. That looks like a butterfly. And his whiskers. I guess that's all on him.	(Top detail only.)	D	F+	A	

Response	Inquiry	Loc.	Det.	Content
VII. That looks like somebody's mouth, opened. Guess there's nothing else there.	(Mouth is detail from forehead to mouth of usual lady at left.)	Dd	F+ / M	Hd
VIII. That looks like a butterfly flying.	(Orange and pink.)	D	FM	A
That looks like an animal and an animal, walking up something. That's all to that.	(Usual animals.)	D	FM	A P
IX. That looks like two eyes.	(Two dark spots near center in green. She is unable to say whether they are animal or human.)	Dd	F+	Ad
This looks like a vase. There's nothing else.	"It's shaped like a vase." (S detail in center between orange and greens.)	S	F+	obj
X. V This looks like a flower.	(Gray and pink.)	D	FC	flower
And that's a spider.	(R blue.)	D	F+	A P
That looks like an animal walking, and that.	(Center yellow.)	Dd	FM	A
And this looks like a little flower and the stem on it.	(Side yellow plus brown.)	D	FC	flower
These are two leafs.	(Side greens.)	Dd	FC	plant
And a frog.	(Side brown.)	D	F+	A

Card most liked: X. "It has all different colors on it."
Card least liked: IV. "'Cause it's all black."

Sample Record of 6-Year-Old Girl M.W. (*Continued*)

RESPONSE	INQUIRY	SCORING
R = 19		
		9A, 3Ad = 63%A
2W₁		1H, 1Hd = 10%H
2W₂ = 21% W	10F = 42%F	2 object
	9F+, 1F± = 95%F+	1 plant
10D = 53%D	1M, 1 tend. M, 5FM	2 flower
4Dd	3FC	
1S = 26%Dd		5P = 26%P
	1M : 1½∑C	

COMMENT This is probably a very feminine and perhaps a somewhat talkative little girl, though there is no compulsive verbalization such as we have seen in some earlier protocols and will see again later. She is highly intelligent and though her intellectual processes may not be too orderly, she is practical and realistic and able to observe well. She has good capacity for inner creative experience and responds pleasantly to external stimuli.

Although the FM responses outnumber the M, suggesting considerable dependence, as might be expected at this age, both animal and human movement are active, if not always dynamic.

There is evidence of some oppositional tendencies in the space response at IX. The rather unusual response at VII—"somebody's mouth opened"—may be indicative of "space

shock" or "white shock." Such a tendency occurring at this card has been interpreted as indicative of conflict with the mother. A response such as "eyes" which we see at Card IX is often interpreted as indicative of feelings of anxiety or guilt. High stereotypy and the high number of popular responses indicating a high consciousness of the demands of the culture and the environment, may well implement such feelings.

Her perceptions are, as with the boy of this age, more detailed than those of most of her contemporaries, and the quality of her color responses indicates a high degree of adaptability. This projection toward maturity, implying an increase of social consciousness, may also serve to induce some anxiety in her. In general, however, this appears to be a rather mature and equilibrated child.

Sample Record of 6-Year-Old Boy J.C.

	RESPONSE	INQUIRY		SCORING	
I.	A mask.	"Eyes and the teeth. A nose. Ears." (Whole, with space details as eyes and teeth.)	WS₁	F+	obj	P
II.	< A dog. Some spots around the dog. Looks like red spots. Ears, nose, tail of dog. Feet. Oh, and an eye.	(Dog is black only. The "red spots" are the red fading into the black; red details are not included in response.)	D	F+	A	P
III.	(Laughs) Ears, nose, eyes, cheeks.	"An animal's face." (Eyes are usual men's heads, nose is center black, ears are side red.)	W₁	F±	Ad	
IV.	(Laughs) Feet, ears. Let's see now, there's some. I don't know what that looks like (strokes upper middle shaded part). That's all I can find out in this picture.	"Some kind of an animal's." (Feet are usual boots, ears are usual arms. He does not see an animal, only details.)	Do D	F+ F+	Ad Ad	
V.	The whole animal looks like a bat. It has these here eyes, wings, feet.	(Whole. Demonstrates feelers with fingers on his head.)	W₁	F+	A	P
VI.	Uh, whiskers.	(Usual whiskers on top D.)	Do	F+	Ad	
	Um, a nose. That's all I can tell in this. I don't know what these are here (feathers).	(Rounded top of upper D.)	Do	F+	Ad	

Sample Record of 6-Year-Old Boy J.C. (Continued)

RESPONSE	INQUIRY		SCORING	
VII. The whole thing can be some clouds.	"Because they have like lumps, the little white parts and little black parts."	W_o	F(C)	nat
VIII. A bush with flowers on it. It looks like a pretty flower.	(Lower orange and pink.)	D	CF	plant
V The other way it looks like a pretty flower.	(Same detail.)		repetition	
< Is this a fish, or is it a polly-wog? Must be a pollywog, because nothing else has feet like a fish.	(Usual animal.)	D	F+	A
These couldn't be leaves that are teared up here, could they? That's all I can tell on this one.	(Center blue and gray.) "They are torn like there and it looks funny like." (Indicates white spaces in detail.)	D	F+ m	plant
IX. V∧ A stem.	"Because it's straight and it's green." (Midline)	Dd	FC	plant
Part of a hat over here.	(Lower pink.) "Part of this here, part of a hat like Santa Claus' hat and it's red. All you have to do is put the top over there."	D	FC	obj
There's some holes here.	(Slits in middle space D.)		S remark	
X. V Bugs.	"Cause some got wings like that." (Lower green.)	D	F+	A

Um. Some clouds over here. (Side orange.) "Two of them, cause some of them are pink and there's orange clouds sometimes." — Dd · CF · nat

There's another bug. With wings. (Center orange.) — Dd · F± · A

Part of leaves. (Top green.) — Dd · CF · plant

Branches over here, branches they look like. (Side brown.) "Cause they're brown and they look like them." — D · CF · plant

A stick. (Top gray.) "It's brown and it's shaped like a brown stick." (Calls gray "brown.") — D · CF · obj

That's all I can think of.

Card most liked: VIII. "Because it's pretty—the colors."
Card least liked: VI. "It hasn't got many things on it—all it has is a nose and two whiskers like that."

$R = 20$

$1W_0$
$3W_1 = 20\%W$
$9D = 45\%D$
$4Dd$
$3Do = 30\%Dd$

$12F = 60\%F$
$10\ F+,\ 2F\pm = 91\%F+$

1 tend. m
$2FC,\ 5CF$
$1F(C)$

$0M : 6\Sigma C$

5A, 5Ad = 50%A
3 objects
2 nature
5 plant

$3P = 15\%P$

COMMENT This boy's motivation probably stems largely from external influences, and his reaction is in general pleasant. At present he shows very little capacity for inner creative experience (no movement response, either animal or human). However, his rather expansive reactions to external stimuli are somewhat tempered by an inner control, as indicated by the shading response at VII, suppressive tendencies indicated by the Do response at IV and VI, as well as the "mask" response at I.

He tends to observe details more readily than most of his contemporaries and he may be somewhat compulsive. Stereotypy is high and he probably enjoys routines and regulations. The response at VIII, "torn leaves," may indicate a tendency to masturbation, and may be another symptom of the restriction and suppression under which he is operating.

CHAPTER EIGHTEEN

Seven Years

R = 18.3	52%F	7.6A = 42%A
	82%F+	2.6H = 14%H
51%W		2.7 object
41%D	1.4M 1.9FM .8m	1.5 nature
8%Dd	.7FC 1.3CF .8C	.9 plant
	1.1F(C) .5Clob	.7 fire
		.5 architecture
	1.4M : 2.9ΣC	
		3.7P = 27%P

Qualitative Description

At seven years of age there occurs a definite inwardizing of experience. M occurs here more than at any age to date, and also more than at the following age. The average number of M responses is 1.4 per child. FM is also high, in fact higher than at any other age in the first ten years, with an average of 1.9. m too is higher than at any other age with an average of .8, suggesting not only inwardizing but also suppressed aggressive tendencies. Also more children give M responses than at any other age in the first ten years.

The nature of M is of interest here. Flexor and passive M responses occur more than at any other age. Two humans may simply exist or simply watch each other, and flexor responses occur here outstandingly. FM is considerably more active than M. Marked empathy seems to be felt by children of this age for movement seen in the cards. Children experience people's or animals' feelings to the extent that they frequently try themselves to portray the emotions or activities mentioned. "See, like this," is a frequent comment, the child proceeding to twist his face into a horrible snarl, or to open his mouth as wide as it will go, or even to stand up, bend over, and lift his arms above his head—becoming for the moment a menacing giant.

Along with the marked increase in introversivity, comes a general narrowing down, expressed in the Rorschach by a definite decrease in

206

variety of content. The number of different content categories employed at this age is extremely low—only 13. However this is one of the two highest ages for productivity, the average child giving 18.3 different responses, and one of the lowest ages for refusals, with a mean of .3.

Inwardizing tendencies are also suggested by the inwardizing of experience indicated in the high percentage of Clob responses given at this age. Later, at 8 years for example, the child projects unpleasant feelings aroused by the test cards outward, complaining about the blots or the examiner. At this age he inwardizes unpleasant experiences and gives an average of .5 Clob responses, an all-time high. Furthermore, nearly half of our subjects give the morbid and gruesome responses which are commonly scored as Clob. Thus we may expect to find in a typical 7-year-old record such descriptions as: "Gorilla skin, blood gushing out," "Dinosaurs pulling up bloody skeleton," "A buried bat all torn up," "Screeching with pain," "Fox has sore leg, it should be chopped off." There are more of these "horrible" responses in boys than in girls, and they are more extreme in boys than in girls. Outstanding among such responses are references to dead and poisoned things.

Decay, damage, and mutilation are conspicuous themes. Many of the people or animals are headless or beheaded. Parts or limbs are torn off or chopped off—"Looks like a book that somebody's torn up, like a book that could have been all burned up." Objects have holes in them or are torn or broken. Bones are decaying—"It looks as though the bone started to deteriorate, like rot over here." Both color and dark shock occur at this age.

Even when responses are not gruesome or morbid, we find such adjectives as a "freak" cat, a "strange" animal. There is also a great deal of confabulation. Thus to Card III one boy says, "This is a little bit of smoke and a little bit of fire. Maybe the little bomb just bursted over here where the people are fighting." (In answer to a question about what people, he indicates that the people are not seen in the picture but are armies vaguely seen or assumed in the white spaces.) "They're dropping bombs and somebody's closing in on them."

Another example of a confused, somewhat confabulated response is the story told by one boy about Card IX:

"Ooh, every time you give me another one it's harder." [Laughs.] "Gee, it looks something like a totem pole but I wouldn't say all like a totem pole. ∧ This looks like a—ugly thing that spins around, and there's hinges, like couplings here [between pink and green], and I think it spins around, there's oil, and it goes down here [through midline] and comes out here [at bottom]. Looks as though it's going down into the earth, sucking up oil or putting it down. And over here it looks like it's made of rock, and this looks like it's cement [rock is orange, cement is green], but they, the Indians, put some kind of a coloring in it. There are holes in it [slits in middle] like if there's a war they can get behind and shoot their bows and arrows out of here. And stop the oil from running. And they could use that oil to make bombs like, dry up the oil and make some kind of hand-grenade or something. And here is some more places [upper whites, just under pink]. If they get up to here they could put a telescope through there. And if this is a ———— looks as though this is one of those teepees, like, with that round thing going around, this here is the teepee, and they have this for their fire. [Teepee is triangular part of orange and green.] And it's the chief's. Like if another tribe is fighting some cowboys, the other Indians would think it's just a part—and they could be looking out of those peepholes. And whoever wins, like there's a door up here, and they shoot out these holes. This looks as though it's a mat—like a doormat only it's outside [claws of orange]. And it looks as though this is an Indian's feather sticking up here, and the Indian's way over here [feather is gray between orange and green]. You can just see the feather."

Sometimes included in confabulatory responses and sometimes given without confabulation are things, people, and animals not actually seen in the blot, as puppies standing on an elephant "which isn't there"; a tiger "not there," or unseen armies, fighting.

At this age F% is only 52%, the lowest of any age in the first ten years. This results from, or results in, not only a very high M but also an usually large ΣC. The average ΣC at this age is 2.9. The CF responses lead among color responses with an average of 1.3. C exceeds FC. The frequent pure C responses are often combined with a tendency to m, and we find blood gushing, fire burning someone, paint splashed. Fire responses are especially prevalent. SEVEN goes out of his way to explain incongruous color. Thus the pink animals on VIII are described as "mice under some kind of treatment—some kind of X-ray, ultraviolet stuff, a ray that makes things turn red." Or unnatural color may be handled as "a lobster that somebody painted," or "a pink animal that people have never seen."

Perseveration occurs in more than half the cases at this age, but it is most often a dynamic perseveration rather than the static type found at the earliest age levels. An example of dynamic perseveration is found in the subject who gives cat responses on the first three cards, and bat responses on Cards V through X. The cat is just a cat on Card I. The next response is, "Looks like pieces of the cat," and the next, "Looks something like the inside of the cat." The bat is first just a bat. On the next card, "Looks like the bat split in half." Then, "Looks like a bat with something in the middle tooken out"; then "Looks like if the bat was buried." Then, "Same bat, breaking up more," and lastly, "Looks like it's broken up still more."

Another subject has "A big gun, shooting" on Card II; "Two monkeys shooting fire at each other" on Card III; "Fire shooting down," on VI; "Red bullet shooting" on VII; "Orange fire with a bullet shooting through it" on VIII; "Two bullets coming out of there" on IX; and "A red flame to show rage and two rats, fire-headed" on X.

In other instances of perseveration, the object seen changes from card to card, but the descriptive adjective may remain the same. Thus everything may be described as broken up, decayed, or with holes in it.

Seven is the high point for shading responses. Differentiation of detail within the blot and texture responses are the outstanding types. In keeping with the prevalent feeling-tone of SEVEN, many of the shading responses are of a decidedly unpleasant character. Several children mention the weight of the cards, "Whew! These are heavy!"

Seven also appears to be an age of extremes. Red things are prominent but so are black; both fire and ice responses occur; FC is high but so is pure C. Or good and exact designs alternate with things that are "all torn up."

The 7-year-old remains relatively docile within the situation, in spite of such initial comments as "Eeh!" "Whooh hooly!" "Yikes!" "Sheez!" He may greet the situation with considerable enthusiasm and there is considerable friendly laughter, though some do complain that the cards get harder as they go along. However for the Examiner the test situation may be difficult at this age because subjects, boys in particular, tend to give long, complicated responses and to speak so rapidly that verbatim recording is difficult. The child may choose rare and hard-to-see parts of the blot, and his combinations and confabulations often make scoring difficult. The child of this age can help somewhat in the scoring because he can often give his reason for choosing a concept. Though he may be somewhat surprised at the question, "What reminded you of ———?" he will think about it for a while and often can explain his answer. When he is not sure, he may alibi, "We haven't had that yet," or "I guess a butterfly's wings would be like that—I don't look at them too much."

Seven is the high point for WS responses, i.e. whole responses based on the white area of the card. Space responses are often incorporated into the whole response as eyes, nose, and mouth, not only on Cards I and II but on III, VII, and VIII as well. White spaces also are frequently given as responses by themselves. Though the more customary use of the spaces as holes, tunnels, caves, and water forms still appears, for the first time a full reversal of figure and ground takes place and the spaces themselves are seen as actual objects: tops, fishes, and ducks, rocket ships, bellows.

Seven years also is a high point for combinatory responses. The 7-year-old can handle several discrete details at the same time, building them into a whole response, or combining them below the global level. He may combine the details successively, but often he is able to take them all in at a glance and to respond quickly. With his ability for quick organization he often cuts across the usual boundaries of a blot to organize it into a whole form. On Cards II and III, for instance, where the most customary response is two people or animals in profile, SEVEN pulls the sides together, fills in the white spaces, and produces a single face. Scenes occur more at this age than at any other.

This is a transition age so far as semantics is concerned. At 6 years naming the blot is by far the outstanding method of identification. At 8 years comparing the blot to the concept is the chief method. At 7 years the transition from naming the blot to comparing the concept to the blot is taking place.

Also aside from 4½ years when qualified concepts appear very frequently, this is the first age where qualification is strong. Use of such phrases as "It might be," "It could be" is very frequent. Also such phrases as "Looks something like," and "If you cut this off it would look like" are conspicuous, for the first time. The 7-year-old is highly critical of the difference between the actual shape of the blot and his concept, and he may attempt to adapt the blot to his specifications by verbally adding or removing various portions. An example of this appears in one boy's response to Card III:

"These could be fitted into a monkey, like. Without this space here. His face here—it couldn't be much of a monkey with a point there, but if the point was taken off and this here was all filled in at his leg here, and all this white, right up to here, fill that up. And have a little leg down this way. If this wouldn't be such a point, like, and this was all filled in here, and it had a little leg here, with the kind of hand here and the leg here, leaning against something. And this would be filled in here."

Along with qualification is the beginning of denial and changing of concept. Thus: "Snakes or something. No I don't think snakes." "This is some kind of an animal. I don't even think it is an animal." Or, "Bears climbing up an icy mountain. That isn't an icy mountain to me too much." While the number of refusals has decreased since 6 years, the number of complete denials has increased but is still low, an average of .14 denials.

Interest in the supernatural is indicated by very frequent references to witches and giants. Skeletons are also prevalent. Interest in people is increasing. H%, which was only 11% at 6 years, is now 14%.

The number of popular responses is the highest to date. P% is 27%, its highest point, though A% has decreased from 48% to 42%. At this as at other introversive ages, behavior trends appear strong and clear-cut, behavior being surprisingly similar from child to child. An example is the case of a girl and a boy at this age who give very similar responses to Card III: "These are two men. A bow and balls of fire and two big stones. Men standing like this and their legs going like that and they were leaning over the fire." "Two men fighting and a bow on fire between them and burning one of their hands off." Other examples are the considerable amount of perseveration which makes one record resemble another even though the object perseverated on may be different; the very large number of children who see things that are morbid and gruesome, decayed or broken; and the large amount of verbalization.

Individual Determinants

Number: The number of responses at 7 years is higher than at any other age except 9 years. The average number of responses per child is 18.3.

Area: W% (51%) is much higher than D (41%). Dd occurs to the extent of 8%. D has increased over what it was at 6 years, at the expense of Dd, which is low at this age.

Form: F% is at 7 years the lowest of any age, only 52%. F+% is 82%.

M, FM, m: M is the highest of any age to date, and higher than at surrounding ages. Average number of M is 1.4; and the percentage of children using it is also higher than at any age except 10 years. The average FM is 1.9 per child, higher than at any other age. m is also higher than at any other age, an average per child of .8.

Of the M responses, moderate extensor movements are the leading type. However, flexor responses occur here more than at any other age except 10 years. Just two people existing is the leading single item. Next in order come holding, lifting, carrying, sitting, placing something, cooking. In FM strong extension leads and the outstanding items are climbing and flying. Of the m responses, upward activity definitely leads, especially upward movement of flames and smoke. However downward activity is conspicuous, and shooting occurs here more than at any other age.

Color: As to color responses, ΣC is higher here than at any other age, an average of 2.9. CF is the leading type with an average occurrence of 1.3; C is next and FC third. Pure C reaches its high point here, an average of .8 per child. Of the CF responses, flower and fire and tree or leaf lead; of the C responses, nature and fire responses predominate.

Shading: Like several of the other determinants, shading responses at 7 years reach an all-time high, an average of 1.1. Differentiation of fine details within the blot is the leading type of shading response. However texture responses also occur conspicuously.

Clob: At this age there are more Clob responses than at any other age, an average per child of .5.

Content: The number of different content categories given by all 7-year-olds is small compared to surrounding ages, only thirteen. The average number used by any individual child, however, is high—5+. The leading content categories are animals, humans, objects, and nature. Architecture and anatomy are also conspicuous. A% is low, 42%; H% is the highest of any age to date—14%. Feet are emphasized in over one-third of the cases. There are many fire responses, many scene responses. Designs occur often in girls.

Length: The average record, particularly in the boys, at this age is very long, about 400 words.

Semantics: Merely naming the blot is for the last time the outstanding type of response. However qualification is coming in. Both the phrase "Looks something like" and the suggestion that "If you cut this off," etc. "it would look like" occur frequently. "Might be" or "Could be" are commonly occurring phrases.

Cards Preferred: Girls and boys at this age both prefer Card X. The cards least liked by girls are II and VI; by boys, X.

Typical Adjectives Used: Cracked, torn, bloody, burning, decaying, smeared, broken, dying, dead, poisonous, wicked, cruel, black, flaming, rotten, terrible, flabby, monstrous, worried.

By Cards:

Card I: Nearly all W responses.

Large number of W_s, as "Two girls and a frog," "Two men and a lady."

WS very strong, mostly faces, especially cat's face.

Things seen are torn, ripped, or have holes.

Card II: Many clouds and many skeletons.

Card III: Two persons doing something to object in middle.

Card IV: Much mention of blackness.

The adjective "big" is used frequently.

The majority of responses are W_1.

Big men and giants predominate.

Affect tends to be unpleasant: monster, giant, scarecrow, skeleton, ghost.

Card V: Butterflies and bats predominate. Bats' and butterflies' wings are consistently torn, broken, jagged.

Sex Differences

Sex differences are quite marked at this age—probably more so than at any other age in our range—with respect to many different aspects of the Rorschach response. As to number of responses, boys give many more than do girls, an average of 21.3 for boys, of only 15.2 for girls. Furthermore, girls' responses tend to be neat, concise, and generalized. The boys' records are often long and involved; their comments and explanations are complicated and rambling; and their elaborations are often confabulated.

Girls give more W responses than do boys; boys give more D and many more Dd responses. Amounts are respectively: girls—8.2W, 6.2D, .8Dd; boys 8.1W, 9.6D, 3.6Dd. Boys find responses in barely visible specks on the cards. Or they may for example pick out from the "ribs" on Card VIII just one rib and give it a name. Boys, however, give more W_s responses than do girls.

There are more M and more FM responses in boys than in girls and both M and FM are more active in boys than in girls. Boys also give more m than do girls.

As to color—ΣC is larger in boys than in girls. FC occurs more in girls than in boys. Other kinds of color responses occur more in boys than in girls.

An equal number of girls and boys give shading responses (52% in each case), but twice as many shading responses are given by the boys. There are many more Clob responses in boys than in girls, and in general boys are much more preoccupied with decay, damage, and mutilation, either in process or already having taken place, than are girls. The bat in V has, most frequently for the boys, ragged wings, for example.

Conspicuous sex differences occur with regard to several content categories. There are more plants in boys than in girls. (.5 in girls, 1.2 in boys); more nature responses in boys (.8 in girls, 2.1 in boys); more architecture responses in boys (.2 in girls, .8 in boys); more blood responses in boys (.0 in girls, .2 in boys), more fire responses in boys (.5 in girls, 1.0 in boys). There are many more design responses in girls (.6 in girls, .0 in boys). As to animal responses, there are more in boys than in girls (138 in all in girls, 198 in boys) and more different kinds of animals in boys than in girls (35 in girls, 45 in boys). Flying animals definitely exceed in boys but at this age wild animals occur slightly more in girls than in boys. There are slightly more human responses in boys than in girls.

As to total length of record, boys' records are much longer as a rule than are girls'. Most of the girls' records fit neatly onto one typed page; boys' frequently run to five pages.

Comparison of Rorschach and Developmental Findings

DEVELOPMENTAL	RORSCHACH
Introversive. Absorbed. Assimilating. Withdraws from difficult situations. Inner life active. Inwardizing of experience.	An average M of 1.4, more than at any age to date. M is frequently passive or describes flexor movement. FM and m also very high at this age. High Clob.
Quieting down, calmer. Less expansive.	Fewer content categories for group as a whole. However, ΣC as well as M increases.
Brooding, sad, complaining, sulky, morbid, unhappy.	Very high Clob. High use of morbid and gruesome concepts.
Inner tensions. May be in equilibrium with the world but in disequilibrium with himself.	Very high Clob, highest of any age. Largest number of m of any age. Largest number of shading responses of any age. Color shock and dark shock.
Attachment to and interest in persons. Increasingly sensitive to and aware of attitudes of others.	H% increases. Marked empathy shown in physical postures and expressions of the child himself as he responds to the cards.

Comparison of Rorschach and Developmental Findings

DEVELOPMENTAL	RORSCHACH
New critical ability.	F+% high.
	Qualifies concepts and suggests changes in blots to make them fit his concepts.
	May question or deny own responses.
More ability to generalize.	Much combination and confabulation in area of response.
Perseverative, but not from inability to modulate as much as from desire to continue and improve on a satisfying behavior.	The high point for "dynamic" perseveration in which the response changes, but there is some constant thread: a noun, adjective, or verb, running through all answers.
An age of extremes.	Black and red; fire and ice; FC and C responses about equal.
Self-centered.	CF responses predominate.
	Child changes blot to fit *his* concept.
Interest in magic and the supernatural.	Large number of witches and giants.

Sample Record of 7-Year-Old Girl M.V.

RESPONSE	INQUIRY		SCORING	
I. ∨ (Pause) Is it this way or the other way? This way it looks like a pumpkin with some things cut out here—the eyes, the mouth. These are like air holes so it can burn.	(Whole minus angular wing and top projection.) "This isn't part of it."	W̌S₁	F+	obj P
II. ∨ This looks like a top and it's going round, and this is the wall part in back.	(Center space detail is spinning top, black is wall.)	W̌Sₓ	m	obj
III. ∨ Part of a frog. This part wouldn't be in it [side red].	"Don't see his eyes. Just where his shoulders come." (Black is body of frog up to "shoulders.")	W̌₁	F±	Ad
Looks like a skeleton too. I think it's a skeleton.	"This part where the eyes are." (Points out eye sockets in lower center heads.) Remind you? "Well the hair and everything." (Gray in lower center around heads. She sees only the skeleton head.)	D	F±	anat
IV. (She flicks out her tongue.) Looks like a scarecrow. Its legs look like legs. And the stick. The head's kinda small though. The way the arms come. Sometimes skeletons have straight arms.	Skeleton? "Scarecrow, I meant." (Whole)	W₁	F+ m FClob	obj

Sample Record of 7-Year-Old Girl M.V. (Continued)

RESPONSE	INQUIRY		SCORING		

V. A butterfly. The way his wings come. Part off of it—some pieces are broken off of it. The way pieces are broken off butterflies—from hitting everything and trying to get away.

(Whole)

W_1 F+ A P

VI. (Long pause.) A sign. (Now turns card to inverted position.) This is the grass and sticks, and this is the sign. It's a broken piece of wood.

(Feathers on top D are grass and sticks. Sign is lower D.)

W_2 F+ obj
F(C)

VII. ∨ Hair. With some parts off of it. The part in the middle (center of third tier) and the hair comes all down here.

Remind you? "The way it looks here, the shape and the part." (Whole)

W_1 F+ Hd
F(C)

VIII. (Pause) This could be a knick-knack of a bear. It could be a statue of mountains with like a reflection—something in front of it. The bears must be climbing up it.

Knick-knack? "Real bears aren't pink." (Bears are usual animals, mountain is blue and gray, reflection is pink and orange.)

W_3 FM (A) P
FC

IX. A lot of colors in it. (Extended pause.) I don't know—I can't get anything on that one.

(Further questioning does not elicit a response.)

Refusal

X. This could be some birds.   D   FC   A

Leaves.   D   FC   plant

(Side yellow.) "Canaries, they're the only kind I know that are yellow." (Side green.) "The way they look."

This could be like the insides of a hellgrammite. That's about all.   D   F(C)   anat

Hellgrammite? "That you put on a line for fishing. They're black. You fish with them, they pinch. That looks like the inside." (Top gray.)

Card most liked: X. "This one's pretty—got all different colors. Reminds me of a wedding cake with all different colors, decorations." (V is nice too.)

Card least liked: VII. "This doesn't look like anything."

R = 12

5W$_1$
1W$_2$
1W$_3$
1W$_x$ = 67%W
4D = 33%D

7F = 58%F
5F+, 2F± = 85%F+
1FM, 1m, 1 tend. m
2FC, 1 tend. FC
1F(C), 2 tend. F(C), 1 tend. FClob

0M : 1ΣC

2A, 1(A), 1Ad = 33%A
1Hd = 8%H
4 object
2 anatomy
1 plant

3P = 25%P

COMMENT This girl is probably more restrained than most 7-year-olds (low R, refusal at IX) and she probably finds it difficult to express herself adequately in difficult or emotionally charged situations. She appears to be quite adaptable (2FC) but there is a good deal of caution and restraint in her adaptation [1 F(C)+2→F(C)] and she lacks spontaneity.

Although she is more responsive to external than to internal stimuli (0M : 1ΣC), there is probably more interest in herself (2 anatomy, 1 reflection) than interest in others. There are indications of suppressed aggressivity and a good deal of unemployed energy and feelings of frustration (1m+1→m, plus her interpretation at Card V "a butterfly . . . the way pieces are broken off of butterflies from hitting everything and trying to get away.") There are also possible feelings of guilt (? red shock at II).

The most marked characteristics of this age are evident in this protocol in such remarks as "some pieces are broken off of it" at V; "a broken piece of wood" at VI; and "parts off of it" at VII. Responses such as these are often interpreted as indications of masturbation. Whether this is an age at which this behavior appears more strongly, or whether such responses are indicative of some other psychic and emotional change is yet to be determined. The signs of difficulty which occur here as both age and individual characteristics may well support the possibility of masturbation, such a behavior being only another sign of the inner tensions present at this age.

The inversion of five of the cards indicates initiative and independence of action as well as some resistance to and conflict with the environment. This is supported by the WS responses combined with extratensivity. The individual responses such as those at VI and VIII are extremely interesting in revealing supplementary facets in this child's personality.

Sample Record of 7-Year-Old Boy B.S.J.

RESPONSE	INQUIRY		SCORING		
I. A bird. A bat. With some part of its wings torn off. And here's his paws. It got ripped in the bottom of its wings. All ripped off.	(Whole. "Paws" are top center details. He indicates uneven edges as "torn" and "ripped.")	W₁	F+ m	A	P
II. Looks like—these look like two chickens—they're red chickens.	(Top red.)	D	FC	A	
And this looks like a jet-propelled plane.	"Cause it has like this on the back—the fire coming out." (Lower red.) "And like a rocket front." (Usual hands.) "This white part is the plane, this black part is the smoke. It's not straight and it looks black." Elaboration of initial response.	WS₃	m CF ClobF	obj	
III. This looks like a bow tie that somebody took some bites out of, cause there's little round circles in it. Looks like somebody took a bite.	(Center red.)	D	F+	obj	P
Except these are two roosters.					
This looks like the top of a duck.	(Head of usual men. See elaboration below.)	W₃	FM	A	
This looks like the branch of a tree.	(Legs of usual men.) "Cause it looks like a branch, and somebody sawed some of this off."	D	F+	plant	

Sample Record of 7-Year-Old Boy B.S.J. (Continued)

RESPONSE	INQUIRY		SCORING		
And this looks like a little pan they have. And these look like little brooms. This is their mops that they clean things with.	(Pans are center black; brooms, which at once become mops, are side red.) "Long stick, the bottom thick and like a mop." (Ducks have now been enlarged so that usual men are ducks.)	W₁	M	H	P
IV. Looks like the back of an old man who has a club down there. And here are his hands —he has the mouth like that [demonstrates with hands forward]. Great big feet and a club down there. Here's his head, but he's turned around the other way.	(Head of man top center, usual hands and feet, club is lower center.) "Maybe he's gonna get somebody— he's chasing them. Maybe he's got his club through his belt."	W₁	FM FClob	A	P
V. (Pause) Looks like a bird that has some bites on his wings— a black bird. Legs, front part, and there was a round part here, but somebody bit it off. Maybe a bluejay or a dog or a cat bit it. He's flying.	(Whole. Notches in top edge of wing are "bites.")	W₁			
VI. That looks like a little plane that I have home—my brother ripped some pieces off the	(Whole. Midline is "where the men are." Wings are lower D and feathers of top D.)	W₁	m	obj	

wing. He broke it [sadly]. And this part is the little front wing. And this is the line down here where the men are. And these are the wings right here. Pieces off all along the edge. Musta crashed, and the parts broke off, and they're flying back to get another plane.

VII. (Pause, turning card.) Looks like an old broken bridge this way [card inverted]. An old ancient bridge, and part of the cement's broke outa there and it's broke here. A long, long time ago. Lot of fire and fights, and parts of the bridge was broken [despairingly]. But it was still there. Made of cement, that color—gray.

(Whole. Cement is broken in middle of third tier, and at joints between tiers.)

W₁   F(C)   arch
     m

VIII. Looks like a little tree that they painted part here. And there's two animals climbing up it. Two red foxes. And a butter-fly down here. I heard of red foxes, but they'd be darker red.

(Whole. Tree is blue and gray. Foxes are usual animals, butterfly is orange and pink.) Butterfly? "It's lived a long, long time and it's old and it flew over near the tree."

W₃   FM   A   P
     FC

Sample Record of 7-Year-Old Boy B.S.J. (Continued)

RESPONSE	INQUIRY		SCORING	
IX. This looks like somebody scribbled some colors—the whole thing. Some little boy who didn't know how to color. He just scribbled some colors. Nobody big would scribble colors like that. Must have been on paper that had a building on it. And there's the building right down there. That's all that's left—in the middle.	(Whole. Building is dark midine projection of blue-green. Windows are central slits. Scribbled colors surround "all that's left" of the building.) "Looks tall and looks like it has windows in it." (Side blues.)	WS$_x$	CF	obj
X. These look like lobsters that somebody painted.	(Side blues.)	D	F+ FC	A P
And these look like flowers.	(All yellows and oranges.)	D	CF	flowers
And two leaves.	(Top green.)	D	FC	plant
And weeds.	(Lower center green.)	D	FC	plant
This looks like a plate that I have—like a trade mark of somebody—two half animals and a chimney, and there's some rope down here and they must have got their heads caught. That's all.	(Top gray. Lines down center are "rope.")	D	F+ FM	obj

Card most liked: IV. "Cause I like to play giant—get a lot of kids and run all around the yard and I run after them."

Card least liked: X. "Hard to think what they are." VI. "Nobody would want an old broken plane."

R = 17

5F = 29%F
5F+ = 100%F+

1M, 3FM, 1 tend. FM, 2m, 2 tend. m
3FC, 2CF, 2 tend. FC, 1 tend. CF
1F(C), 1 tend. FClob, 1 tend. ClobF

1M : 3½ΣC

6A = 35%A
1H = 6%H
5 object
3 plant
1 flower
1 architecture

7P = 41%P

5W₁
3W₃
1Wₓ = 53%W
8D = 47%D

COMMENT This boy has rather expansive extratensive reactions though he responds easily to both external and inner stimuli. He is sympathetic, imaginative, readily empathetic and identifies easily with both the animate and the inanimate. The 2m responses imply suppressed aggressivity though the "jet-propelled plane" at II suggests more direct aggressive response. Considering the space responses plus extratensivity, one would suspect that this boy is quite capable of rather active and direct aggression when a situation prompts it.

The response at Card IV indicates that he may be working out for himself some of his fears and conflicting attitudes. The "old man with the club" who is "gonna get somebody— he's chasing them," followed by "I like to play giant—get a lot of kids and run all around the yard and I run after them," suggests identification with the adult whom he probably regards as somewhat menacing and powerful. But in the kind of activity which he suggests, he may be making a satisfactory resolution of the conflict which it implies.

Again we see concern with things "broken" and "ripped off," but with this boy there is also some concern and empathy with things that are "old." Of Card VI he says sadly, "Nobody would want an old broken plane," and at VII there is "an old broken bridge." It is at VII that he turns the card for the first time, and there is a longer pause. If this implies some shock it may indicate concern with problems of birth and/or death. The "bridge" interpretation itself, however, implies a desire to resolve conflict.

This boy is quite conscious of the color interpretations as something "somebody painted," indicating a sophistication which is more mature than that of most of his contemporaries. At Card IX he finds an interpretation difficult, and though he is still quite conscious of the colors, he takes refuge in a space detail. This suggests that when emotional difficulties become too great for him, he probably exhibits oppositional tendencies.

He dislikes Card X because it is "hard to think what they are." The pressure of external stimuli probably disturbs his perfectionist demands (F+% 100) and for that reason he finds them disturbing even though he responds more spontaneously to them at present.

This boy is well endowed both intellectually and emotionally and shows imagination, sympathy and adaptability. He shows strong aggressive tendencies but has a desire to resolve conflict and with his capacity and maturity, he is probably working out many of his own difficulties.

Sample Record of 7-Year-Old Boy G.R.

RESPONSE	INQUIRY		SCORING		
I. Two bears.	(Whole with bear on each side.)	W₂	F+	A	
Crab.	(Top center detail.)	D	F+	A	
II. Fire.	(Top red.)	D	C	fire	
Two witches.	(Whole)	W₂	M	(H)	
Fire.	(Bottom red.)	D	C	fire	
III. Two monsters.	(Usual figures.)	W₂	M	(H)	
Monster's hat between.	(Center red.)	D	F±	obj	
Fire to burn their home.	(Side red.)	D	C	fire	
IV. Funny clown.	(Whole minus lower center D.)	W₁	F+	(H)	P
Big stick, has prickles on it.	(Lower center D.)	D	F+	obj	
V. Big bird.	(Whole)	W₁	F+	A	P
VI. Funny cat, face is inside, and whiskers.	(Top D.)	D	F+ / F(C)	A	
Big wings, just wings, not of anything.	(Lower D.)	D	F+	Ad	
VII. Two funny men.	(Top two tiers.)	D	F+	H	
Seesaw.	(Bottom tier.)	D	F+	obj	
VIII. Beavers.	(Usual animals.)	D	F+	A	P
Hard man—monster what kills nearly all the animals.	(Face and head in blue and gray.)	D	F+	(Hd)	
IX. Two bad men trying to get themselves undone from here.	(Orange)	D	M	H	
Wings.	(Green)	D	F±	Ad	

X. Crabs. (Side blue.)
Piece of monster. (Top gray, head of monster.)
Goat's horns. (Lower green.)
Two birds. (Side brown.)

D	F+	A	P
D	F±	(Hd)	
D	F+	Ad	
D	F±	A	

Card most liked: X. "Nicest one I ever saw."
Card least liked: IV. "Big bird monster."

R = 23

2W₁
3W₂ = 21%W

18D = 79%D

17F = 74%F
13F+, 4± = 88%F+
3M
3C
1 tend. F(C)

3M : 4½ΣC

7A, 3Ad = 43%A
2H, 3(H), 2(Hd) = 30%H
3 fire
3 object

4P = 17%P

COMMENT This additional protocol is included, not so much to indicate individual characteristics of the boy in question as to point up age factors. Through our developmental studies which preceded our use of the various projective techniques, we have already considered Seven as an essentially thoughtful and pensive age, an age at which the child is shy, musing, brooding, less explosive and less impulsive than at Six. These seem to be the characteristics he presents to the world in his overt behavior.

The Rorschach responses reveal many of these characteristics, but they also supply for us a clue to the thought content of this pensive, musing child. This thought content seems sometimes quite startling in its gory detail and pleasurable horror. There is apparently a good deal of inner turbulence in the withdrawn and shy 7-year-old. His musing seems to be filled with "witches," "monsters," "fire," "blood," and "scary" things which may have an almost compulsive fascination for him.

This boy illustrates the presence of all these factors with the exception of "blood," and he gives his responses in a very matter-of-fact, unemotional manner. (Some SEVENS are prompted by their interpretations to long and exciting confabulations.) However, although these qualities may appear disturbing to our more adult and pacific (!) point of view, this expression of horror, danger and violence may be a very normal way for the 7-year-old to pursue his emotional path through the disturbing contradictions of the culture and his own personal drives.

CHAPTER NINETEEN

Eight Years

R = 15.9	58%F	7.3A = 45%A
	87%F+	2.6H = 17%H
55%W		2.2 object
37%D	1.3M 1.5FM .4m	.9 anatomy
7%Dd	.5FC .9CF .4C	.7 nature
	.9F(C) .2 Clob	.6 plant
	1.3M : 1.8ΣC	3.7P = 24%P

Qualitative Description

The 8-year-old child is, on the surface at least, quite different from his 7-year-old self. He is no longer withdrawn and melancholy, and is much less likely to inwardize his experiences and to brood about his imagined wrongs. He is expansive and evaluative and much more outgoing than at 7 years.

Evidences of this lessening of inner turmoil are seen in several aspects of the Rorschach response. Clob responses are reduced sharply from an all-time high of .5 per child at 7 years to a low of only .2 per child at 8. The number of children giving Clob responses is also reduced, from 41 per cent to 22 per cent, and the incidence of shading responses is reduced from an all-time high average of 1.1 per child to .9 per child. m also is reduced, from an average of .8 per child to an average of .4. All of these changes are in the direction of a much less troubled psyche.

Eight years, however, does appear to be a high point for qualification and uncertainty combined with a great demand for accuracy. The Rorschach blots are chiefly identified by such statements as "Looks like," in which the blot is compared to the concept, but this phrase is commonly modified to, "It looks *something* like." Or, the child may go even farther and suggest changes in the blot in order to make it more closely resemble his concept. Such phrases as, "If you cut this part off" occur more frequently at 8 years than at any other age. More qualifying statements are made at 8 than at any other age except at 9 years. Other common qualifying phrases are: "Might be," "Could be," "I think," or "I guess." "Probably" is a characteristic adverb.

Temporizing is frequent. "Well, it might be," "Well I think maybe." Such statements as, "Doesn't look like anything," "I don't think it looks like anything to me," "I don't think any of these look like anything," "I can't say anything about this," are frequent. Such statements are usually followed by good responses, but complete refusals are also high. Some question the Examiner or themselves with such phrases as, "What are these things?" "What on earth is this?" or "Now what could that be?"

In addition, this is the high point for denying own responses. In this behavior we see the combination of uncertainty and yet demand for accuracy which appears to characterize this age. The child does not make statements lightly—he hesitates till he is certain. He questions himself. He alibis that he can't see anything. He does not phrase his responses, "That is," as earlier, but "That looks something like," "That could be." And then having given his response he frequently tends, in search of greater accuracy, to deny his own response. "A rat, no, a moth," "A fighting elephant, no not a fighting elephant." The considerable emphasis on orientation of the card, "Does it go this way?" "You handed it to me upside down," etc., is probably a further aspect of this demand for accuracy.

In spite of all these factors, the response tends to be more clear-cut and less confused than at 9 years of age, since denials are usually direct and concise.

With their need for exactness, children at this age seem to feel, as do some 4-year-olds, that the blots actually represent something, and that there are right and wrong answers. They say, "I can't guess," or "Did I guess right?"

Eight-year-olds show considerable aggressivity toward the cards, the situation and even toward the Examiner. Initial exclamations such as "Eeh!" "Yike!" "Bah!" "Wow!" "Oh golly!" "Judas!" are frequent. Negative criticisms of the cards include such statements as "Oh those. They're too confusing!" or "I hate these!" The child makes rude remarks to the Examiner, though less rude than at 9 years: "Don't ask me too many or I won't tell," or "Don't ask me all these crazy questions."

The child is, however, somewhat interested in the recorder and the recording, if these are visible. He asks, "Are you writing all these down?" or sometimes even slows down in his response so that the recorder can keep up with him. The characteristic 8-year-old interest in other people is also expressed by an extremely high H%, and by questions as to what other children have said.

Disparagement of the blots is further expressed by such adjectives as

"Dumb," "Crazy," "Old," "Funny" with which the child describes his concepts.

Unpleasant feelings which the blots engender are suggested by the fact that nine children (18 per cent) either say outright that the cards are "horrible," or give gruesome details such as: "man's legs bleeding and bones of his face," "raggedy old bird falling to pieces, nothing left," "hog's body cut out as a rug, blood coming out." "Blood" is a frequent color response. However, as indicated above, horrible or gruesome responses are much fewer than at 7 years. It may be that in the extraversive manner which has been considered typical of the 8-year-old the child instead of being inwardly shocked by the blots (or by other things which he perceives) takes out his reaction of unpleasantness by attacking the objects, or those about him.

Scarecrows occur in 6 per cent of the cases; skeletons and witches are each mentioned by 20 per cent of the children. Anatomy responses for the first time constitute one of the leading content categories. There is also strong interest in the oral, especially in teeth; and figures without heads appear frequently.

The response of this age is extremely global in character. The expansive 8-year-old gives on the average 55% global responses—detail responses falling to 37% and tiny details occurring less than at any age since 3½ years. Wholes are for the most part immediately seen wholes, not of the DW variety. In spite of this, good form is high—an average of 87%.

EIGHT is generally considered to be a more expansive, less inwardized age than is SEVEN. Reduction of introversive tendencies is suggested in the Rorschach by a slight reduction in number of all types of movement responses. Fewer in number, movement responses are nevertheless vigorous in character. Human movement responses are conspicuously extensor; and violent extensor movements, as at 4 and 5½ years, exceed moderate. Dancing and fighting responses are prominent. In animal movement, strong extension also leads—climbing, walking, flying, all being conspicuous forms of activity. There is less flexor movement than at surrounding ages. Thus we find in the nature of movement responses, indication of the active inner life of the 8-year-old.

Emotions are expressed in a somewhat more modulated fashion than at 7 years. Though egocentric CF responses predominate here as at most ages, FC responses definitely exceed pure C. Of the C responses, fire is the leading type, blood comes second. Blood may be splashed, paint is spilled, fire is burning.

Thus, in summary, in relation to immediately preceding and succeeding ages, responses at 8 years, though still frequently gruesome and indicative of inner turmoil, are much less so than at 7 years. Though very frequently qualified and uncertain, they are more clear-cut than they will be at 9 years, in spite of the numerous qualifications and denials.

Individual Determinants

Number: There are only 15.9 responses on the average at this age, less than at either 7 or 9 years.

Area: Number of W is very high (an average of 5.7 per child). This high number of W is exceeded at only one age, 3½ years. W% is also very high, 55%. Both D and Dd are lower than at surrounding ages.

Form: F% at 8 years is lower than at any other age but one, 7 years. This indicates that the response is not constricted. F+% is higher than at any other age except 10 years.

M, FM, m: The actual average number of M, 1.3, is slightly lower than at surrounding ages, but the percentage of total responses is slightly higher. FM as usual is slightly higher than M. Of M responses, extensor movements lead and strong to violent extensor movements exceed moderate. Holding something, fighting, dancing, and standing are the outstanding types of human movement.

Of FM responses, strong extension also leads, climbing, putting noses or paws together, sitting, walking, flying or pulling something being the outstanding kinds of activity.

m responses are somewhat fewer than at immediately surrounding ages. Falling is a prominent m response as is also upward activity.

Color: ΣC is relatively less than at 7 years. CF predominates but FC is greater than C. As to CF responses, tree or leaf is the outstanding response; flower and anatomy responses share second place. Of the C responses, fire is the leading type, blood comes second.

Pure C responses occur most on Cards II and VIII: fire, paint, blood on II; fire, rainbow, colored ice on VIII. Blood occurs most, then paint, then fire. Blood may be splashed, paint spilled, fire burning. There is no color naming.

Shading: Shading responses are higher at 8 years than at any other age except 7 years. Leading types are differentiation of fine details within the blot, and texture responses.

Clob: The number of Clob responses is lower than at preceding ages though the average FClob% is only exceeded at two ages—5½ and 7 years.

Content: Number of different categories found at this age is high—15. Number of different categories used on the average by the individual child at this age is, however, only 4.7, slightly lower than at surrounding ages. A% is 45%, about average for the total range, but H% is unusually high, 17%. Animals are, as at all ages, the outstanding content category, but at this age for the first time humans rise to second place. Other outstanding categories are objects and anatomy. Of animal responses, the "butterfly-bird" category is the leading one.

Length: In boys especially this is one of the wordiest ages, even though the total number of responses is low. Records average about 300 words.

Semantics: At this age for the first time, comparing the blot to the concept by use of such phrases as "Looks like" is the outstanding method of expression. Qualifying phrases are very frequent, i.e. "Looks something like." Suggestions for changing the blot, i.e. "If you cut this off," etc., occur more at 8 years than at any other age.

Refusals and Denials: There are .5 refusals per child; .3 denials. This is an all-time high in denials.

Best and Worst: Card X is liked best by both sexes; Card IV least.

Sex Differences

The outstanding characteristics of the age seem to come out a little more strongly in girls than in boys. Girls deny and qualify their responses more, make more initial exclamations, are more aggressive against the Examiner and against the cards, suggest more changes in the cards.

Girls give more W responses than do boys, boys more D and Dd responses than girls. Boys give more FM and more M responses than do girls. Boys and girls give about equally active M responses; boys are a little more active than girls in FM. More boys than girls give m responses.

ΣC is greater in girls than in boys as are numbers of FC, CF, and C responses.

More boys than girls give shading responses. Many more girls than boys give Clob responses.

Sex differences in content are not noteworthy.

Comparison of Rorschach and Developmental Findings

DEVELOPMENTAL	RORSCHACH
Evaluative.	Denying own response, effort to achieve accuracy: "A rat, no a moth." Or refusal when not certain. Use of "Well," "probably," "something like." Accuracy suggested by F+% higher than at any age but 10 years.
Expansive.	F% low.
	Higher global than at surrounding ages.
	Large number of different content categories.
Very strong interest in adults.	Highest H% of any age except 9 years.
Close but complex interpersonal relationships with adults.	Interpersonal with Examiner beginning to come in strongly, expressed especially in rude remarks to Ex. Also in interest in recorder's activity, "Are you writing down what I'm saying?"
Feelings easily hurt, sensitive, self-critical.	Shading responses occur more than at any other age except 7 years.

Comparison of Rorschach and Developmental Findings

DEVELOPMENTAL	RORSCHACH
Dramatic and explosive.	Initial exclamations, "Yike!" "Wow!"
Emotionally impatient, demanding, tearful, egocentric.	CF predominates and is almost twice FC.
Children much more outgoing and extraversive than at 7 years.	No clearcut findings to indicate this, but it may be reflected in less Clob and inward shock and more projecting outward with attacks on the blots and on Ex. Also reduction in all types of movement response.
Aggressive.	Aggressive against cards in initial exclamations; describing cards as "crazy," "dumb"; such remarks as "I hate these." Also aggressive remarks against the Examiner.

Sample Record of 8-Year-Old Girl M.L.

RESPONSE	INQUIRY		SCORING		
I. It looks like an eagle. That's all.	(Whole) "The head and the wings and also the whole thing makes it look like that. That spoils it though, the two little mouths."	W₁	F±	A	P
II. How come red? Do you have one for everybody? Two little heads screaming at each other. Two little people peeking out of something. No, two little people screaming at each other. That's all.	(Whole) (Sees usual figures.) "The body and here are two legs."	W₂	M	H	
III. I hate these. I have had this. It's easy. Two people.	(Usual men.) "I see heads, body, muff, legs and feet of course. Oh yes, their arms and they have something in their hands." (Center red.)	W₂	M	H	P
With a bow in the center. And they have something in their hands, some muffy things in their hands. Are you writing down what I'm saying?		D	F+ elaboration	obj	P
This sort of looks like a river.	(S detail between lower center gray.) "Not exactly river, sort of a little pond. Doesn't that look like it? Remind you? "The white. The rest looks dopey. Those two things [people], put 'dopey' on them."	S	F±	nat	

Response	Inquiry	Location	Determinant	Content	P
IV. I can't say anything about this except that it looks like a dead animal.	(Whole) Remind you? "That, the head right there." (Lower center head.) "That's all I can say about that."	W_1	F+ FClob	A	P
V. A bee or butterfly, either one. It looks more like a butterfly.	(Whole) "The wings and this and this, the whole thing. What else do we do in here?"	W_1	F+	A	P
VI. I don't know. Might be a fly with wings chipped off. That's all.	(Top D.) "There are wings chipped off, and there's the fly part. The head and around here the neck. Sort of cuckoo though, the darning needles." (Dark midline of top D.)	D	F+	A	
VII. It looks like two little chipmunks sitting on two stones—sitting on stones, except for this spoils it. You know the ears are too long.	(Whole) (Top two tiers as chipmunk, bottom tier as stones.) "The body and the head. I can't see any legs though."	W_3	FM	A	P
VIII. Is this meant to be ink too? Looks like an insignia, just color not shape, not counting the shape.	(Whole)	W_x	CF	obj	
IX. Doesn't look like anything. Just this is the only part I can name and that's meant to be the tail of the airplane, that's all I can name.	(She indicates the whole blot as an airplane, though the orange as the tail is the only part she can identify.) Remind you? "The shape."	W_x	F±	obj	

Sample Record of 8-Year-Old Girl M.L. (Continued)

RESPONSE	INQUIRY	SCORING
X. These look like two bees or beetles.	(Top gray animals.)	D F± A
This looks like a rabbit's head, but not counting these. And that's all I can think of. What did David name these?	(Lower center green, usual rabbit's head, not including green projections.)	D F+ Ad

$R = 13$

$9F = 69\%F$
$5F+, 4F\pm = 78\%F+$

$2M, 1FM$
$1CF$
1 tend. FClob

$3W_1$
$2W_2$
$1W_3$
$2W_x = 61\%W$

$4D = 30\%D$

$1S = 9\%Dd$

$2M : 1\Sigma C$

6A, 1Ad $= 53\%$A
2H $= 15\%$H
3 object
1 nature

$6P = 46\%P$

COMMENT   Judging from the configuration of scoring, this appears to be a typical 8-year-old subject. However, she is more responsive to inner than to outer stimuli ($2M : 1\Sigma C$) and probably more intellectual than emotional in her approach to any problem. She may tend to evade or to dismiss as quickly as possible any disturbing emotional situations either profound or peripheral.

She tends to worry and to be over-critical as do many 8-year-olds. This is typified in such remarks as "this spoils it though," "sort of cuckoo though," and "the rest looks dopey."

Remarks such as "I hate these," followed almost immediately by "It's easy," are indicative of feelings of ambivalence. The movement response, "Two little people screaming at each other" seems to indicate some interpersonal conflict while the S response combined with introversivity, plus the qualifying remarks, probably indicates feelings of doubt in herself and some feelings of insecurity.

Sample Record of 8-Year-Old Boy H.R.

RESPONSE	INQUIRY		SCORING	
I. What in the ——! Bat. Could that be it? Butterfly.	(Whole) Remind you? "Those claws there." (Top center detail.) (Whole) "Just sort of looks like one."	W_1 (same)	F+	A P
II. A volcano or something.	(Black is volcano, red is lava.) "Cause a volcano has lava."	W_x	CF	nat
III. Good grief! Skeleton family. It looks so ugly.	(Usual men.) "These two, they look awful. I can't make out what those are."	W_2	F+	anat
IV. If these were in color I could tell better. (Look like?) Like a map. And that's all. Looks something like a giant with his head chopped off.	(Whole, with surrounding white as water.) (Whole)	WS_1 W_1	F± F+	map (H) P
V. Cow or something. It's upside down, isn't it? It looks like a bird.	(Whole) "A cow has four legs. Sort of skinny too." (Whole) Remind you? "Beak, and the way it's shaped."	W_1 W_1	F− F+	A A P
VI. Carved statue of some ugly thing.	(Whole) "The whole business." (Cannot specify what the "ugly thing" is.)	W_1	F(C) FClob	obj
VII. Two dogs. Looks like an awful looking thing. It would be better if you folded it.	(Top two tiers.)	D	F+	A P
VIII. Looks like a jaw or something. Somebody's mouth. Here are the teeth, the tongue, good gravy—a lion's in it! Ahhh, it's a funny thing.	(Whole. Each side is a jaw, mouth open, holding the lion in the mouth.)	W_x D	F± M CF F+	anat A P

Sample Record of 8-Year-Old Boy H.R. (Continued)

RESPONSE	INQUIRY	SCORING	
IX. A flower, pollen spraying. Flowers and the leaves and then a pink bottom.	(Whole. Pollen is orange spikes, green is leaves.)	W_x	CF flower m
X. (He inverts the card.) What's it so—? Doggone. I couldn't tell what that is. (He continues to turn the card, but Ex. can elicit no response.)		Refusal	

R = 12	9F = 75%F	5A = 41%A
1 refusal	6F+, 2F±, 1F− = 77%F+	1(H) = 8%H
		2 anatomy
6W₁	1 tend. M, 1 tend. m	1 nature
1W₂	2CF, 1 tend. CF	1 flower
3Wₓ = 83%W	1 F(C), 1 tend. FClob	1 object
		1 map
2D = 17%D	0M : 2ΣC	5P = 42%P

COMMENT. The most outstanding characteristic of this record is the disturbance that any new situation apparently causes this boy. Signs of initial, red, Clob, and color shock are all present. He regresses easily to less mature and poorly conceived reactions, and seems to find himself at the mercy of constantly fluctuating forces when he copes with disturbing situations. (See progression of response for all ten cards with a refusal on the last card. Also note progression on the darker cards, IV, V and VI; or on the color cards, VIII, IX, X.)

His interpersonal relationships are probably not satisfactorily developed (the only H response is "giant with head chopped off"). He probably finds it quite difficult to deal with his strongly diffuse and rather vague emotional reactions, and may at times react in an explosive and unpredictable manner.

CHAPTER TWENTY

Nine Years

R = 18.6		8.7A = 48%A
	67%F	2.9H = 16H%
	84%F+	2.5 object
42%W		1.2 anatomy
48%D	1.4M 1.6FM .5m	1.1 nature
9%Dd	.7FC .7CF .7C	.6 plant
	.8F(C) .2Clob	
	1.4M : 2.1ΣC	3.9P = 22%P

Qualitative Description

It has been said of NINE that at this age "many of the behavior trends of EIGHT come to clearer issue" (Gesell & Ilg, 28). We find this to be especially true in the Rorschach. Outstanding among these trends is the tendency to qualify any given response. Nine years is the high point for the whole age range for qualifying responses. The child says, "It looks something like," "It could be," "It might be," "I guess it's ———," "In a way it looks like," "I was thinking maybe that was," "I'd say that would probably be." Others qualify even further: "Well, I don't know. It only looks something like it might be a butterfly. I don't know what it *is*!" "Hm! Doesn't look like much. Never seen anything like it before. Bug or something, maybe." Quite a few go so far as to say, "It doesn't remind me of anything."

Suggestions for changing the blot to make it more closely fit the concept are also very prominent at this age. "Well, if this weren't here, this might look like a giant's feet and it might also look something like a monkey if the hands were better"; "Cat's face without these. Without these knobs up here. And make it circular sort of like in here and cut this off."

Denying own response is another 8-year-old behavior which occurs conspicuously at 9 years. 18% of the subjects give responses and then deny them. However denials at this age are not as concise and clear-cut as at 8 years. Now the response tends to be confused and confusing. Responses are often difficult to score because it is frequently difficult to tell what the child means. "Oh this is a Viking's head; no I don't think it's a Viking's head. Map of Wonderland because I can't think of anything else." "Looks like a butterfly in a way, not too much, but in a way." "That might be his tongue. No! Oh well it might be. It's not quite big enough." "Complicated. That would be an owl's head down to here, and let's see what the rest would look like. Maybe a leaf? Owl? Because he's got two black eyes." "The head is like a frog and the part here like a cat's whiskers. This part is like a butterfly's wing. Don't know what it is." "This part gets me all mixed up."

In the denial and hesitation, we see beginning signs of TEN's balancing of responses: "In a way it looks like part of an animal and in a way it doesn't."

Accuracy of response, as indicated by $F+\%$ is less than at surrounding ages.

Card turning occurs in only 51 instances, less than at surrounding ages, but the considerable amount of verbal reference to the position of cards, i.e. comments as to whether cards are upside down or right side up, or statements that "If you turn it like this then it looks like . . ." are part of the same effort at clarity and accuracy aimed at by the numerous denials.

We find an example of these factors just described in the response of one girl to Card I:

"Can I hold it and turn it upside down and everything? They sort of remind me of the Alps mountains, in a way they do. This way, here, sort of looks like the face of Buddha. We're studying China in school. This reminds me of people—this looks sort of like a tent. And these right here remind me of sort of wings and this reminds me of windows. That's all I can think of."

Nine years is a very variable age, and individual differences usually stand out in a clear-cut manner. We note this characteristic variability in the responses to the Rorschach. There occur, in all, 17 different content categories, more than at any other age. The average number of different content categories used per child is only equalled at one other age—7 years. Percentage of popular responses is slightly less than at surrounding ages.

Many at this age appear to be looking to outside sources for information and confirmation. Such comments as "I've seen them in pictures before," "I saw a picture like that in a book," "I know because I saw some in Peabody Museum," "I've seen a lot of pictures cause my father's a doctor." This need for outside confirmation may result from a strong tendency at 9 years to deprecate self. We see this tendency during the Rorschach when the child says, "I'm not very good at figuring," "I haven't got the imagination that some kids have."

Nine years is sometimes considered to be a somewhat neurotic age, more so than the immediately surrounding ages. We see signs of this in the

Rorschach response. In addition to feeling the need to qualify his statements, to support them with outside authority, and to verbalize about his own inadequacy, the child shows strong concern about himself in the relatively large number of anatomic responses which he gives. The 9-year-old gives on the average 1.2 anatomic responses, more than at any other age; and also gives at this age the highest average number of human responses (2.9), which are usually considered to show an interest both in oneself and in others. Concern about body parts and functions is shown not only by this large number of anatomic responses, but by the unusually large number of human details which, at this age only, far exceed the customary ratio of 2 human responses to 1 human detail. Here we find an average of 1.2 whole human responses per child and 1.0 human detail response.

Map responses, often considered evasive, reach a high point at 9 years. Other possible indicators of somewhat neurotic temperament are high number of shading responses, rather high number of Clob responses, and a higher number of Dd responses than at any surrounding ages. The average number of Do per child is .6, greater than at any other age, suggesting suppressive tendencies. Interest in immediate practical detail is indicated by the fact that at this age only, D responses exceed W. 48% of responses are now in the practical detail category—an all-time high. W% has conversely fallen to 42%, an all-time low.

Emotions appear to be increasingly well controlled. Of the various types of color response, adaptive, FC responses now occur as frequently as CF or C responses. The average number of M at this age is 1.4, the highest total number to date, though the percentage of M responses to the total response is lower than at 8 and 10 years. Animal movement is slightly more frequent than, and slightly more active than human movement. Human movement responses tend to be rather static.

Initial exclamations, antagonistic comments about the cards and rude comments to Examiner are found conspicuously at 9 years as at 8. Comments such as, "Oh bunk!" "Oh gush!" "Oh how tiresome!" "We *would* have those things!" "They look dumb!" "Don't ask me, ask yourself," "Confusing!" "Looks like a crazy goon, like a four-eyed nut," "Two jerky dwarfs," "I don't want any more of them. I'm not going to do the others" are characteristic and represent the less-than-cooperative attitude which we frequently meet in the 9-year-old.

Productivity is high at 9 years, higher than at any other age through 10 years.

Individual Determinants

Number: The average number of responses at this age is 18.6, more than at any other age in the first ten years.

Area: At this age only, D% is greater than W%, there being on the average

48% of the responses in the D area, 42% in the W area. Dd% (9%) is also larger than at the surrounding ages. Thus both D and Dd occur rather extensively, at the expense of W.

Form: F% is 67%, higher than at any other age from 5 to 10 years. This suggests a certain amount of constriction at this age. F+%, however, is only 84%, lower than at the surrounding ages.

M, FM, m: The average number of M per child is 1.4, the highest of any age to date, but the percentage of M responses in the total response is lower than at 8 or 10 years. FM is just slightly more frequent than M with an average occurrence of 1.6 per child. m occurs on an average of .5 per child, more than at any age except 5½ and 7 years.

As at 8 years, in the M responses, strong to violent movements lead. Holding or carrying something and dancing are prominent single items. Sitting or two people just existing, however, are also prominent. In FM, strong extension also leads, with climbing, fighting, putting noses or paws together, and hanging from something, being the outstanding single items.

m responses are relatively high at this age, hanging being the outstanding item.

Color: ΣC is very high, an average of 2.1 per child. FC, CF, and C responses occur with nearly equal frequency.

As at 8 years, of the CF responses, tree or leaf, flower and anatomy responses are the most common with tree or leaf leading. Blood comes in as a leading C response, with fire second.

Color naming is virtually nonexistent.

Shading: Next to 7 and 8 years, this age provides the most shading responses. Differentiation of details within the blot and texture responses are the main types of shading response, texture responses now equalling differentiation of details.

Clob: Occurs to about the same extent as at 8 years. Monsters, ghosts, and animals are the most frequent Clob responses.

Content: There are 17 different content categories used at this age—the highest of any age. The average number of different categories used by any one child is high—the highest in fact of any other age but 7, which equals it with an average per child of 5.2 different categories. However A% is high, 48%. H% (16%) is higher than at any age but 8 and 10 years which it equals. Objects, anatomy, and nature are three other categories which occur conspicuously in that order of frequency. Of animal responses, the "butterfly-bird" category is the leading one, but wild animals also occur very prominently.

Length: Records are lengthy, about the same as at 8 years (300 words), and longer than at 10 years.

Semantics: As at 8 years, comparing the blot to the concept, chiefly by use of such a phrase as "looks like," is the most common method of identification. However 9 years is the high point for qualification of responses. "Looks something like" occurs more here than at any other age. "Might be" or "could be" or "I guess," "I think," are very frequent, and suggestions for changing the blot to fit the child's concept are stronger than at any ages except 7 and 8 years.

Refusals and Denials: The average refusal per child is .5. The average denial is .2, more than at any other age except 8 years.

Best and Worst: Card X is liked best by both girls and boys. Card IV is liked least by both sexes.

Sex Differences

Sex differences are not outstanding at this age. There is no important difference in the number of answers given. As to area, boys definitely give more W and DW than girls, slightly fewer D and Dd. Boys also give fewer Do and S than do girls.

In girls, FM is more active than M. In boys, both are about equally active. Boys in FM give "hanging onto things" responses not seen in girls, and give fewer fighting responses than do girls. FM is more active in girls than in boys; M is more active in boys than in girls.

ΣC is larger in girls than in boys, but differences in color responses are actually not marked. There are slightly more CF responses in girls than in boys. In girls, flower responses lead, in boys anatomy. In girls, C and CF responses appear about equal, whereas in boys CF predominates over C. There are more C responses in girls than in boys. Fire and blood are the outstanding C responses for both sexes.

Shading responses are about the same in both sexes, a little more frequent in girls.

As to content, there are more architecture, anatomy and map responses in girls than in boys. Of animal responses, large wild animals are more in boys, small wild animals more in girls. More flying animals (butterflies and bats) in boys.

Comparison of Rorschach and Developmental Findings

DEVELOPMENTAL	RORSCHACH
Self-deprecation, lack of self-confidence.	"I haven't got the imagination that some kids have," "I'm not very good at figuring." Also seeks confirmation of response by saying he has seen pictures like this in a book, etc.
Interest in self, and self-appraisal.	One of the three highest ages for shading responses.
Wrapped up in self and own concerns. Anxious and apprehensive both about self and own health.	Anatomic responses highest of any age; Hd nearly equals H.
Sensitivity which may approach the neurotic.	Very high Dd and Do. Many Clob responses. Qualification of own responses. Confused answers; uncertainty.

Comparison of Rorschach and Developmental Findings

DEVELOPMENTAL	RORSCHACH
Complaining.	High Dd.
Individual differences becoming more marked.	P% less, though only slightly less, than at surrounding ages.
	Largest number of different content categories and largest average number of content categories.
	The phrase, "It looks *to me* like" reaches its peak here.
Very variable mood. Expansive. "Deepening" of emotions, less "shallow" than at 8 years.	Very high ΣC with CF and pure C predominating.
Resists adult supervision.	Very rude and resistant remarks to Ex.
Evaluative and more discriminatingly evaluative than earlier.	High F(C); high Dd.
Very critical of others.	
"At 9, many of the behavior trends of 8 come to clearer issue." Child is expansive, sensitive.	All of these factors are expressed in the Rorschach.
Is uncertain and finds it difficult to make choices or decisions.	The high point for qualification of response.

Sample Record of 9-Year-Old Girl D.L.

RESPONSE	INQUIRY		SCORING		
I. That looks like (pause) a bat in some cases.	(Whole)	W_1	F+	A	P
Sometimes it looks like a mouse, if it didn't have the wings. If it was plain, it might have looked like a bat. A mouse if the tail was a little longer.	(Each side figure without the wings is a mouse.) (Questions response.) (Questions response.)	Dd	F±	A	
This part looks more like a beetle.	(She settles for the center part which looks like a beetle "because of the shape.")	D	F+	A	
II. (Inverts card.) If I turn it up this way, it looks mostly like a design.	(Whole)	W_0	F+	design	
The only thing, here it looks like sort of a lobster, I don't know.	(Lower red.) "The spikes remind me."	D	F+	A	
And this way it might look like part of pincers—a bug that pinches.	(Center hands.)	Dd	F+	A	
III. That looks sort of like a basket if it's filled in here, and these might be a bottle falling out of it.	(Outline of black figures makes the basket. Side red are bottles.)	W_s	F± m	obj	

Sample Record of 9-Year-Old Girl D.L. (Continued)

RESPONSE	INQUIRY		SCORING	
IV. Well if this weren't here, this might look like a giant's feet.	(Usual boots.)	Do	F+	(Hd)
And it might also look something like a monkey if the hands were better.	(Whole)	W₁	F+	A P
V. (Laughs) That's a bat. This is part here, and the wings.	(Whole)	W₁	F+	A P
VI. Might look like a darning needle if—I don't know. I can't think of anything else.	(Top)	D	F+	A
VII. I don't know. (Turns card all around.) I don't know. (Ex. can elicit no further response.)			Refusal	
VIII. That looks something like flowers. (Covers part of figure with hands, looking at it again, but gives no further response.)	(Whole gives impression of flowers because of colors.)	W₀	CF	flowers
IX. Umph! This looks like a pink cloud up here.	(Pink)	D	CF	nat
This down here is a tree.	(Green, because of color.)	D	CF	plant
And it looks something like it might be an orange sunset.	(Orange)	D	CF	nat

X. This looks like sumac.

And this looks like there might be all sorts of butterflies and things flying around. That's all.

(Pink) "Well, sumac is something like that, red and fluffy."
(All parts outside of pink are flying insects.)

	D	CF	plant
		F(C)	
	W_x	FM	A

Card best liked: X. "Well, I don't like a plain picture. I like them more colorful."

Card least liked: VII. "Because I can't see anything in it."

R = 17
1 refusal

$2W_0$
$3W_1$
$1W_8$
$1W_x = 41\%W$

$7D = 41\%D$

2Dd
1Do = 18%Dd

11F = 64%F
9F+, 2F± = 91%F+

1FM, 1 tend. m
5CF
1 tend. F(C)

0M : 5ΣC

9A = 53%A
1(Hd) = 6%H
1 design
1 object
2 plant
1 flower
2 nature

3P = 18%P

COMMENT A girl who is strongly extratensive and who seems rather well equilibrated except for expressions of the extreme uncertainty and indecision which characterize the age. The constant qualification of interpretations with "if," "sort of," "something like," and "something like it might be" is outstanding at Nine, and this girl shows it up well. She is quickly responsive to external stimuli and her attitude is pleasant and euphoric. She has a rather rich variety of expression and shows some originality.

Interpersonal relations do not seem too highly developed. The refusal at VII suggests some antagonism to or difficulty with the maternal figure. No human movement appears in the protocol and only one animal movement. This girl is probably quite dependent, perhaps in an attractive feminine manner, with little revealed active inner creative experience potential as yet.

Sample Record of 9-Year-Old Boy W.W.

RESPONSE	INQUIRY		SCORING		

I. (Pause) Doesn't look like much of anything. Looks a little bit of something like a bat—not too much.

Musta been a big pen (to make inkblots).

(Whole)

W₁ · F+ · A · P

II. This way or that way? This looks like a bear and that looks like a bear, but I couldn't tell what those red spots were.

(Black only.) "They look as if they're putting their noses together, like."

D · FM · A · P

III. Well, sorta looks like—not much —but a little like two people sitting down—or standing up —two women standing up.

(Usual figures.) "Looks like they're putting their hands on something, but I don't know what that was."

W₂ · M · H · P

That looks like a bow.

(Center red.) "Looks like a bow."

D · F+ · obj · P

IV. That looks like a—. (Turns card.) Looks like something, but I just can't—I don't know what. A little bit like a—. (Now inverts the card.) Some animal skin hanging up like. Like a bear skin.

(Whole) "Well, looks like that's flapping over like that and looks like it's hanging up on a wall like. Just looks like a bear skin."

W₁ · m · obj

Response	Inquiry	Loc.	Det.	Content	
V. Uh—looks something like a butterfly.	(Whole) "Well, it looks like a butterfly—head and feet and its eyes out there."	W_1	F+	A	P
VI. Looks like a dead cat hanging up—but—	(Whole. Top D is head.) Idea? "Well, the face up here—really isn't a face but—." Idea dead? "Well, doesn't look much alive—its feet are spread out and cats don't sleep with their feet out." (Cat is hanging, head up.)	W_1	m	A	P
VII. Looks something like two bunnies sitting up on two rocks. That's all there is in the picture.	(Bunnies are two top tiers, bottom tier is rock.)	W_s	FM	A	P
VIII. Doesn't look like anything much alive—I don't know what it could be. Those look sorta like two little animals climbing to something up there.	(Usual animals.)	D	FM	A	
And that looks something like a rock. (Turns card to side.) Those really look like little animals if you put it up like that.	(Pink and orange.) "The way it looks."	D	F±	nat	
IX. I wouldn't know what that [softly]—looks like sorta two persons underground and something on them. I don't know what is on the persons lying on the ground.	(Lower pink is persons with rest of blot "lying on them.")	W_x	M, m	H	

Sample Record of 9-Year-Old Boy W.W. (Continued)

RESPONSE	INQUIRY		SCORING	
			M	(H)
Those look—not really, but just a little—like two witches up there.	(Orange) "Leaning sideways on the rocks, and the rocks are on top of the people. Maybe they don't look too much like rocks." (Greens are rocks.)	D	M	(H)
And those look like rocks.		D	F±	nat
X. They look like they're all little insects.	(Whole)	W_x	F±	A
That looks like the head of a fox.	(Top gray with tube as snout.)	D	F+	Ad
That and that looks like two crabs.	(Side blues.)	D	F+	A P
That and that look like two fish hanging onto something.	(Side brown.)	D	FM	A
And that looks a little like the head of a grasshopper.	(Usual rabbit's head with side projection as legs.) "Sort of like a grasshopper with green legs and face." Else? "There is something else, but I don't know what that would be." (Pink)	D	FC	A

Card most liked: V. "Well it looks more like a real live animal."
Card least liked: I. "It really doesn't look like anything."

R = 18

$4W_1$
$1W_2$
$1W_3$
$2W_x = 44\%$
$10D = 56\%D$

8F = 44%F
5F+, 3F± = 81%F+

3M, 4FM, 2m, 1 tend. m
1FC

$3M : \frac{1}{2}\Sigma C$

10A, 1Ad = 61%A
2H, 1(H) = 17%H
2 object
2 nature

8P = 44%P

COMMENT   A striking characteristic here is the number and quality of the movement responses—M, FM, and m. The human movements range from barely active (women sitting down . . . standing up . . . putting hands on something) to passive (witches leaning sideways on rocks) to acted-upon (persons lying on the ground, something on them). The animal movements, though gentle, depict more animation and more sharing (bears with noses together, bunnies sitting up on rocks, little animals climbing to something, fish hanging onto something [dependent or predatory?]).

The M seems to suggest a conscious self view as passive, submissive, and powerless, which differs from his more spontaneous impulses and images of activity and sharing and perhaps initiative. His least acknowledged fantasies (m of animal skin hanging up, dead cat hanging up) involve feelings of dependency and frustration that appear similar to his image of the people seemingly buried alive, who eventually have both rocks and witches on top of them.

Like the hopefulness in his animal movements, one also finds hope in this very introversive boy's response to color—it is just one FC, to a cool color, and saved up for his very last response, but still it is color.

The general picture which emerges of a boy with extensive fantasy, who feels hampered, even possessed, and who is in conflict over passive and active impulses, certainly prompts one to try and see how he can be helped. While not withholding help, one might well withhold a diagnosis of "neurotic" or "disturbed" until a retest at a later time can help one to separate age and individuality characteristics.

CHAPTER TWENTY-ONE

Ten Years

R = 16.3	63%F	8.1A = 49%A
	89%F+	2.8H = 16%H
52%W		2.2 object
40%D	1.7M 1.7FM .4m	.7 anatomy
8%Dd	.5FC .8CF .3C	.6 nature
	.6F(C) .1Clob	
	1.7M : 1.5ΣC	3.8P = 25%P

Qualitative Description

TEN is the first age when the basic experience balance is introversive—
1.7M : 1.5ΣC. An interesting correlate of this increased introversivity is
that now instead of suggesting change in the blot if it does not fit his concept, the child changes his concept, stating that he has changed his mind.
"Little fire or something here. No, that wouldn't be fire. . . . I said it but
I changed my mind." Not only is the experience balance slightly introversive at this age, but also we find a much larger percentage of subjects giving
M responses than giving any of the color responses. Movement responses
at this age are predominantly vigorous and extensor.

Along with increased introversivity of the individual child at this age,
we find a general narrowing down and drawing in, and so far as the group
as a whole is concerned, more similarity in response from child to child,
less variety of response and less individual variation. We find, for instance,
a decreased productivity. The child gives on the average only 16.3 responses as compared to 18.6 at 9 years. The total record tends to be
shorter than at 9 years. And furthermore there is a marked narrowing
down of content. The total number of different content categories used in
all is only 13 as it was at 7 years, making 10 years one of the most restricted ages so far as spread of content is concerned, in comparison with
8 and 9 years when the total number of content categories was 15 and 17
respectively. Also the average number of different content categories used
by any one child is only 4.8, lower than at 9 years.

Central tendencies in M are also seen more strongly—there is much less variety from child to child. The high A% of 49% suggests considerable stereotypy, and P% is higher than at the preceding two ages.

Not only is the child narrowing down in his response, but he is also calming down, achieving a better equilibrium. There are markedly fewer signs of disturbance: low F(C), only an average of .6 per child; low Dd%; Hd only about half of what it was at 9 years. Clob occurs less than at any other age since 4 years, m less than at any age since 5 years.

ΣC is lower than at any age since 4 years. The high average of .7 pure C responses of 9 years has dropped to a low of .3. CF now leads among color responses with FC in second place.

The increased critical ability of the 10-year-old is suggested both by the highest F+% to date (89%F+), and also by an average of .6 refusals per child. This is the highest amount since 3 years, and now probably has a somewhat different connotation than in the preschool years when it frequently implied unwillingness or inability to respond. Now it may mean that the child wishes to be clear and accurate even though he may not actually be so. He may refuse when he is not certain that he can give an accurate response.

Greater critical ability is also suggested by interpretation of facial expressions. "Gorilla, it looks so fierce," "Sort of the expression you know like they were mad fiery people and might be very quick tempered, smiling at each other," "Someone cross."

Several subjects show great confidence in the accuracy of their responses. Ten is the highpoint for extra positive identification: "Without this that would be a perfect lamb." "This one looks very much like a bat." Others speak as if answers must be definitely right or wrong: "I am sure that's wrong," "Oh my God! None of these are right of course."

In spite of the apparent demand for accuracy, general uncertainty of response continues to be characteristic. The child gives a response, questions it, returns to the first idea, tempers his response with "sort of." He says, "Maybe it is, and maybe it isn't." He says "No—yes—no." At this age qualification seems frequently to represent more the characteristic balancing of TEN rather than the neurotic confusion of NINE. TEN says, "In a way it looks like two people dancing and then in another way it looks like bears growling at each other." "Bears. Not bears. Something like bears." "They're talking they look like. Not like talking but—." "Deers fighting, fawns, no not fawns, deers."

Some show more than a normal degree of vacillation and uncertainty, giving responses such as "Looks like a—let me see—a—looks like something—looks like—two people. . . . Faces look odd—look—kinda hard to explain." "That looks like a face—no—kinda uneven though. Face of—I don't think it's an animal."

Though there is less qualification at 10 years than at 8 and 9, this is one of the three leading ages for the use of qualifying phrases. "Looks something like" is frequent, and "Might be" or "Could be" occur more here than at any other age.

The hypochondriacal tendencies of TEN are suggested in the strong emphasis on anatomic responses. Anatomical responses fall within the four leading types of content, occurring here more than at any other age except 8 and 9 years. Bones, hands, body, chest, stomach, pelvic region all are mentioned frequently. Headless animals or people occur often and, conversely, heads alone are also prominent.

The supernatural comes in for frequent mention, reflecting an interest in magic and supernatural forces. Witches appear nine times, ghosts five, skeletons eight, ogres six, dragons four—more in girls than in boys.

Increased ability to generalize is suggested by the fact that whole responses once again definitely exceed detail responses. There is also description of the nature of the whole card. "A cheery looking picture," "A funny one," "A most peculiar looking one." Abstract responses are occasionally given, as "Spring" for Card X.

A rather unusual characteristic of this age is the fact that many children appear to confuse people and animals. The following are typical comments: "In a way it looks like people and in a way it looks like bears," "Looks like somebody with a beak," "I can't describe what they look like but they're in the comics too. Some people look like this, look more like frogs," "Two girls. No an elephant trunk," "Looks like a face of—I don't know, think it's an animal." Several ask, "Does it have to be an animal?" even though they may have already given other types of response.

Another rather unusual characteristic, also noted at 7 years, is the mention of things not actually seen. Thus: "They'd look like the wind if you could see it. Well I just thought it would look like the wind if you could see it." "Hunter opening up an animal." (Hunter?) "The hunter isn't there." "Looks like a house, too, only no one's building it. Like the beginning—maybe the people have gone away, or the frogs that were building it, and left it like that."

There is a strong emphasis on Twoness—"Two heads as though they were arguing," "Two big animals knocking into a lady." Twoness is also implied by the very frequent phrases "each other"—"People looking at each other," "Two rabbits' tails bumping each other," "Two dogs kissing each other."

In this same vein of interest in relationships of two persons or animals is the marked emphasis on things being *attached* or *pulling apart*. We have such responses as: "A person that isn't attached here," "Sort of like people if they were attached," "Two people dancing, aren't attached to each other." Or, "Two men pulling apart a clam," "All kinds of fish pulling apart a whale," "Old rag doll with funny looking animals pulling her."

Orientation seems to be a matter of some concern. Card turning occurs a great deal—more than at any other age. Furthermore even though the subject may hold a card in the customary orientation, he frequently makes such comments as, "Two upside down boys," "Upside down house," "Spring because it's upside down."

Shading responses are few at this age, only .6 such responses per child. Texture responses for the first time constitute the leading type of shading response. "Wax, shines the way wax does," "Satin," "Wet fur," "Fuzzy stuff like cotton."

Size also appears to be important—"Sort of oversized crabs," "Oversized butterfly," "Two big animals knocking into a lady, she has big horns."

There are at 10 years fewer initial exclamations and almost no rude comments against the cards or against Examiner. Criticism is largely confined to such comments about the cards as that they are "Funny looking," "Funny," or "Peculiar."

Individual Determinants

Number: There are fewer responses here than at the preceding age. The average subject gives 16.3 responses.

Area: The average number of W is relatively high, 7.8 per child. D is slightly less, an average of 7.0 per child. Dd is less than at many ages, an average of 1.6. W% is rather high, 52%; D is less, 40%; Dd is 8%.

Form: 63% of responses are determined by form alone. F+% is the highest of any age to date—89%.

M, FM and m: There is here the largest number of M to date, an average per child of 1.7M. FM is now no higher than M, 1.7FM. m is lower than at any time since 5 years, an average of .4.

Of M responses, extensor movements predominate, and of these, strong to violent extension exceeds moderate. Holding, lifting, carrying, dancing; shaking, touching or posturing hands; and looking, are the outstanding types of human movement. Hands, mostly engaged in some type of action, are mentioned by 27 out of 50 cases, or 54 per cent of subjects.

Of FM also, strong extensor movements predominate. Climbing leads, fighting comes second, putting noses or paws together third. Standing and flying also occur. Of m response, upward activity predominates.

Color: ΣC is low at 10 years, only 1.5, lower than at any age since 4 years. CF responses predominate, followed by FC and C in that order. Pure C is extremely low, an average of only .3 per child.

As to CF, flower responses lead, anatomy responses come second. Of the C responses, fire leads. There is virtually no color naming.

Shading: Shading responses are relatively very infrequent, only an average of .6 per child, less than at any age since 5½ years. This is the first age at which texture responses are the leading type of shading response. Differentiation of details within the blot is the second most prominent type.

Clob: Clob responses now occur only on an average of .1 per child, less frequently than at any age since 4 years.

Content: Total number of different categories found at this age is very low, only thirteen. Average number of categories per child is also rather low, 4.8. A% is 49%, high; H% is 16%, also fairly high.

Animals are the leading content category, humans come second, objects are third, and anatomy fourth. Nature responses are lower than at most preceding ages but flower responses are higher. Of animal responses, "butterfly-bird" is the leading category.

Length: Records tend to be shorter at this age than at 9 years, about 230 words.

Semantics: Comparing the blot to the concept, chiefly by use of the phrase "looks like," is the leading response. This is a high point for use of qualifying phrases such as "might be," "could be," or "looks like," though slightly less so than the preceding age.

By Cards: WS responses are outstanding on *Card I*. They occur in 9 girls out of 25, in 9 boys out of 25. Hallowe'en mask or cat is the most common of these WS responses. Bat or butterfly is also very frequent on Card I, occurring in 23 children.

Responses to Card I tend to be of a much less pleasant nature than those to *Card II*. Characteristic of Card I are such comments as: "torn leaves," "ghosts or witches with glaring teeth," "cracked head with two bumps on it," "female without head," "crab with holes in the shell." On Card II we get people or animals dancing, kissing, putting noses together, or such ideas as "sun rising."

On *Card III*, especially, the attachment or lack of attachment of the two "people" is mentioned. On *Card VII* "each other" is a common phrase; that is the two people or animals are often doing something to each other.

Best and Worst: Card X is the most preferred by both sexes. Carl IV is disliked most by both boys and girls. Boys also dislike Card VI. Card II is most frequently omitted by girls; Card VI by boys.

Sex Differences

Boys give slightly more responses than do girls. Boys give an average of 16.6 responses; girls 16.0.

The average number of W is much higher in boys than in girls. Boys have an average of 8.6W, girls only 6.9. The W% also is higher in boys (54%) than in girls (50%). D is higher in girls, an average of 7.4 compared to an average in boys of 6.6. Dd is very similar in both, slightly higher in girls.

There are twice as many shading responses in boys as in girls, and more than twice as many boys as girls give such responses.

There are few conspicuous sex differences in regard to content. Anatomy responses occur more in girls than in boys. Boys give the greater variety of animal responses and the greater number. Large wild animals are definitely more in boys. Bat occurs more in boys. Water animals occur more in boys but snakes more in girls. Supernatural forces occur more in the records of girls than of boys.

There are no conspicuous sex differences in M, FM, or m. As to color, however, ΣC is higher in boys than in girls and each of the types of color response occurs more in boys than in girls.

Comparison of Rorschach and Developmental Findings

DEVELOPMENTAL	RORSCHACH
Introversive.	1.7 M : 1:5ΣC. Less ΣC than at any preceding age since 4 years. Fewer responses than formerly. Fewer different content categories.
Straightforward and matter-of-fact, uncomplicated, direct. Sincere. In good equilibrium. Less neurotic than at 9; has self better in hand.	Low F(C), only an average of .6 per child. Low Dd and low Hd. Do and S less than at 9 years. Clob least of any age since 4 years. Pure C much lower than at 9 years.
Behavior rather stereotyped and somewhat predictable.	A% is 49%, high. P%, 25%, higher than at 8 and 9 years. Less variety of M from child to child than at most ages.
Not too loquacious.	Total length of record is conspicuously less than at 9 years, as well as fewer responses.
Compares and matches, balances answers: "Sometimes I do and sometimes I don't."	Gives a response, questions it, then returns to first idea. "Bears. Not bears. Sort of like bears." "In a way it looks like people and in a way it looks like bears."
Increasing critical ability.	Highest F+% to date—89%. Appears to refuse card if not certain—.6 refusals per child.
Magic is important; child is superstitious. In general, accepts adult directives. Relatively docile. Conforming and agreeable with adult.	Many (9) witches, 5 ghosts, 8 ogres, giants or devils, 4 dragons. CF leads but FC is second as to extent of occurrence. Fewer initial exclamations and very few attacks on cards or on Examiner or situation, beyond calling cards "peculiar."
Emotions: anxious to please but wholehearted. On the surface. Lack of hidden undercurrents of later ages.	FC now second leading category, CF first. Pure C has dropped to third place. Clob least of any age since 4 years; F(C) least of any age since 5½.
New emotions coming in, suggested by use of such words as "humiliated," "embarrassed."	Now describes facial expressions of people or animals seen.
Somewhat hypochondriacal.	Anatomic responses higher than at any age except 9 years, average of .7 per child.

Sample Record of 10-Year-Old Girl B.L.

RESPONSE	INQUIRY		SCORING		
I. (Laughs) Nothing. (Long delay.) Might be an eagle. No, it couldn't be an eagle because it hasn't got a head. Butterfly. Right?	(Whole. But then she rejects the response.)				
	(Whole) "Shape and dots [S details] in there."	WS_1	F+	A	P
I see a girl without a head. Right? That's what it looks like to me.	(Center figure.) "Shape."	D	F+	H	
II. Two dogs.	(Black only.) "Looks like a poodle, long skinny thing and nose."	W_2	F+	A	P
A butterfly down here.	(Lower red.) "Shape and features."	D	F+	A	P
An arrow.	(Usual hands.)	Dd	F+	obj	
And I can't make out—oh, this is a dotted line.	(Dotted line below hands.)	Dd	F+	obj	
Rhinoceros.	(Black only.) "Shape with horn—there are two."	D	F+	A	
III. (Long delay.) Skeleton—no, not—a bone.	(One of the usual figures.) "Shape and features in it."	D	F+ F(C)	anat	
A bow over here.	(Center red.) "Shape."	D	F+	obj	P
Two chicken legs.	(Usual legs.) "Shape and lighter down here."	D	F+ F(C)	Ad	
Two sheep—lions.	(Side red.) "Shape and long tail and features."	D	F±	A	

Response	Inquiry	Loc.	Det.	Content	Pop.
IV. (Turns card.) Is this how you look at it? (Puts face close to card. Long delay.) Say it's a rabbit.	(Whole. Head of rabbit is lower center.)	W₁	F±	A	P
(Turns card to ∧ position.) Looks like something this way. Looks like somebody doing back bending—I see their head.	(Whole. Head is at top with body bent back.) "Shape and features."	W₁	M	H	P
V. Butterfly. That's all I can make out of it.	(Whole) "Shape."	W₁	F+	A	P
VI. Whew! What is this? Oh gosh! This looks like a skin hanging up on a wall.	(Whole)	W₁	m	obj	
And it looks like the emblem eagle down here.	(Top D.) "Way it's made."	D	F+	A	
VII. This is—I don't know. Two girls—no, an elephant trunk. Something up here. Who made these ink blots—you? Look at it. Oh my God. None of these are right, of course.	(Rejection of response.) (Top tier.)	Do	F+	Ad	
VIII. Bones.	(Center ribs.)	S	F+	anat.	
Two bears.	(Usual animals.)	D	F+	A	P
A pair of pants.	(Central blue is pants.)	D	F+	obj	
With a jacket, no a sweater.	"Shape." (Pink and orange is sweater.)	D	F+	obj	
IX. Oh my gosh. ∨ A map.	"Two maps." (Each side is a map.)	Wₓ	F±	map	
A tree.	(Green)	D	CF	plant	

Sample Record of 10-Year-Old Girl B.L. (Continued)

RESPONSE	INQUIRY	SCORING			P
X. You write down everything I say. Spider.	(Side blues.)	D	F+	A	
Two bugs quarrelling.	(Top gray animals.)	D	FM	A	
Two snakes looking at a rabbit.	(Bottom green.)	D	FM	A	
Two lions.	(Center yellow.)	D	F+	A	
Two crabs.	(Side brown.)	D	F+	A	
I can't make out what they are.					
Two sea horses.	(Pink)	D	F+	A	

R = 29

5W₁	24F = 83%F	15A, 2Ad = 68%A
1W₂	21F+, 3F± = 94%F+	2H = 6%H
1Wₓ = 24%W	1M, 2FM, 1m	6 object
18D = 62%D	1CF	2 anatomy
	2 tend. F(C)	1 map
2Dd		1 plant
1Do	1M : 1ΣC	
1S = 14%Dd		8P = 27%P

COMMENT This girl reverses the perceptive type of most 10-year-olds with 62%D and only 24%W. This may be indicative of a characteristic which Klopfer terms "escape into reality," as well as an affinity for thinking which is based more on the concrete and the factual than on the more abstract and synthetic. This possibility is supported by the high F%, which surpasses that of most of her group.

She is highly conscious of authority (see "eagle" responses at Cards I and VI) and the indication of initial shock on Card I may suggest some conflict with paternal authority. The quality of the M, FM, and m responses is interesting: "Somebody doing back bending," "Two bugs quarrelling," "Two snakes looking at a rabbit," and "Skin hanging up on a wall." This last suggests strong feelings of dependency and frustration; the animal movement is suggestive of a feeling of being spied upon and of interpersonal conflict, while the "back bending" suggests a tendency to dynamic resistance and retreat. These difficulties combined with high banality (8P) and high stereotypy (A%=68%) as well as a desire to make a good impression (2 anatomy), probably serve to make her conform or retreat rather than providing outlet for her frustration and conflict.

Sample Record of 10-Year-Old Boy B.T.

RESPONSE	INQUIRY		SCORING		
I. Some kind of ghost or witch.	(Whole) Ghost? "I didn't see any ghost." Witch? "Well sort of like a witch. All of it." Remind you? "First of all the eyes. Just saw the head."	WS₁	F+	(Hd)	P
No, no, a cat, a cat, a cat. With his glaring teeth. (Opens mouth wide to demonstrate.)	(Whole) "I saw the mouth and the eyes and these things like ears sticking out."	WS₁	F+ FM	Ad	
II. Oooh, gee, that's bad. Is it the right way? ∨ Looks like two dogs kissing each other (chuckles). Very much so.	(Black only.) "This and this shape and the whole business and . . ."	W₂	FM	A	
∧ And it looks like two foxes kissing. Both people are kissing each other. Awful funny (chuckles).	(Black only.) "The shape and the little ears sticking back—no, no, the lamb would be much more. Without this thing that would be just a perfect lamb, with little tiny button ears." (Sees head of animal only.)	W₂	FM	Ad	P
III. To me looks like two monkeys, doesn't it? (Shows it to Ex. and turns card, then turns it back.) That's very good. See, there are the two monkeys and their tails are both down and here are their heads and their feet.	(Usual men.)	W₂	F+ FM	A	

Sample Record of 10-Year-Old Boy B.T. (Continued)

RESPONSE	INQUIRY		SCORING	
∨ And turn it this way and they're looking away from each other and their tails are —see that's their nose here and their big nose sticking out, and turn it around and they're sticking out the other way (chuckles). **Awfully funny.**	(Black figures with heads lower center.)	W₂	F+ FM	A
IV. That to me looks like a bear skin. Doesn't it? I think so. This is his tail and these are his legs and these are his front paws.	(Whole)	W₁	F+	obj
∨ Looks like a bat that **way,** doesn't it?	(Whole)	W₁	F+	A
V. This one looks very much like a bat. That's definitely a bat this way. Definitely.	(Whole) Remind you? "This kind of thing with the ears and great big wings on either side."	W₁	F+	A P
VI. (Regards for some time, then turns the card sideways, then upside down, regarding for 16"). Doesn't remind me of anything. Does it remind you of anything? Well, what does it remind you of? But I want to know your . . . (Total regard 37"). (Ex. can elicit no further response.)			Refusal	

Response	Inquiry	Location	Determinant	Content	P
VII. This looks like two little tiny rabbits, baby rabbits, and these are their little heads and long ears. And these are their tails bumping into each other, and this is part of their body. (Yawns)	(Whole. Rabbits are looking toward one another with paws up and tails bumping. Tails are bottom tier.)	W_2	FM	A	
VIII. Oooh gee, that's a funny one. That looks like the insides of some animal. I think so, don't you? These things look like ribs sticking out.	(Whole with usual center ribs.)	W_x	F± CF?	anat	
And it looks like the inside of a huge animal's mouth. And then this is the roof of his mouth and his tongue. And the orange part is his tongue and this pink stuff is his teeth —lower teeth. This is the roof of his mouth up here. How many more have I got to go?	(Whole with space details between blue and gray as teeth, central pink as lower teeth, orange as tongue.)	WS_x	CF CF–	anat	
IX. Oh gee, this looks like two dragons. Two dragons.	Remind you? "This part here, this part here." (Orange) "The head and this part here except —sort of sea dragons."	D	F+	(A)	

Sample Record of 10-Year-Old Boy B.T. (Continued)

RESPONSE	INQUIRY		SCORING	
V Let's see, and this looks like the atomic bomb explosion, very much. See, first this part and then the cloud of dust, and then this part on top.	(Whole, with pink at top as smoke.)	W$_x$	m F(C)	nat
X. (Yawns) Looks like a plain design.	(Whole)	W$_o$	F± CF?	design
This little part up here looks like sea horses.	(Top gray animals.)	D	F±	A
These look like crabs in here.	(Side blue.)	D	F+	A P
And this thing looks like a sea plant.	(Side green.)	D	FC	plant
And these are—this is a hard shelled crab—these two here.	(Side brown.)	D	F+	A
And these are little baby sea horses and this is just seaweed, seaweed, seaweed.	(Same as above.)	Repetition		

Retrial of VI:

RESPONSE	INQUIRY		SCORING	
That looks like the dead body of a cat which has been strung up by his nose—isn't a very nice thing. We saw a cat in the hotel—he was hanging by his tail and his feet.	(Whole) Remind you? "This nose and this part here."	(W$_1$	m FClob	A)

V And let's see what this looks like. This way it looks to me like this is all ground, this is an oil pit going down and this is oil. And this is the ground surface, and just this top part, and there's a pool in here and the oil is bubbling out.

(Whole. Oil pit going down is midline, ground surface is lower D.)

$(W_x \quad m \quad nat\,)$
FClob

Card best liked: "The two cards?" Just one. "I can't really tell you the card—I like them all. Well, if I could choose three, I'd choose this one and this one and this one." (II, III, VII.)

Card least liked: VI. "I don't like the idea of that." (No difficulty in making this choice.)

$R = 19$

$1W_0$
$5W_1$
$5W_2$
$3W_x = 74\%W$

$5D = 26\%D$

$13F = 68\%F$
$10F+, 3F\pm = 88\%F+$

3FM, 1m, 3 tend. FM
1FC, 1CF, 2 tend. CF?
1 tend. F(C)

$0M : 1\frac{1}{2}\Sigma C$

9A, 1(A), 2Ad $= 63\%A$
1(Hd) $= 5\%H$
2 anatomy
1 nature
1 plant
1 design
1 object

$4P = 21\%P$

COMMENT Here is an interesting example of the additional responses (retrial of VI) revealing more of the difficulty and the individual characteristics of the subject than do the initial responses. From the original responses, we have a picture of a strongly dependent child with a good deal of suppressed aggressivity and with feelings of frustration. The "dead cat strung up by the nose" and the "bubbling oil" responses given on the retrial of Card VI confirm this and in addition, the strong Clob tendency of both of these responses gives us the feeling that here is a boy whose profound emotional reactions are easily disturbed but who attempts to hide this from himself as well as from others.

He is more responsive to external than to internal stimuli though his responses at VIII are of poor form. (Loosli indicates DW CF− as a sign of dishonesty.) The WS CF—at Card VIII may confirm a tendency to evasiveness or a desire to make a good impression, but on too grand a scale, so that the whole response becomes poor and the structure shaky.

He may tend to be somewhat of a bluffer though the evidence of red shock at Cards II and III (indicating guilt feelings) may indicate that he is more honest with himself than with others. The only H response is at Card I and is a "witch," possibly indicating a not too satisfactory state of interpersonal relationships.

We also have evidence from the repetition of response (see Cards III and X), from the perceptive type (W : D ratio of 14:5), and from his attempts to get confirmation from the examiner by such questions as "Doesn't it?"—which usually occur more at 5 years than at 10—that this boy is somewhat immature. It may be that this emotional immaturity combined with a good intellect is one of his great sources of difficulty.

The FC response and the high stereotypy (A% of 63) indicate good potential for adaptability, but his frustrations and antagonism probably contribute to some explosive, nonadaptable behavior. This is an instance where unemployed energy needs to be guided toward more productive use, which at the same time may tend to increase the emotional maturity.

CHAPTER TWENTY-TWO

Normal Expectancies of an Adult Rorschach Record

N = 20 to 50	F% = 50% or less	A% = 35–50%
	F+% = 75% or more	H% = 10–15%
W% = 20–30%		3–4 other categories
D% = 50–70%	2–3M, 1–2FM,	
Dd% = 10%	About 3FC, about 1CF,	5–6 popular responses
	2–3F(C)	

Expected ratios:
W:D about 1:3   FC:CF about 3:1   A:H about 2:1
W:M about 2:1   M:FM about 2:1
Optimum succession is orderly.

COMMENT The percentages presented above represent an amalgamation of figures given by leading investigators in this field. They are presented not as a picture of ideal adult performance but merely as a standard of comparison in order that the reader may determine the extent to which performance at the several early ages resembles that of a representative adult.

A series of papers by one of the authors (Ames, 4, 5, 6), which views Rorschachs at a succession of ages throughout the life span, in a semilongitudinal design, helps to place children's Rorschachs in a broader perspective. And, on the other hand, acquaintance with children's records can help in understanding of adults with impaired functioning. A book by all the present authors, *Rorschach Responses in Old Age* (11), describes the responses of 200 persons aged 70 to 100 years. As people age, their records in some respects develop new characteristics, not seen earlier, and in other respects they again show responses characteristic of childhood.

Part Three

CHAPTER TWENTY-THREE

Longitudinal Findings: Individual Consistency and Developmental Trends

The 650 records analyzed in this book come from a mixed cross-sectional-longitudinal sample. Most of the subjects, by far, are represented by a single record but some contributed records at as many as three ages. Our analysis has so far treated the data entirely cross-sectionally, but we have often written as if the findings were longitudinal: we have referred not only to age group *differences* but to age *changes*. We obviously have inferred (and implied) that the individual child who showed a particular Rorschach constellation at age 6 is likely to show a somewhat different constellation at age 7, and that the difference is partly predictable.

While a cross-sectional approach is very useful for plotting out growth trends, for certain questions concerning both stability and change a longitudinal design offers the best—or only—possibility of answers. To determine the extent to which particular children follow the "typical" trends we have proposed, and the extent to which particular children maintain the same relative scoring position within a group at different ages, requires that we follow some particular children over time.

We have managed to follow 22 boys and 11 girls long enough to make longitudinal treatment possible. More than half of these 33 children contributed a record before their third birthday and only three of them began as late as 5 years. Over the 13 age levels between 2 and 10 years (half-yearly up to 6, yearly thereafter), individual subjects contributed series of six to eleven records, the median subject contributing ten. This small, hardy band not only produced 295 records by age 10; about two thirds of them continued contributing records beyond that age. Some of these later records have helped to give a longer-range perspective to our analysis.

Results from portions of this longitudinal sample have been reported in some detail in several papers (Ames, 3, 4, 5, 6). Some of these results are summarized here and several new analyses are presented. It is important to note that no more than three records from any one longitudinal subject were included in our main sample of records, and all those included were at preschool ages. Thus, after age 5, findings from this sample are independent of those presented earlier in this book, and can be fairly taken as cross-validating.

Individual Consistency

Scoring Variables

If a child produces relatively many movement or color or rare-detail responses at age 2, is it likely that he will still be scoring above average on this variable at age 4? Is it possible that his early scoring trends will still be appearing at age 10, or even later? (The answer, for this sample, turns out to be clearly yes for several variables.)

For 16 main Rorschach variables occurring with enough frequency to permit the calculation, product-moment correlations were run between all

TABLE 34.　NUMBER OF SUBJECTS AT EACH PAIRING OF AGES
IN LONGITUDINAL SAMPLE

	Age					
Age	*4*	*6*	*8*	*10*	*12*	*14*
2	16	17	16	15	10	9
4		29	27	26	19	17
6			31	30	22	21
8				28	20	20
10					22	21
12						21

possible combinations of even-numbered ages from 2 to 10 years.* At 2 and 4 years, when a child had a record at 2½ (or 4½) and lacked one at 2 (or 4), the half-year record was used; when he had records at both 2 and 2½ (or 4 and 4½), the earlier record was used. Many children also had given records at 12 and 14 years, and these were included in the matrix.

Table 34 presents the number of subjects at each pairing of ages.

---

* Here, and throughout this chapter, we included secondary occurrences ("additionals," "tendencies to") as well as primary ones in tabulating individual children's totals for color and shading responses. This helped statistically, by increasing totals of infrequently occurring determinants. It also helped to reflect more sensibly children's actual responses when they were multiply determined. For example, if a child on II said, "Two people dancing around a red fire," it would be foolish to say he had used no color, though none would be tabulated if only the primary determinant, M, were counted.

About half of the 33 children had records at 2 years overlapping later records, and about two thirds had records at 12 and 14 years overlapping earlier ones. In the main body of the comparisons, from 4 to 10 years, close to 30 subjects appear in each pairing.

Table 35 presents the inter-age correlations. If one is used to seeing inter-age correlation matrices for large samples and for such relatively stable variables as IQ scores or height, he may be struck by the irregularities in these 16 matrices. But, considering that the sample is small and that Rorschach scores have some quirky statistical properties, patterns do emerge rather clearly—some common to nearly all the variables and some descriptive of particular groups of variables.

Some help in discerning these patterns is offered by Table 36, which summarizes parts of Table 35. It presents, for each variable, averages computed for different groups of correlations. The first column gives the average of all the values within each matrix, with the exception of correlation with age 2 (since the Rorschach at 2 is such a chancy affair). It offers the broadest summary of total intercorrelation. The following four columns give means for four successive six-year spans. The final column averages the three values at the top of the age range, when the highest correlation might be expected.

As a general finding for most variables, the usual inter-age pattern appears: in the individual matrices the values tend to decrease from left to right and to increase from top to bottom. That is, the greater the time interval between the ages compared, the less the correlation between them; and, given equal time intervals, the older the subjects the higher the correlation. (The middle four columns of Table 36 show this in their steady median increase.)

Differences between the variables are striking. Age-to-age correlations for different Rorschach scores range from nil to quite substantial, either throughout the whole age span or during the later four or six years of it. Findings can be presented most easily in four general groups.

1. At least one variable, F+%, shows no inter-age consistency to speak of, even among the oldest ages. It is, of course, the most subjectively scored variable, and by the older ages its range of variation was not great —many subjects were pushing against a ceiling of 100% F+. Whatever the reasons, a high or a low F+% at an earlier age foretold nothing about F+% at later ages in this sample.

Two other scores showed little self-predictiveness through most of the age range: F(C) and CF. They did appear to be showing an increase in correlations toward the end of the age range, but these remained quite modest.

2. For two variables—FM and FC—substantial inter-age consistency is evident from their first occurrence and continues throughout the age

TABLE 35. INTER-AGE CORRELATIONS FOR RORSCHACH VARIABLES
(Values underlined differ significantly from zero at the .05 level)

Score	Age	Age in years					
		4	6	8	10	12	14
R	2	.35	.01	.25	−.04	−.14	.08
	4		.27	.28	.22	−.07	.07
	6			.15	.28	.47	.19
	8				.64	.44	'.36
	10					.55	.52
	12						.65
W%	2	−.04	−.01	−.23	−.37	−.66	−.58
	4		.12	.12	.05	.21	.22
	6			.38	.21	−.01	.10
	8				.69	.61	.54
	10					.70	.65
	12						.78
D%	2	−.03	.18	−.26	−.28	−.63	−.68
	4		−.02	.22	.16	.20	.22
	6			.35	.16	−.04	.08
	8				.73	.48	.46
	10					.61	.61
	12						.71
Dd%	2	−.16	−.15	−.15	−.16	−.24	.08
	4		.02	.00	−.17	−.36	−.15
	6			.31	.12	−.06	−.18
	8				.69	.44	.52
	10					.71	.78
	12						.76
F%	2	.18	.17	.09	−.09	−.18	.04
	4		.45	.59	.10	.04	.39
	6			.54	.34	.26	.13
	8				.58	.31	.60
	10					.68	.71
	12						.71
F+%	2	.01	.45	.06	.12	.33	.00
	4		.16	.01	.12	−.52	−.05
	6			.57	.16	.15	−.07
	8				.27	.43	−.09
	10					.40	.17
	12						.20
M	2	....	....	....	....	....	....
	4		.25	.44	.47	.41	.20
	6			.36	.40	.45	.23
	8				.68	.57	.35
	10					.79	.71
	12						.80
FM	2	.43	.70	.57	.31	.68	.25
	4		.59	.57	.32	.18	.06
	6			.69	.43	.51	.15
	8				.66	.76	.31
	10					.69	.48
	12						.60

TABLE 35. INTER-AGE CORRELATIONS FOR RORSCHACH VARIABLES
(continued)

Score	Age	Age in years 4	6	8	10	12	14
m	2	.60	.12	.44	.00	.00	.00
	4		−.05	.25	.33	.20	.00
	6			.55	−.12	.21	.28
	8				−.14	.36	.21
	10					.34	.50
	12						.68
M+FM+m	2	.77	.77	.70	.57	.77	.50
	4		.50	.58	.50	.35	.45
	6			.65	.55	.56	.55
	8				.77	.73	.54
	10					.75	.64
	12						.75
F(C)*	2	−.28	−.04	−.05	−.41	−.31	−.20
	4		.37	.44	.07	−.23	.24
	6			.03	−.01	−.36	−.09
	8				.29	.01	.13
	10					.45	.43
	12						.39
FC*	2	....	....	....	....	....	....
	4		.82	.06	.73	.65	.84
	6			.15	.45	.71	.72
	8				−.02	.21	.44
	10					.82	.62
	12						.76
CF*	2	.54	−.30	.12	−.25	−.42	−.15
	4		.10	.33	−.02	.11	.09
	6			.44	.20	.43	.37
	8				.20	.12	.15
	10					.35	.43
	12						.51
ΣC*	2	.23	.07	.28	−.12	−.17	.83
	4		.45	.48	.19	.60	.49
	6			.16	.19	.51	.38
	8				.17	.06	.32
	10					.48	.40
	12						.60
A%	2	.14	−.07	.46	−.65	−.78	−.69
	4		.44	.05	.03	−.22	−.40
	6			.39	.25	.03	−.42
	8				.40	.21	.10
	10					.53	.57
	12						.56
P	2	.27	.15	.04	.22	−.04	.00
	4		.45	.30	−.09	−.23	−.26
	6			.48	.19	.08	.08
	8				.26	.25	−.04
	10					.66	.68
	12						.69

* Includes both primary and secondary ("additional," "tendency") occurrences.
.... No child gave M or FC responses at 2 years.

range. M shows moderate but significant early inter-age correlations, which increase steadily with increasing age to reach the highest levels of stability of any of the variables. Interestingly, a score summing across all varieties of movement—M+FM+m—shows the highest, most consistent correlations for the entire age span, and its stability is already fully apparent at 2 years. This seems important not only because the added-together scores have such predictability but because it shows how addable the three scores are. That

TABLE 36. MEAN INTER-AGE CORRELATIONS FOR SELECTED AGE RANGES
(from Table 35)

| Variable | *Ages grouped* | | | | | |
	4-14	*2-8*	*4-10*	*6-12*	*8-14*	*10-14*
Number of ages paired	15	6	6	6	6	3
Mean age interval in years	4.7	3.3	3.3	3.3	3.3	2.7
R	.35	.22	.32	.44	.53	.58
W%	.40	.06	.28	.47	.67	.71
D%	.36	.08	.31	.41	.61	.65
Dd%	.28	−.02	.19	.41	.67	.75
F%	.45	.35	.45	.47	.61	.70
F+%	.22	.23	.23	.34	.24	.26
M	.50	....	.44	.56	.67	.77
FM	.49	.60	.56	.64	.60	.60
m	.26	.34	.15	.22	.35	.52
M+FM+m	.61	.67	.60	.68	.70	.72
F(C)	.15	.09	.21	.07	.29	.42
FC	.59	....	.43	.45	.53	.74
CF	.26	.22	.21	.30	.30	.43
ΣC	.38	.29	.28	.27	.35	.50
A%	.18	.25	.27	.31	.41	.55
P	.26	.29	.27	.34	.46	.68
Median r	.36	.24	.28	.41	.53	.62

Note. Means computed through Fisher's z'.

is, in some important way the three scores are interrelated, to the point that they are somewhat interchangeable—in that early high scores on any of them (at ages when FM is more common) predict high later scores on any of them (at ages when M is more common). All evidently share in some common pool of meaning.

It is, of course, gratifying that the variables with the earliest emergence of stability are those at the heart of the Rorschach: movement and FC.

3. Five or six scores show essentially zero inter-age correlations during the earlier years; then quite abruptly they jump to sizeable values. R, Dd%, and F% all show a striking shift between 6 and 8 years, P and m show shifts between 8 and 10 years. Correlations for ΣC are much more irregular, but may be increasing around 10 years.

These scores, along with the three in the next group, suggest a stabilizing of certain functions shortly before or shortly after age 8. The child goes from unpredictability of response to a quite consistent tendency to use the particular variables much or little. This occurs at a time when most children have moved from Piaget's stage of intuitive intelligence to his stage of concrete intellectual operations. And most of the scores can be considered as reflecting essentially cognitive activity: R, W%, D%, Dd%, F%, A%, and P.

4. The final group of three variables—W%, D%, and A%—resembles the preceding group in shifting from mostly negligible consistency at 4 and 6 years to sizeable consistency at 8 or 10 years and thereafter. It differs in that scores at the very earliest ages and the latest ages are not just unrelated—they are *negatively* related, significantly and substantially so. This does not mean that the children in general changed in amount of W% or A% from 2 to 14 years; rather, those children who gave low A% at 2 years tended to give high A% from age 10, and vice versa.

The source of this intriguing reversal of children's scoring statuses is probably not the dynamic or compensatory one that may first spring to mind—not a "got-it-out-of-their-systems" vs. "seeking-restitution" formulation. If one looks over a batch of 2-year-olds' records, one sees that animals are a good kind of response for a 2-year-old to give, as compared with the very miscellaneous assortment of other responses given at that age (windows, trees, meat balls, paint, sidewalks, etc.). It is the more mature, brighter 2-year-olds who have high A%. By 10 years, high A% is no longer an asset; it is given by the less advanced children. The negative inter-age correlation, then, is via a third variable. W% and its complement, D%, appear to follow a similar pattern. Two-year-olds' W responses tend to be diffuse and blob-like, not the sign of intellectual strength that they tend to have become by age 12 or 14. The correlations would indicate that A%, W%, and D% must actually have a different interpretive significance at the earliest and the later ages.

To generalize from the above four groups: for the entire group of 16 Rorschach scores, regardless of whether their early inter-age correlations were high or low or negative, by age 8 or 10 and thereafter all but three scores reached mean inter-age correlations of at least .50. And more than half reached mean correlations in the .60s and .70s.

Constancy of content

The records of 29 of the preceding subjects were inspected to determine the extent to which responses of essentially identical content recurred in particular children's series. (The identity considered was not just of the content scoring category, such as Animal or Human, but involved repetition of the specific concept, such as alligators or butlers.) A concept was counted as being used consistently if a substantially identical content was produced for any given card for a minimum of four consecutive age periods.

Both boys and girls were found to produce consistently recurring responses on a mean of 3.9* cards during the 2- to 10-year-old age span. Most of the repeating responses were found to start at 5 years or later.

As might be expected, many of the responses repeated year after year were popular responses. Of all the repeated responses tabulated, 74 per cent were P. (Thus even if artificial "age series" were assembled randomly, with different children representing each age, a moderate "mean consistency" score might appear, produced by all the bats on V, bears on VIII, and so forth.) The cards producing the most consistent responses were, predictably, V, VIII, and III.

Though many children's repeated responses were unelaborated populars, given year after year with no apparent recognition of this sameness, some of the repeated responses were original responses of considerable specificity. These often had apparent personal significance to the subject, and he was more likely to remember them from year to year. (Example: Card IX, ∨ "A candy tree near a candy fudge pool, with all fudge squirting up.")

Following are two sets of examples, each presenting all the responses of one child to a single card at a succession of ages.

Girl A. L., responses to Card VII:

Age   3½   Looks like a girl; two girls. (Tiers 1 + 2).

Age   4   Two deers on two rocks. Nothing else.

Age   5   That looks like two bunnies hopping on two stones.

Age   6   These look like two funny bunnies.

Age   7   Looks like two rabbits talking together. They're going like this. (Demonstrates turning away, then twisting head back over shoulder.) And they're turning their heads.

---

* Constancies were tabulated by cards and only one per card was tabulated, even when more than one occurred. Three girls and three boys repeated more than one concept on particular cards.

Age 8   Now this looks like two rabbits, bending around looking at each other. All I can get out of it. (Bottom part is part of the rabbits, but "it comes off.")

Age 9   Oh I know—this looks like two bunny rabbits and they're turning around looking at each other.

      ∨Oh yuh, here, two girls looking at each other. (Faces are inside profile of top tier.) Other arm and other leg, don't know where it is.

Age 10   Oh—this looks like two bunnies looking over backward to see each other.

      ∨Oh, and this one—you know those dancers with their hair up? —this one looks like they're dancing and turning to see each other. Skirts out here.

Boy P.S., responses to Card II:

Age 3   That looks like an elephant. Oh dis (opposite side) is an elephant too.

Age 4   Red and black. (Look like?)
      Elephant. Baby elephant and mamma elephant in circus.

Age 5   Two elephants.
      Two sea lions (top reds).

Age 6   (Laughs) Oh, this looks like some of those tunnels with a steeple up here (S between blacks, with "hands" detail).
      This looks like a mountain right here. (Idea?) Just looks sort of like a mountain (side blacks).
      Oh, I know something—two elephants.
      Fireman's hat (top reds). (Idea?) Looks like them.

Age 7   (Sighs) People dancing. Heads and hair sticking up.
      Elephant ears. (All side blacks are ears; head is inner white.)
      Looks like seals (top red).

Age 8   Two elephants.
      Two butterflies (top reds; no color elicited).
      One butterfly (bottom red). (Idea?) Looks like a swallowtail.
      They're maple seeds (top red; evidently a correction of his first concept, butterflies, not an alternative idea).

Age 9   This looks like two elephants' heads, trunks going up. (?) Holding trunk together.

This looks like a butterfly. I think that's the same thing I said last year (lower red). (Idea?) Wings around here and some butterflies have that tail.

Age 10 \/Looks like a head of a scotty dog, without this red stuff (all black areas). Kind of bushy eyes there, kind of shape of his head. Two dogs.

(Sighs and comments as he sees next card, "Wish I could find something different from last year.")

How much children's recollections of their responses contributed to the stability of scores reported in the preceding section on correlation is not possible to say. At the earliest ages there appears to be little awareness of having given the same concept at an earlier age or even having seen the same card before. Even at the older ages, many subjects go on giving the same response without comments implying recognition. But by the older ages it appears that most subjects recall at least a few earlier responses ("There's my soldering iron," "Still looks like a coyote skin").

That is not to say, though, that children tried to remember responses so that their scores would not change. On the contrary: though some children had a few pet responses they enjoyed looking for, many more reported that they were trying to give new and different responses. Boys more often complained about, and girls more often apologized for, the persistence of responses. Experientially, the sameness did not look like something children were trying for.

Further, it often happened that while the same content was maintained for many years, determinant scoring changed from year to year, movement or color appearing or dropping out at different ages. The following sequence illustrates some of the variations in one boy's scoring on Card II.

Age 5	W₂ F+ A P	Two elephants. (?) There and there. (Else?) The red pieces. (Look like?)
	D C blood	(Long, long regard) Blood.
Age 7	W₃ FM A P	It looks like two bears fighting and some
	D m nat	and some and some water splashing (all red parts). (Water?) It looks as if it's water.
Age 8	W₃ FM A P	Two bears fighting and bleeding; fighting for
	CF	fish (center "hands" detail). (?) Because it's red there.
Age 9	W₂ FM A P	Looks like two bears slapping their hands together like this (demonstrates). And kicking their feet together.

Age 10 W₂ FM A (P) Looks like two bears crashing their heads to-
        CF   gether. Heads jumping off in a bloody mass.
        m   And crashing their feet together in a bloody
                  mass.

It has struck us that subjects who have relatively high persistence of responses from year to year tend to fall into two groups. Some subjects repeat popular or unenlivened responses from age to age seemingly automatically, expressing little of a unique, original individuality. One feels that the blots somehow force these responses on them and they can do little but respond with what is "given" to them. The other group of consistent responders gives the impression of imposing their own rather strong ideas upon the blots. Their repeated responses tend to be original and personally meaningful. These subjects, especially by the time they reach adolescence, seem to be expressing a solid core of individuality which does not change markedly in its expression from age to age.

Whatever the "practice effect" may be on the Rorschach, it is not a simple one. Unlike ability tests, where once one learns an answer or solves a problem he can apply the solution from then on, the Rorschach invites (or at least permits) a fresh solution to the task on each testing. Subjects differ considerably in their willingness and their ability to accept this invitation. All, to some degree, show a persistence in characteristic ways of approaching and solving the Rorschach tasks.

Developmental Trends

Developmental trends on the Rorschach, we suggest, can be divided into two kinds: overall, general trends, in which scores show a more or less steady increase or decrease from age 2 to age 10; and age-specific trends, in which scores go up and down (and other qualities appear and disappear) as children pass through successive "stages" of growth. The latter trends can be viewed as superimposed on the former, rather than alternative to them; for example, M in general increases over the age span but it especially increases at certain ages and fails to increase or slightly decreases at others.

Though differing in detail, researchers who have worked with children's Rorschachs quite generally agree concerning trends of the first sort, the overall trends.* The more specific age trends, such as those we describe

---

* As this book goes to press, a study has appeared by Levitt & Truumaa (52), which presents composite trends for 15 Rorschach scores, derived from means reported in 15 published studies. It gives a most comprehensive picture of general trends from 5 to 16 years. Since the trends were determined by regression analysis, all are presented as straight lines or smooth curves, and no age-specific changes were considered.

in this book, are more controversial. The question is raised whether they represent genuine age changes or largely chance fluctuations in scoring of the samples at the different ages. Our longitudinal data offer the chance of testing this in a sample independent (after age 5) of our cross-sectional sample.

Most basically, we view the age-to-age changes not so much as mean changes of groups of children but as ways in which individual children are likely to vary around *their own* standards. We would expect a child at an "outgoing age," for example, to be likely to be more outgoing than he usually is, but that might well not be very extraverted. We have used this individual model in analyzing age-specific trends in our longitudinal sample.

For each child's age series, for each Rorschach variable, we partitioned his scoring into two parts: his "usual" behavior (including overall trends) and his variations from his own standard. The first was determined simply by regression analysis. In effect, for each subject we plotted his scores for a particular variable by age and then found the straight line that gave the best fit for the whole array of scores.* Figure 8, as an example, depicts one boy's scores for R, plotted by age. The straight line passing through the array of his nine R scores is one which gives the best fit (the smallest mean of squared deviations), and so serves to define his "usual" or "expected" R.

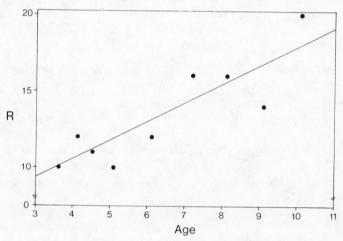

FIG. 8. Number of Responses by Age for One Boy, and His Best-Fit Line for R.

---

* The assumption of a straight line seemed best, for the small number of values each child had for each variable—6 to 11. Levitt & Truumaa (52) found straight lines to provide the best fit to the *mean* values for most of the variables they tested for ages 5 to 16, and their remaining curves appear approximately straight over their 5- to 10-year-old segments.

Two-year-olds produced so many maverick scores, deviant from the rest of the child's own series, that this analysis was done only for ages 3 to 10. The analysis gave for each child two scores for each Rorschach variable: one, beta, describing the slope of his line (how much the variable changed each year); the other, alpha, relating to its overall level. In Figure 8, the boy's regression line increases each year by 1.2 (his beta score for R).

The second, age-specific portion of each child's scoring was determined as the deviation of his actual scores at particular ages from his "expected" scores at those ages, as determined by the regression line. The alpha and beta values were used to predict his score for each age, and this predicted score was subtracted from his obtained score. In Figure 8, the deviations are represented by the vertical distance of each plotted point from the regression line. (Note that this boy gave equal numbers of responses at 7 and 8 years, but the 8-year-old value is the less deviant because his overall trend is one of increasing R.)

If it is true that fluctuations around the general, overall trend are just scatter, due simply to chance, then for all the children who have positive deviations at 7 years, say, there should be an equal number who have negative deviations. Only if there are valid age-specific trends should the mean deviations by age differ from zero.

Following are results for this two-part analysis.

Overall trends

Although there is general agreement about the usual overall trends of the different Rorschach scoring variables, that does not mean that these are well matched by *individual* overall trends in those same variables. Table 37 presents some findings for the slopes of the 33 subjects' regression lines for 16 Rorschach variables. Ten of the variables show enough child-to-child similarity to have mean slopes that differ significantly from zero. That is, on the average the children showed a significant overall increase in R, F+%, P, all movement scores, F(C), and FC, and an overall decrease in F%. Though the values for mean change per year appear small, when they are projected to the full age span (in the last column of Table 37) many appear more substantial. These values correspond to the means of what, in Figure 8, would be the difference between the height of the regression line at age 3 and its height at age 10. That boy gained 8.5 R from 3 to 10. The average series showed a gain of about 5 R between 3 and 10, a gain of 27 points in F+%, a loss of nearly 30 points in F%, and so forth.

These significant values are all much as would be expected, except that W% does not decrease nor D% increase consistently enough to show a significant trend. What seems more interesting is the very wide range of individual children's values for each Rorschach variable—this despite the fact that each child's value is itself based on six to eleven observations of the variable and so has considerable stability. For all but two variables, individual children's trends range from clearly positive to clearly negative, regardless of whether the *average* trend is significantly positive or negative.

TABLE 37. BETA COEFFICIENTS OF SLOPE (MEAN CHANGE PER YEAR)
FOR RORSCHACH VARIABLES IN 33 LONGITUDINAL SERIES
Range, Mean Score, SD, and Cumulated Change, 3-10 Years

Variable	Range Low – High	Mean	SD	Change, 3-10 years
R	−2.1 – 4.1	.7**	1.3	4.8
W%	−8.5 – 10.7	−.5	5.0	
D%	−9.5 – 7.7	.1	4.3	
Dd%	−3.7 – 9.0	.4	2.7	
F%	−13.0 – 6.4	−4.1**	4.1	−28.8
F+%	.1 – 8.7	3.8**	2.1	26.8
M	.0 – 1.3	.3**	.3	2.2
FM	−.7 – 1.7	.4**	.5	3.0
m	−.5 – .4	.1**	.2	.8
M+FM+m	−.5 – 2.5	.8**	.7	5.8
F(C)	−.4 – .5	.1*	.2	.6
FC	−.3 – .3	.1*	.1	.5
CF	−.3 – .5	.1	.2	
ΣC	−.5 – .5	.0	.3	
A%	−5.6 – 9.5	1.1	3.6	
P	−.6 – 1.6	.6**	.5	4.0

• Differs significantly from zero, by t-test, at .05 level.
•• Differs significantly from zero, by t-test, at .01 level.

For example, though the general trend was clearly to increasing R, some children decreased overall in R—one by over 14 R between 3 and 10 years. Similarly, some children gained overall in F%, and so forth. Only for F+% and M did no child decrease in his overall trend.

What children are like whose overall trends are consistently "against the rule" on particular variables is an interesting area for future study.

Age-specific trends

For the 16 Rorschach variables, the mean deviations were computed for each age and the differences among the means tested by one-way analysis of variance.* The seven variables that showed more variation than

---

* Since only two children had observations at all 11 ages, a repeated-measures design could not be used and so the variates at each age were treated as independent observations. This seems legitimate because inter-age correlation among scores of individual subjects was removed when their regression values were subtracted (if there are no age-specific trends). If the deviation scores are not, in effect, independent, the test used is presumably too conservative and some real age-specific variation may have been missed.

could be accounted for by chance are listed in Table 38. The variation is of individual age group differences entirely independent of general age trends—quite a stringent test.

The variables that showed significant variation from straightline developmental trends are movement and color, number of responses, form accuracy, and popularity. In the case of R, there is some suggestion that the observed values might have been better fitted by curves than by straight lines; this is not the case with the other variables. The significant variation in the determinant scores was not produced by their correlation with R; apparently this correlation was eliminated when the overall developmental

TABLE 38. MEANS OF DEVIATIONS FROM INDIVIDUAL SUBJECTS'
REGRESSION LINES FOR VARIABLES WITH SIGNIFICANT INTER-AGE VARIATION

Age group	R	F+%	M	M+FM+m	CF	ΣC	P
3	−.7	−8.4	.1	−.2	.1	.2	−.5
3½	.9	7.4	−.1	−.5	.1	.1	.1
4	−1.2	−3.3	−.2	.0	−.4	−.5	−.2
4½	−.4	3.2	−.2	−.5	.1	.0	.3
5	.5	−1.5	.1	.3	−.1	−.4	−.3
5½	1.8	1.0	−.1	−.6	.2	.6	−.1
6	1.1	−2.9	.0	.4	.5	.4	.1
7	1.9	2.1	.6	1.0	−.1	−.1	.4
8	−.7	1.8	−.1	−.3	−.2	−.1	.3
9	.6	1.6	−.3	−.2	−.1	−.2	.1
10	−.8	−2.9	.0	−.4ʹ	.1	.1	−.5
$F_{10,257}$	2.18	3.32	2.35	1.86	1.97	2.06	2.12

trends were partialled out. (P shows a correlation of .40 between its mean deviation scores and those of R—not significant if N is taken as 11, but suggestive of a possible association.)

By variables: R suggests its overall curvilinearity by a succession of high values at 5½, 6, and 7 years, with negative values earlier and later. Ages 5½ and 7 appear as inflection points in development of R. Form accuracy appears to develop by a series of spurts, most noticeable at 3½, 4½, and 7, with periods of little growth at 3, 4, 6, and 10. (All but one of the negative F+% values are exceeded by the positive mean slope of F+%, so children mostly do not "go backwards" but just advance very little in F+% at those ages.) In P, the only moderate gain is at 7 years, the only moderate low points at 3 and 10, all ages that show corresponding highs and lows in R.

In movement—both M alone and M+FM+m—it is clear that the one age most deviant from straightline growth is age 7, when much movement is produced. In the color scores—CF and ΣC—a similar spurt occurs at 5½ or 6. Other high or low points are much less striking.

By ages: Since characteristic values for the different variables of Table 38 differ in scale, it is difficult to read it by ages (rows) rather than by variables (columns). Therefore, the ages at which the three highest and three lowest mean deviations occurred for each variable were determined. These are listed by age in Table 39.

TABLE 39. AGES AT WHICH RORSCHACH VARIABLES ARE RANKED
HIGH OR LOW
(Highest three and lowest three ages for each variable, from Table 38)

Age	Low	High
3	F+%, P	M, ΣC
3½	M+FM+m	F+%
4	R, F+%, M, CF, ΣC	
4½	M, M+FM+m	F+%, P
5	ΣC, P	M, M+FM+m
5½	M+FM+m	R, CF, ΣC
6	F+%	R, M+FM+m, CF, ΣC
7		R, F+%, M, M+FM+m, P
8	CF	P
9	M, ΣC	
10	R, F+%, P	

Several of the ages show constellations that deserve mention. The children in this sample proved unexpectedly unproductive at age 4, not only of total responses but of movement and color. The sequence from 5 to 7 seems important and it clearly parallels our earlier cross-sectional findings (as well as our ideas about characteristic behavioral changes). Five years is relatively high in movement and low in color. Five-and-a-half reverses this with increased color and lowered movement. At 6, both movement and color are higher than the overall trend would predict. And at 7, growth in movement is at its peak while color is unexceptional. (Only this moderate color at 7 contradicts our earlier findings.) Nine years suggests a slowing of development of more emotional characteristics, while 10 years suggests a slowing of development of more cognitive ones, R, F+%, and P.

It is difficult to compare these longitudinal trends systematically with those described for the cross-sectional sample, since the latter mixes evaluations of overall trends with age-specific ones (and so, for example, has many ages described as "the highest age to date for M," including ages whose gain is less than the average, overall trend for **M**). Subjectively, the main surprise we found was age 4, which appeared livelier in the cross-sectional analysis, more restricted in the longitudinal one. The middle four ages—5, 5½, 6, and 7— strike us as quite confirming of our cross-sectional findings.

CHAPTER TWENTY-FOUR

Socio-Economic Status
and Rorschach Scores

The distributions of socio-economic status (SES) and intelligence for our main sample are clearly not representative of the U. S. population as a whole, as Tables 2 and 3 show. This has raised questions concerning the extent to which SES and intelligence affect Rorschach scores and what standards to use in evaluating children from other groups.

We can offer some answers to these questions by comparing Rorschach scores in three additional samples. Other authors have, of course, provided findings from other samples, but these three allow the most useful comparisons because their records were administered and scored in the same way as were those in our main sample.*

Table 40 presents the distributions of SES levels for the three samples, compared with our main sample, along with the mean for all four groups. The sample designated Suburban I consists of 313 children from a school in an eastern Connecticut residential suburb of New York City. The Suburban II sample consists of 350 children from two schools in a residential and manufacturing town adjacent to New Haven. The Inner-city sample consists of 219 children, all black, from a New Haven school in a black, working-class neighborhood. The SES distributions for the four samples— our main sample, Suburban I, Suburban II, and Inner-city—are distinctly different, with modal fathers' occupations being professional, managerial, skilled trades and retail business, and slightly skilled, respectively. Mean IQ levels for the groups differ correspondingly: 116 for our main sample, 110 for Suburban I, 105 for Suburban II, and 93 for Inner-city.†

---

* For all three samples, all the records were obtained and scored by L.B.A.

† IQ values for our main sample are from the appropriate section of Table 3. All subjects in the Suburban I sample were tested individually on the WISC at the time of their first Rorschach testing. IQ for the Suburban II sample is estimated from a subsample of 50 children, distributed equally over ages 6 to 10, tested on the WISC. For the Inner-city sample, only 10-year-olds were tested, individually, on the Slosson Intelligence Test.

Both the Suburban I and Suburban II samples were mixed cross-sectional-longitudinal samples, in which most of the children were tested on three occasions, starting at different ages. Children in the Inner-city school were tested only once. Numbers of subjects at each age in each sample are presented in the top rows of Table 41.

Table 41 presents for each sample mean scores for each Rorschach variable at each age. In addition, overall means are presented for each

TABLE 40. FATHERS' OCCUPATIONS FOR CHILDREN AGED 5 TO 10 YEARS IN FOUR SAMPLES (Percentage at each level)

Classification	Main sample	Sub-urban I	Sub-urban II	Inner-city	Mean
I. Professional	42	15	5	1	16
II. Semi-professional, managerial	25	51	22	4	25
III. Clerical, skilled trades, retail business	22	24	40	16	25
IV. Farmers	0	0	3	0	1
V. Semi-skilled, minor clerical, minor business	10	8	10	17	11
VI. Slightly skilled	1	1	16	54	18
VII. Day Laborers	0	1	5	8	4
Total, levels I-II	67	66	27	5	41
Total, levels III-VII	33	34	73	95	59

Note.—Unclassified cases prorated through remainder of categories.

sample (across all ages) and for each age (across all samples). Both kinds of overall means were computed by averaging the separate means, rather than pooling all subjects and striking the overall average. (The latter procedure would have produced imbalances due to groups of unequal size; for example, the Suburban I subjects would be overly weighted in the overall means for age 7 and the 7-year-olds would be overly weighted in the overall means for Suburban I subjects.)

Overall growth trends in the groups are, in general, similar and resemble the overall trends described in the preceding chapter, though some gradients are notably steeper or shallower. For example, the Inner-city sample's F+% starts lower but goes up more sharply with age than does F+% of any other group; all three new samples' F(C) growth, on the other hand, is essentially nil. Still, the general trends mostly match earlier findings well.

The more specific age-to-age trends described in the main portion of this book are not clearly in evidence here. Some similarities can be discerned in the new samples, but generally the overall means by age advance

TABLE 41. NUMBERS OF SUBJECTS AND MEAN RORSCHACH SCORES
FOR SAMPLES AT FOUR SOCIO-ECONOMIC LEVELS

Variable	Group	Age in years							Ages com-bined
		5	5½	6	7	8	9	10	
N	Main sample	50	50	50	50	50	50	50	350
	Suburban I	18	58	66	84	42	23	22	313
	Suburban II	50	50	50	50	50	50	50	350
	Inner-city	30	19	50	40	25	33	22	219
	Total	148	177	216	224	167	156	142	1230
R	Main sample	13.9	13.6	15.8	18.3	15.9	18.6	16.3	16.1
	Suburban I	10.7	11.3	12.8	13.7	14.0	12.9	14.8	12.9
	Suburban II	10.8	10.0	13.1	11.0	12.8	11.9	13.5	11.9
	Inner-city	11.0	10.0	10.0	9.4	8.8	10.0	10.0	9.9
	Mean	11.6	11.2	12.9	13.1	12.9	13.4	13.7	12.7
Refusals	Main sample	.6	.7	.5	.3	.5	.5	.6	.5
	Suburban I	1.3	.7	.7	.5	.5	.6	.7	.7
	Suburban II	1.2	1.1	.6	1.0	.4	.6	.5	.8
	Inner-city	1.2	1.6	1.4	1.5	2.1	1.4	1.5	1.5
	Mean	1.1	1.0	.8	.8	.9	.8	.8	.9
W%	Main sample	58	55	51	51	55	42	52	52
	Suburban I	66	73	63	61	60	64	63	64
	Suburban II	66	68	70	67	58	62	58	64
	Inner-city	74	75	71	75	71	67	78	73
	Mean	66	68	64	64	61	59	63	63
D%	Main sample	34	33	34	41	37	48	40	38
	Suburban I	30	25	31	32	35	31	31	31
	Suburban II	30	29	25	28	37	33	36	31
	Inner-city	25	25	25	25	26	30	21	25
	Mean	30	28	29	32	34	36	32	31
Dd%	Main sample	8	12	15	8	7	9	8	10
	Suburban I	4	2	6	7	5	5	6	5
	Suburban II	4	3	5	5	5	5	6	5
	Inner-city	1	0	4	0	3	3	1	2
	Mean	4	4	8	4	5	5	5	6
F%	Main sample	70	62	60	52	58	67	63	62
	Suburban I	75	73	65	67	69	74	72	71
	Suburban II	81	74	73	73	68	70	72	73
	Inner-city	84	91	86	79	81	76	78	82
	Mean	78	75	71	68	69	72	71	72
F+%	Main sample	78	84	81	82	87	84	89	84
	Suburban I	78	83	87	89	89	92	92	87
	Suburban II	75	86	86	92	87	92	94	88
	Inner-city	57	63	78	86	87	90	91	79
	Mean	72	79	83	87	88	90	92	85
M	Main sample	.6	.4	1.0	1.4	1.3	1.4	1.7	1.1
	Suburban I	.7	.6	1.0	1.1	1.0	1.1	1.0	.9
	Suburban II	.3	.6	.4	.7	1.1	1.4	1.9	.9
	Inner-city	.7	.3	.4	.5	.4	.6	.7	.5
	Mean	.6	.5	.7	.9	1.0	1.1	1.3	.9
FM	Main sample	1.1	1.3	1.6	1.9	1.5	1.6	1.7	1.5
	Suburban I	1.0	1.0	1.7	1.7	1.8	.9	1.8	1.4
	Suburban II	.6	.6	1.0	1.0	1.8	1.3	1.7	1.1
	Inner-city	.4	.1	.4	.5	.6	1.0	.7	.5
	Mean	.8	.8	1.2	1.3	1.4	1.2	1.5	1.1

TABLE 41.   NUMBERS OF SUBJECTS AND MEAN RORSCHACH SCORES
FOR SAMPLES AT FOUR SOCIO-ECONOMIC LEVELS *(continued)*

					Age in years				Ages com-bined
Variable	Group	5	5½	6	7	8	9	10	
m	Main sample	.2	.5	.4	.8	.4	.5	.4	.5
	Suburban I	.2	.4	.7	.5	.5	.4	.2	.4
	Suburban II	.3	.2	.1	.7	.4	.4	.4	.3
	Inner-city	.0	.1	.2	.1	.2	.1	.2	.1
	Mean	.2	.3	.4	.5	.4	.4	.3	.4
F(C)	Main sample	.4	.6	.7	1.1	.9	.8	.6	.7
	Suburban I	.1	.1	.1	.2	.1	.1	.2	.1
	Suburban II	.3	.3	.2	.1	.3	.2	.1	.2
	Inner-city	.0	.0	.1	.1	.1	.1	.0	.1
	Mean	.2	.3	.3	.4	.4	.3	.2	.3
FC	Main sample	.2	.2	.4	.7	.5	.7	.5	.5
	Suburban I	.1	.3	.1	.1	.1	.1	.1	.1
	Suburban II	.0	.0	.1	.1	.1	.2	.2	.1
	Inner-city	.0	.1	.0	.0	.0	.0	.1	.0
	Mean	.1	.2	.2	.2	.2	.3	.2	.2
CF	Main sample	1.2	1.4	1.5	1.3	.9	.7	.8	1.1
	Suburban I	.3	.6	.6	.6	.3	.3	.4	.5
	Suburban II	.4	.7	.7	.6	.5	.5	.3	.5
	Inner-city	.1	.2	.2	.6	.6	.5	.6	.4
	Mean	.5	.7	.8	.8	.6	.5	.5	.6
C	Main sample	.2	.5	.3	.8	.4	.7	.3	.5
	Suburban I	.0	.2	.1	.2	.2	.3	.1	.2
	Suburban II	.0	.2	.1	.2	.3	.1	.2	.1
	Inner-city	.3	.2	.0	.1	.0	.0	.0	.1
	Mean	.1	.3	.1	.3	.2	.3	.2	.2
ΣC	Main sample	1.6	2.3	2.2	2.9	1.8	2.1	1.5	2.1
	Suburban I	.4	.7	.9	.9	.6	.8	.5	.7
	Suburban II	.8	1.0	1.0	.8	.9	.9	.6	.8
	Inner-city	.5	.5	.2	.1	.6	.4	.3	.4
	Mean	.8	1.1	1.1	1.2	1.0	1.1	.7	1.0
A%	Main sample	44	41	48	42	45	48	49	45
	Suburban I	59	52	54	55	57	63	67	58
	Suburban II	47	53	52	57	53	55	56	53
	Inner-city	45	58	61	60	71	65	69	61
	Mean	49	51	54	54	57	58	60	54
H%	Main sample	9	11	11	14	17	16	16	13
	Suburban I	13	12	14	15	17	16	16	15
	Suburban II	18	14	16	15	17	20	20	17
	Inner-city	22	13	11	10	5	7	12	11
	Mean	16	13	13	14	14	15	16	14
Content cate-gories	Main sample	4.7	4.9	4.8	5.2	4.7	5.2	4.8	4.9
	Suburban I	3.8	3.7	3.9	4.2	4.4	3.8	3.5	3.9
	Suburban II	4.1	3.7	2.1	3.4	4.5	3.8	4.2	3.7
	Inner-city	3.0	3.6	3.0	3.2	2.6	3.5	3.0	3.1
	Mean	3.9	4.0	3.5	4.0	4.1	4.1	3.9	3.9
P%	Main sample	22	25	23	27	24	22	25	24
	Suburban I	31	32	39	34	36	40	40	36
	Suburban II	23	31	33	38	36	38	40	34
	Inner-city	22	26	31	33	37	40	40	33
	Mean	25	29	32	33	33	35	36	32

much more smoothly than do those of the main sample alone. Since our longitudinal sample confirmed some of the age-specific trends from our cross-sectional sample, we do not view them as essentially sampling fluctuations. Instead, it seems likely that two factors are producing the smoother composite results. First, it has seemed to us that the age characteristics we have described have generally been most apparent in the brightest, most advanced children. Superiority seems to affect the expression of age characteristics more by intensifying them than by accelerating them. The greatest variations certainly appear in the group with the fullest Rorschach productivity. Some timing differences do seem to occur too, and these would make up the second factor tending to obscure specific age-to-age changes. If corresponding developmental peaks tend to occur six or eight months later in one sample than another, then averaging by chronological age will produce a gentle curve without peaks. The greater the heterogeneity and "representativeness" of a sample, the less it can reveal specific developmental trends.

The findings for SES are surprisingly regular: for 17 of the 19 Rorschach variables considered, overall mean scores increase or decrease directly with SES. Means for the following variables show consistent decrease from the main sample to the Inner-city sample: R, D%, Dd%, M, FM, m, F(C), FC, CF, C, ΣC, and number of different content categories. Consistent increases in mean score from the main sample to the Inner-city sample occur in number of refusals, W%, F%, and A%.

It might be expected that Inner-city would show the greatest difference from the other samples, since the gap between it and Suburban II is greater for mean IQ and modal SES than the gaps between Suburban II and Suburban I or Suburban I and the main sample, and also since the group differs racially as well as socio-economically. Such is not the case. The difference between overall mean scores for adjacent samples in Table 41 is greatest between the main sample and Suburban I for 12 variables, greatest between Suburban II and Inner-city for just 6 variables (refusals, F+%, M, FM, m, and H%). Suburban I and Suburban II are consistently similar.

Since the progression from the main sample to Inner-city is so clearly stepwise, with little or no break between Suburban II and Inner-city, there is certainly no indication that race affects Rorschach scores over and above SES effects. The puzzle is rather to explain why our main sample differs from the remaining groups.

The dimension along which the groups have been classified has been labelled socio-economic status, but it is an amalgam of SES and intelligence—both of which are themselves complex composites. Nearly all the children in the main sample had attended a nursery school (which was how we had obtained most of them in the first place). Undoubtedly fewer had done so in the other samples. This is not cited as showing possible beneficial effects of nursery school attendance, but as an indicator of the parents' concern with fostering development. We would guess that they also talked more with their children, paid more deliberate attention to intellectual growth, and generally encouraged open expression of ideas. The children showed it.

An additional factor is situational, hard to evaluate but not negligible in contributing to the differences between the groups. Many of the children in our main research sample knew the examiners, from having come to the Institute on other occasions for other activities which they had enjoyed. They seemed to feel comfortable and to be open with us. Children in Suburban I and II were tested in school settings, with reasonable testing conditions. The examiner, at first a stranger to them, got to be known by them by her second or third year's visit. The children in Inner-city were tested in often noisy, makeshift corners of the school building. Since each child was tested just once, the examiner was always a stranger to them, a white stranger whose own SES was most different from theirs. The fullness of the main sample's response and the increasing relative restriction of the Inner-city children's response may partly reflect differences in their experiencing of the testing situation.

Table 41 should provide examiners with a starting point for knowing how to modify their expectations for a child's Rorschach performance, when the child's background differs from that of the children this book is mostly based upon.

CHAPTER TWENTY-FIVE

The Rorschach and Evaluation

This book, primarily about developmental trends, is intended to provide a background for evaluation, to help with the first steps in sizing up records. We can report two studies that may help with next steps in some instances. One study (2) contrasts Rorschach records of children of normal and disturbed emotional functioning. The other (13) compares early Rorschachs of children who later become good and poor readers.

Rorschach and Emotional Disturbance

We have spent a whole book (several, in fact) in pointing out that many kinds of Rorschach responses considered to be indicators of disturbance or pathology in the adult occur benignly or even normatively in children and adolescents. Even after the preschool period, when it seems least surprising to encounter floridly non-adult thinking, children's records show important qualitative and quantitative differences from those of adults.

If so many of the usual Rorschach indicators of disturbance lose their significance in children, how may children's records be evaluated? To quite a large extent, we think, by adjusting our standards. Most, though not all, of the Rorschach variables seem to have the same essential significance when given by children as when given by adults—a movement response, for example, is an instance of fantasy activity at whatever age it is given. What changes is our judgment of what could constitute *a lot, too much, too little* of one kind of response. Hence the need for age norms.

In our first edition of this book, we also proposed a list of 13 response characteristics that appeared likely candidates for "danger signals": indicators of disturbed functioning in children. Some were quantitative items, others qualitative, and they were presented narratively in sometimes rather loose formulations.

A portion of this sign list was evaluated by Elkins (20) in a study which compared children who had been referred to a child guidance clinic with school children described by their teachers as well adjusted. Forty normal 8-, 9-, and 10-year-olds were individually matched for age, sex, and intelligence with records from the files of the clinic. Their Rorschach records were compared on a checklist derived from our own. Elkins' revised list dropped four of the original 13 items on the grounds that they required subjective judgments (color naming, contamination or confabulation, positional responses, and bizarre responses or actions). Three items were modified explicitly, mainly by splitting up items having several parts to them. And several others were altered implicitly by use of the Beck system for administration and initial scoring of the records. (Though Elkins rescored the records for area and shading, some effects evidently remain for the items involving W%, which runs much lower in Beck's scoring than in ours, and F%, which includes items we would have scored FM or m.)

On her modified list, Elkins found her clinic subjects to show a mean of 2.2 "danger signals," her normal subjects 3.0—a significant difference in the wrong direction. On item analysis, she found only one item to differentiate significantly, again negatively: more normal subjects had A% > 60 than did clinic subjects. Other signs, promising in that they occurred only in the clinic subjects (more than one C, m, or diffuse, dysphoric shading), occurred so rarely that they had little value for screening purposes.

It was hard to know whether to attribute Elkins' negative results to differences in sampling, differences in the lists used, or simply lack of validity of our proposed list. It sometimes strikes us that referral of a particular child to a guidance clinic is rather little related to characteristics lying within the child—many of the children we see clinically do not differ notably from children we see when doing research in school settings. Elkins' disturbed subjects may not have been greatly disturbed, just as her teacher-nominated normals may have been more "good citizens" than robustly healthy. We would presumably have dismissed doubts about the extent of correspondence between her list and ours, or about the nature of the differences between her clinicals and her normals, as just quibbles if her findings had confirmed our proposed list. Since they instead contradicted it, we decided to test our own formulation of the list on a group of children whose disturbance was seen as clear and rather marked.

From the files of our clinical service we drew records of 50 boys, aged 6 to 12, of average intelligence or higher, who had been diagnosed independent of the Rorschach as emotionally disturbed. They make up a sixth of the 301 clinically referred boys of that age in the time period sampled, and so are a fairly extreme group. Each subject was matched individually for age, intelligence, and SES with a subject from our normal research sample (mainly children included in the longitudinal sample described in Chapter 23).

The sign list tested appears in Table 43. It is based on our originally

TABLE 42. Frequency of Occurence of Proposed Danger Signals and Cumulative Percentage Distribution in Disturbed and Normal Subjects

Number of signs	Frequency		Cumulated percentage	
	Disturbed	Normal	Disturbed	Normal
8	3	0	6	0
7	7	1	20	2
6	7	0	34	2
5	13	0	60	2
4	13	1	86	4
3	7	8	100	20
2	0	12	100	44
1	0	22	100	88
0	0	6	100	100

proposed list, with three items added, others subdivided, and standards for scoring modified to accord with our subsequent experience. All modifications were made, of course, before assembling the clinical sample. Incidence of each sign was tabulated for the disturbed and normal boys and the totals for each boy computed.*

Mean number of items for the disturbed boys was 5.0, for the normal boys 1.6, a clearly significant difference (t = 15.9; p < .01 that matched pairs do not differ). As Table 42 shows, the overlapping of scores in the two frequency distributions is remarkably small. The great majority of disturbed boys had scores of 4 or more; hardly any of the normals had scores that high.

Since most Rorschach characteristics show age trends, it seemed important to determine if trends appeared in the sign list. Figure 9 shows the number of danger signals by age for all 100 subjects—the normal boys plotted with black dots, the disturbed boys with white dots. The expected high number of signs at age 7 is suggested in the normal sample but not in the disturbed sample. Each group shows a significant overall decrease in items with age: correlation between age and number of items is —.44 for the normal group, —.29 for the disturbed group. The cutting line, determined by multiple regression as giving the best separation between black and white dots, suggests that 2 danger signals in the record of a 12-year-old would be about equivalent to 4 in the record of a 6-year-old.†

---

* Total possible score was 16; items 1, 2, and 13 were tabulated once when any or all of the subparts were noted.

† The formula (number of danger signals + ⅓ age) provides a better index of disturbance than does number of danger signals alone. Neither the sampling nor the scoring reliability would justify use of such a formula as a psychometric screening device. But it does point out that one should expect fewer of the danger signals to occur with increasing age in either normal or disturbed children.

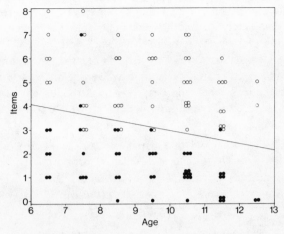

Fig. 9. Total Number of "Danger Signal" Items by Age for Normal Boys (Black Dots) and Disturbed Boys (White Dots).

An item analysis was done to determine which of the signs were contributing most to differentiating the groups. A fourfold table was made for each item, evaluating its presence in each pair of matched subjects (present in both, absent in both, present in normal only, present in disturbed only), and the difference between normal-only and disturbed-only incidence was tested by x^2. The *total* incidence of each sign in each group (ignoring the pairwise relationship) is presented in Table 43, along with results of the significance test.

Eleven of the 20 items show differences at the .05 level between the normal and disturbed subjects and two more are very close to that level. It is interesting that the quantitative scoring items—numbers 1a and 2a through 11 in the list—are most like those tested by Elkins and produce the fewest significant findings here also (three of the 12 are significant, two more are "borderline"). The remaining items—1b and 12 through 16—include those Elkins dropped as being subjective, as well as other behavioral, structural, and content characteristics, all requiring judgment by the evaluator. All tested significant.

The distinction between the objective and subjective groups of items should not be drawn too sharply. The scoring of actual responses, before they are totalled and manipulated as "objective," always involves substantial examiner judgment, and, conversely, the specifications for the more "subjective" items can be laid down fairly clearly. But the general implication is quite clear: a substantial element of judging is called for in effective use of the Rorschach.

To anyone (us, for example) developing a set of criteria, this should serve as a warning of the constant possibility of making self-gratifying, and so self-deluding, judgments. But it should not serve as a deterrent. Anyone interested in completely eliminating judgment from assessment would make a poor choice in picking the Rorschach to work with.

The checklist serves quite well to separate the two sharply different groups of boys we compared. The time when one most wants a prop of this sort is, of course, when the degree of disturbance is *not* clear—when one would expect to find many intermediate scores. A record having three

TABLE 43. PERCENTAGE OCCURRENCE OF "DANGER SIGNALS" IN DISTURBED AND NORMAL SUBJECTS

Item	Disturbed	Control	p*
1a. Fewer than 10 R	30	18	....
b. Excessive card manipulation	24	0	.01
2a. (Dd+S)% exceeds 25	12	8	....
b. More than 1 Do	18	6	....
3. F% exceeds F+%	38	8	.01
4. $m \geqslant 3$ or $m \geqslant (M + FM)$	20	8	....
5. One or more C or Cn	46	24	(.06)
6. Any variation of Clob or C'	16	6	....
7. A% exceeds 70	22	6	(.06)
8. No H or Hd or Hd:H $\geqslant$ 2:1	40	14	.01
9. Anatomy $\geqslant 3$ or anatomy $\geqslant 15\%$ of content *or* any F— anatomy	14	12	....
10. Elimination or sex responses	14	2	.05**
11. *Leaf* or *tree* $\geqslant 3$ or $\geqslant 15\%$ of content	10	4	....
12. Static perseveration	30	0	.05
13a. Bizarre content, F— originals	46	8	.01
b. Troubled content (hostile, anxious)	56	16	.01
c. Personal reference	16	2	.05
14. Contamination	32	2	.01
15. Confabulation	38	10	.01
16. Positional response	16	4	.05**

* Probability of no difference, tested by x^2 corrected for continuity, from the joint distribution for paired subjects, comparing the $+-$ and $-+$ cells.
**Small total frequency of occurrence (Es $<$ 5) makes the test suspect.

items present could equally likely have come from our normal or our disturbed group. Records containing fewer than three items would suggest a good likelihood of adequate adjustment, though some disturbed children with constriction or overcontrol of personality might score low. Children giving records with more than four danger signals would certainly merit careful evaluation. (It is frustrating that the one boy in the normal sample whose record contained more than four danger signals is a boy we have been unable to follow further.)

Even if, for some reason, one only wanted to make the decision, "Disturbed or normal?", use of a checklist alone would not be sufficient. However valid its items, they become fully meaningful only in the larger context of the whole record. (And use of the Rorschach to answer just that question would be wasteful.) But such a list does point out some important elements in evaluation, and should be useful in confirming or raising questions about the evaluator's conclusions.

Rorschach and Reading

Despite the great variety of innovations in curriculum, teaching techniques, and philosophical approaches to education in the past decade, most people continue to view development of skill in reading as a central task—even *the* central task—for the elementary school years. Much research concerning reading has focused, for good reasons, on reading disorder. But from the average through the superior range of reading ability, individual differences in reading skill continue to play an important role in (at least) academic effectiveness. In the case of reading disability, we look to a variety of subject characteristics—perceptual, cognitive, emotional, organizational—for explanation. But from the level of average reading ability on up, it seems that many psychologists attribute individual differences in reading skill either to specific reading abilities or to general intelligence. Are not some of the same factors related to reading disability also associated with reading differences within the non-disabled population?

Research in reading is complicated by the circularity of emotional experience: whether or not "emotional factors" *produce* some reading lags or accelerations, the experience of success and satisfaction or of failure and frustration always has secondary effects. Meyer (55) managed to avoid this problem in his study of good and poor readers at the third-grade level by comparing Rorschach records which had been obtained when the children were in kindergarten and before they had had formal experience with reading. He concluded that these early records

> may not only be used as prognostic tests of reading achievement in the primary grades, but may also be used to provide data on first grade reading readiness, particularly in the areas of intellectual and emotional readiness. Ability to differentiate beyond rather inaccurate, vague, and mediocre perceptions and rapport with the environment are characteristics which seem to differentiate the kindergarten records of those children who make adequate reading progress in the primary grades from those who do not (55, p. 424-425).

On the basis of his comparisons, he developed a prognostic scale of eight items.

We have similarly examined kindergarten Rorschachs of children whose reading was evaluated at a later age. Our study differs from Meyer's in that the children's reading was evaluated later, at the end of fifth grade, when differences in reading ability are more firmly established, and in that the group as a whole is one of superior ability, with virtually no below-grade readers. We asked two questions: (a) Do the pre-reading characteristics proposed by Meyer, or any other Rorschach scoring characteristics, predict later reading ability—not only over a longer time span but at a different ability level? (b) Does any obtained predictiveness of the Rorschach arise mainly by virtue of its association with general intelligence? That is, could one predict the same child's future reading ability as well or better by using intelligence test scores?

For 54 of the children first seen in kindergarten in our Suburban I sample (see Chapter 24), we were able to obtain scores from the reading sections of the Stanford Achievement Test, administered by classroom teachers at the end of fifth grade. The kindergarten Rorschach records were scored for Meyer's signs, and three kinds of comparisons were then made between Rorschach and reading scores. Kindergarten Rorschach scores were compared for children falling in each of the four quartiles of fifth-grade reading ability. Rorschach scores of pairs of children matched on IQ but contrasted on reading scores were compared. And correlations were computed among the reading-prognosis scores, kindergarten IQ scores, and fifth-grade reading scores.

Mean scores for children in the four quartiles of reading ability are presented in Table 44. The high overall reading level of the sample can be seen in that even for the lowest quarter of the group the mean reading score is only slightly below grade level. Mean for the total group was grade 8.2. A number of the Rorschach scores are seen to differ significantly and for the most part systematically for these groupings. The eventually more able readers had at the kindergarten level lower W%, higher D%, lower F%, higher F+%, and more FM. They tended to give more responses altogether and also to give more M. The mean number of prognostic signs (described below) increased successively and significantly from group to group. So also, however, did mean WISC IQ. The results of Table 44 might thus be explained by both Rorschach and reading scores being associated with intelligence scores.

Table 45 indicates that such was not the case. Twenty pairs of children were selected, the pair members having IQ scores within 5 points of each other but reading scores more than two grade levels apart. Mean reading score for the "poorer" members of each pair was a year above grade norm, but that for the better readers was about 4 years above the norm. Mean IQ scores for the groups were virtually identical. When subjects were thus paired, consistent mean differences between Rorschach scores still appeared. Again lower W%, higher D%, lower F%, higher FM, more responses, and more prognostic signs were given by children who were to become better readers. In addition, once IQ was held constant, a tendency for better readers to give more color scores approached significance.

The prognostic score consisted of Meyer's eight signs, plus an additional one found in our own experience to be a useful benchmark of read-

TABLE 44. MEAN KINDERGARTEN IQ AND RORSCHACH SCORES FOR CHILDREN IN EACH FIFTH-GRADE READING QUARTILE

Score	Q_1	Q_2	Q_3	Q_4	$P*$
Fifth-grade reading	5.7	7.8	9.0	10.3	
Kindergarten IQ	101.0	114.9	114.7	119.2	.01
Rorschach score:					
R	9.8	11.6	10.7	13.9	.10
W%	80	77	64	63	.01
D%	19	22	32	35	.01
Dd%	1	2	3	2	....
F%	81	79	75	59	.05
F+%	73	83	91	85	.05
M	.6	.4	.9	.9	.10
FM	.4	.5	.9	2.0	.01
m	.5	.3	.6	.3	....
F(C)	.2	0	.1	.1	....
FC	0	.1	0	.1	....
CF	.2	.9	.1	1.0	....
C	.2	0	0	.2	....
ΣC	.5	.9	.1	1.3	....
A%	54	49	60	55	....
H%	12	12	9	13	....
Number of content categories	3.8	3.9	3.8	4.5	....
P	2.6	3.2	3.6	3.4	....
%(8-10)	28.1	31.4	32.1	35.8	....
Prognostic signs	2.9	3.0	4.5	5.3	.01
N	13	14	14	13	

* P = probability of no difference between groups $Q_1 + Q_2$ versus $Q_3 + Q_4$, by *t* test.

ing readiness and selected as a scoring criterion *before* these Rorschachs were compared. For each of the following criteria fulfilled, the subject had a point added to his total prognostic score.

1. Fewer than seven W.

2. No W_1 or W_2 responses.* These are mostly perseverated, confabulatory, and positional Ws.

3. Fewer than three W_5. These are unelaborated, fairly accurate outline Ws, approaching but below the popular level.

* The W levels are, unfortunately for the reader, different from our own W levels detailed in Chapter 5. They are described briefly here; for fuller definition see Meyer & Thompson (56).

4. Two or more W₆ and W₇; popular Ws or better.

5. D% exceeding 33%. (Klopfer's D + d%, used by Meyer, is quite close to our D%, and the latter was scored.)

6. One or more CF or C.

7. No F? scores. These are noncommittal, essentially shapeless responses.

8. Fewer than 30% of responses on Cards VIII to X.

9. F+% exceeds F% (our own addition to Meyer's list).

TABLE 45. Mean Kindergarten Rorschach Scores for Subjects Matched on Kindergarten IQ but Contrasted on Fifth-Grade Reading Scores

	Reader		
Score	*Poor*	*Good*	*p**
Fifth-grade reading	6.9	9.6	
Kindergarten IQ	111.3	111.4	
Rorschach score:			
R	10.5	12.7	.10
W%	80	61	.01
D%	19	34	.05
Dd%	1	2	....
F%	82	63	.01
F+%	79	85	....
M	.5	.7	....
FM	.3	1.6	.01
m	.5	.4	....
FC	.1	.1	....
CF	.6	.8	....
C	0	.3	....
ΣC	.6	1.2	.10
F(C)	.1	.4	....
A%	50	56	....
H%	14	9	....
Number of content categories	4.1	4.3	....
P	3.1	3.4	....
%(8-10)	32	33	....
Prognostic signs	3.0	4.9	.01

* Probability that mean pair difference is zero, by t test.

Each of these signs was compared for children in the lower two reading quartiles against those in the upper two. The fourfold tables, tested by x^2, showed just five of these to discriminate the groups individually: these are Numbers 2, 4, 5, 7, and 9 in the above list. The other four showed about the same incidence in both reading groups, with one, Number 8, giving differences (nonsignificant) opposite to those suggested by

Meyer. Nevertheless, the total number of signs per individual was clearly associated with later reading, as Tables 44 and 45 show.

Correlation between number of prognostic signs and later reading score is shown, in Table 46, to be significant and of moderate size—nearly

TABLE 46. CORRELATIONS AMONG PROGNOSTIC RORSCHACH SCORE, KIDERGARTEN IQ, AND FIFTH-GRADE READING SCORE

Variables correlated	r
Prognostic Rorschach score versus fifth-grade reading	.53
Kindergarten IQ versus fifth-grade reading	.57
Kindergarten IQ versus prognostic Rorschach score	.15
Multiple R: fifth-grade reading from Rorschach and IQ	.73

the same size as the correlation between IQ and later reading score. Unexpectedly, the prognostic score was insignificantly related to IQ. The two together, therefore, showed a multiple correlation with later reading substantially higher than either alone.

Our results certainly offer support to Meyer's contention that the Rorschach can be useful in predicting individual differences in eventual reading skill. The support is the greater in that the time span was longer and the sample's reading ability was higher in this study than in Meyer's.

While the Rorschach variables associated with reading ability include both location and determinant variables, they tend to fall more in the "cognitive" than the "emotional" sphere of experiencing, insofar as these are separable. The differences among the groups in W% and D%, in F% and F+%, in R, and in quality of W constructions, all reflect differences in clarity, detailing, and accuracy of perception. The variables which differ most for the poorer and better readers are among those which change most in the course of normal development. In every case, the better readers show the more mature scoring. The greater use of color and movement by the better reading groups, concomitant with their lower F%, evidently reflects their greater emotional maturity, more differentiated experiencing, and greater openness to stimulation.

That the poorer reading groups gave higher W% comes as no surprise. It is the dropping out of the preschool global responses—gross, single-object, undifferentiated forms, sometimes perseverated or confabulated—which is a major step in perceptual development on the Rorschach around 4 to 5 years. Relatively many of the eventually "poorer" readers had not taken this step by kindergarten age.

The slight relationship of these perceptual and cognitive aspects of maturing to those reflected in an IQ score was unexpected. Indeed, they are much more closely related to a reading test given some five years later than to an intelligence test given in the same semester. The overall level of this sample of children may well contribute to this finding. We have speculated that brightness and maturity are less closely linked in the upper range of intelligence than in the lower range. That is, the finding of children who are bright but immature seems a commonplace; the finding of children who are dull but mature is a rare event.

In any case, the low association between the prognostic score and the IQ score, together with the moderate relation of each to later reading, allows both to contribute different kinds of information to prediction and results in a quite substantial multiple correlation.

The usefulness of the findings presumably does not lie in their employment specifically for predicting fifth-grade reading scores. Rather, they indicate that the Rorschach is capable of assessing important individual characteristics which correlate with behaviors basic to school success. And they suggest that these characteristics may profitably be viewed within a developmental framework.

Bibliography

1. ALLEN, ROBERT M. Nine quarterly Rorschach records of a young child. *Child Developmn.*, 1955, *26,* 63-69.
2. AMES, LOUISE B. Further check on the diagnostic validity of the Ames Danger Signals. *J. Proj. Tech.,* 1959, *23,* 291-298.
3. AMES, LOUISE B. Constancy of content in Rorschach responses. *J. Genet. Psychol.,* 1960, *97,* 145-164.
4. AMES, LOUISE B. Longitudinal survey of child Rorschach responses: Younger subjects. *Genet. Psychol. Monog.,* 1960, *61,* 229-289.
5. AMES, LOUISE B. Changes in experience balance scores in the Rorschach at different ages in the life span. *J. Genet. Psychol.,* 1965, *68,* 247-307.
6. AMES, LOUISE B. Changes in Rorschach responses throughout the human life span. *Genet. Psychol. Monog.,* 1966, *74,* 89-125.
7. AMES, LOUISE B. (assisted by Judith August). Rorschach responses of Negro and white 5- to 10-year-olds. *J. Genet. Psychol.,* 1966, *109,* 298-309.
8. AMES, LOUISE B. and ILG, FRANCES L. *Mosaic Patterns of American Children.* New York: Hoeber, 1962.
9. AMES, LOUISE B. and ILG, FRANCES L. The developmental point of view with special reference to the principle of reciprocal neuromotor interweaving. *J. Genet. Psychol.,* 1964, *105,* 195-209.
10. AMES, LOUISE B. and ILG, FRANCES L. The Gesell Incomplete Man Test as a measure of developmental status. *Genet. Psychol. Monog.,* 1965, *68,* 247-307.
11. AMES, LOUISE B., MÉTRAUX, RUTH W., RODELL, JANET L. and WALKER, RICHARD N. *Rorschach Responses in Old Age.* Revised edition. New York: Brunner/Mazel, 1973.
12. AMES, LOUISE B., MÉTRAUX, RUTH W. and WALKER, RICHARD N. *Adolescent Rorschach Responses.* Revised edition. New York: Brunner/Mazel, 1971.
13. AMES, LOUISE B. and WALKER, RICHARD N. Prediction of later reading ability from kindergarten Rorschach and I.Q. scores. *J. Educ. Psychol.,* 1964, *55,* 6, 309-313.
14. BECK, SAMUEL J. The Rorschach test in problem children. *Am. J. Orthopsychiatr.,* 1930, *1,* 501-509.
15. BECK, SAMUEL J. The Rorschach test as applied to a feeble-minded group. *Arch. Psychol.,* 1932, *136,* 84.
16. BECK, SAMUEL J. *Rorschach's Test.* Vol. I and II. New York: Grune & Stratton, 1944.
17. BINDER, HANS. *Die Helldunkeldeutungen im psychodiagnostischen Experiment von Rorschach.* Zurich: Art. Institut Orell Fussli, 1932. English summary in *Ror. Res. Exch.,* 1937, *2,* 37-42.
18. BOCHNER, RUTH and HALPERN, FLORENCE. *The Clinical Application of the Rorschach Test.* New York: Grune & Stratton, 1945.
19. COTTE, SIMONNE. Etude statistique sur le registre de perception dans le test de Rorschach des enfants impubères de 7 a 11 ans. *G. Psichiat. Neuropat.,* 1955, *83,* 781-794.
20. ELKINS, ELISE. The diagnostic validity of the Ames "Danger Signals". *J. consult. Psychol.,* 1958, *22,* 281-287.

21. FONDA, CHARLES P. The white-space response. Chapter 4 in Rickers-Ovsiankina, M.S. *Rorschach Psychology.* New York: Wiley, 1960.
22. FORD, MARY. *The Application of the Rorschach Test to Young Children.* Univ. of Minn. Inst. of Child Welf. Monograph Series No. 23, 1946.
23. FOX, JACK. The psychological significance of age patterns in the Rorschach records of children. In Klopfer, B. (Ed.) *Developments in the Rorschach technique,* Vol. II. Yonkers: World Book Company, 1956.
24. FRANCIS-WILLIAMS, JESSIE. *Rorschach with Children.* New York: Pergamon Press, 1968.
25. FRANK, LAWRENCE K. *Projective Methods.* Springfield: Charles C. Thomas, 1948.
26. GESELL, ARNOLD. Growth potentials of the human infant. *Scientific Monthly,* 1949, *68,* 4, 252-256.
27. GESELL, ARNOLD, ILG, FRANCES L. and AMES, L. B. (In collaboration with J. Learned). *Infant and Child in the Culture of Today.* Revised Edition. New York: Harper & Row, 1973.
28. GESELL, ARNOLD and ILG, FRANCES L. (In collaboration with Louise B. Ames and Glenna E. Bullis.) *The Child from Five to Ten.* New York: Harper, 1946.
29. GESELL, ARNOLD, ILG, FRANCES L. and BULLIS, GLENNA E. *Vision: Its Development in Infant and Child.* New York: Hoeber, 1959.
30. HALPERN, FLORENCE. *A Clinical Approach to Children's Rorschachs.* New York: Grune & Stratton, 1953.
31. HERTZ, MARGUERITE R. The reliability of the Rorschach ink-blot test *J. Appl. Psychol.,* 1934, *18,* 461-477.
32. HERTZ, MARGUERITE R. Rorschach norms for an adolescent age group. *Child Developmn.,* 1935, *6,* 69-75.
33. HERTZ, MARGUERITE R. The method of administration of the Rorschach ink-blot test. *Child Developmn.,* 1936, *7,* 237-254.
34. HERTZ, MARGUERITE R. Scoring the Rorschach test with specific reference to the "normal detail" category. *Am. J. Orthopsychiatr.,* 1938, *8,* 100-121.
35. HERTZ, MARGUERITE R. Scoring the Rorschach ink-blot test. *J. Genet. Psychol.,* 1939, *52,* 15-64.
36. HERTZ, MARGUERITE R. The shading response in the Rorschach ink-blot test: a review of its scoring and interpretation. *J. Genet. Psychol.,* 1940, *23,* 123-167.
37. HERTZ, MARGUERITE R. Evaluation of the Rorschach method and its application to normal childhood and adolescence. *Character and Personality,* 1941, *10,* 151-162.
38. HERTZ, MARGUERITE R. Validity of the Rorschach method. *Am. J. Orthopsychiatr.,* 1941, *11,* 512-520.
39. HERTZ, MARGUERITE R. *Frequency Tables to Be Used in Scoring the Rorschach Ink-Blot Test.* (Revised edition.) Cleveland: Western Reserve Univ. Press, Dept. of Psychology, 1942.
40. HERTZ, MARGUERITE R. Rorschach: Twenty years after. *Psychol. Bull.,* 1942, *39,* 529-572.
41. HERTZ, MARGUERITE R. The scoring of the Rorschach ink-blot method as developed by the Brush foundation. *Ror. Res. Exch.,* 1942, *6,* 16-27.
42. HERTZ, MARGUERITE R. Personality patterns in adolescence as portrayed by the Rorschach ink-blot method.
  I. The movement factors. *J. Gen. Psychol.,* 1942, *27,* 119-188.
  II. The color patterns. *Ror Res. Exch.,* 1941, *5,* 30-61.
  III. The Erlebnistypus. *J. Gen. Psychol.,* 1943, *28,* 225-276.
  IV. The Erlebnistypus. *J. Gen. Psychol.,* 1943, *29,* 3-45.
43. HERTZ, MARGUERITE R. and EBERT, E. H. The mental procedure of six and eight year old children as revealed by the Rorschach ink-blot method. *Ror. Res. Exch.,* 1944, *8,* 10-30.
44. KIDD, ALINE and RIVOIRE, JEANNE L. *Perceptual Development in Children.* New York: International Universities Press, Inc., 1966.

45. KLOPFER, BRUNO. Personality diagnosis in childhood. Chapter in Lewis, N. D. C. and Pacella, B. I. *Modern Trends in Child Psychiatry.* New York: International Universities Press, 1945.

46. KLOPFER, BRUNO, AINSWORTH, MARY D., KLOPFER, WALTER G. and HOLT, ROBERT R. *Developments in the Rorschach Technique,* Vol. I. Yonkers-on-Hudson, New York: World, 1954.

47. KLOPFER, BRUNO, FOX, JACK and TROUP, EVELYN. Problems in the use of the Rorschach technique with children. Chapter 1 in Klopfer, *Developments in the Rorschach Technique,* Vol. II. Yonkers-on-Hudson, New York: World, 1946.

48. KLOPFER, BRUNO, MARGULIES, H., MURPHY, LOIS B. and STONE, L. JOSEPH. Rorschach reactions in early childhood. *Ror. Res. Exch.,* 1941, *5,* 1-23.

49. KLOPFER, BRUNO, SPIEGELMAN, MARVIN and FOX, JACK. The interpretation of children's records. Chapter 2 in Bruno Klopfer, *Developments in the Rorschach Technique,* Vol. II. Yonkers-on-Hudson, New York: World, 1956.

50. LANG, ALFRED. *Rorschach Bibliography, 1921-1964.* Berne und Stuttgart: Verlag Hans Huber, 1966.

51. LEDWITH, NETTIE. *A Rorschach Study of Child Development.* Pittsburgh: University of Pittsburgh Press, 1959.

52. LEVITT, EUGENE E. and TRUUMAA, AARE. *The Rorschach Technique with Children and Adolescents.* New York: Grune & Stratton, 1972.

53. LOOSLI-USTERI, MARGUERITE. *Le Diagnostic Individual Chez l'Infant au Moyen du Test de Rorschach.* Paris: Hermann & Cie, 1948.

54. LOOSLI-USTERI, MARGUERITE. L'Homme 'Normal' Vu à Travers le Test de Rorschach. *Arch. psicol. neurol. e psichiat.,* 1949, *10,* 119-125.

55. MEYER, GEORGE. Some relationships between Rorschach scores in kindergarten and reading in the primary grades. *J. Proj. Tech.,* 1953,*17,* 414-425.

56. MEYER, GEORGE and THOMPSON, JACK. The performance of kindergarten children on the Rorschach test: A normative study. *J. Proj. Tech.,* 1952, *16,* 86-111.

57. NORLAND, EVA. Children's Rorschach responses: developmental trends from 3 to 20 years. *Pedagogisk Forskning* 1966, *2-3,* 124-149.

58. PAULSEN, ALMA. Personality development in the middle years of childhood: a ten year longitudinal study of 30 public school children by means of Rorschach test and social histories. *Amer. J. Orthopsychiat.,* 1954, *24,* 336-350.

59. PIOTROWSKI, ZYGMUNT. A comparison of congenitally defective children with schizophrenic children in regard to personality structure and intelligence type. *Proc. Am. Assn. Ment. Def.,* 1937, *61,* 78-90.

60. PIOTROWSKI, ZYGMUNT. Rorschach records of children with a tic syndrome. *Nerv. Child.,* 1945, *5,* 342-352.

61. PIOTROWSKI, ZYGMUNT. Rorschach Compendium, revised edition. *Psychiatr. Quart.,* 1950, *24,* 545-596.

62. PIOTROWSKI, ZYGMUNT. *Perceptanalysis.* New York: Macmillan, 1957.

63. PIOTROWSKI, ZYGMUNT, and LEWIS, NOLAN. A case of stationary schizophrenia beginning in early childhood, with remarks on certain aspects of children's Rorschach records. *Quart. J. Child Behavior,* 1950, *2,* 115-139.

64. RABIN, ALBERT I. and HAWORTH, MARY R. *Projective Techniques with Children.* New York: Grune & Stratton, 1960.

65. RAPAPORT, DAVID, GILL, MERTON M., and SCHAFER, ROY. *Diagnostic Psychological Testing,* revised edition. Ed. by Robert R. Holt. New York: International Universities Press, 1968.

66. RORSCHACH, HERMANN. *Psychodiagnostics.* Berne: Verlag Hans Huber, 1942.

67. SCHACHTEL, ERNEST G. *Experiential Foundations of Rorschach's Test.* New York: Basic Books, 1966.

68. SWIFT, JOAN W. Reliability of Rorschach scoring categories with preschool children. *Child Developmn.,* 1944, *15,* 207-216.

69. SWIFT, JOAN W. Matching of teachers' descriptions and Rorschach analyses of preschool children. *Child Developmn.,* 1944, *15,* 217-224.

70. SWIFT, JOAN W. Rorschach responses of eighty-two preschool children. *Ror. Res. Exch.*, 1944, *9*, 74-84.
71. SWIFT, JOAN W. Relation of behavioral and Rorschach measures of insecurity in preschool children. *J. Clin. Psychol.*, 1945, *1*, 196-205.
72. THETFORD, WILLIAM N., MOLISH, HERMAN B. and BECK, SAMUEL J. Developmental aspects of personality structure in normal children. *J. Proj. Tech.*, 1951, *15*, 58-78.

Index